"the Guru of all screenwriters"
—*CNN*

"the first prophet of writing for the screen"
—*The Los Angeles Times Magazine*

"A true Hollywood character…no one sees films quite
the way Field does. An engineer's report on film construction
and the view of an original thinker worth appreciating."
—*Kirkus Reviews*

"The most sought after screenwriting teacher in the world."
—*The Hollywood Reporter* on Syd Field

"If I were writing screenplays… I would carry Syd Field
around in my back pocket wherever I went."
—Steven Bochco, writer/producer/director, *L.A. Law*, *NYPD Blue*

"Full of common sense, an uncommon commodity."
—*Esquire*

"Syd writes both with passion and an astute understanding."
—Hanz Zimmer, film composer, *Thelma & Louise*

"Impressive… His easy-to-follow step-by-step
approaches are comforting and his emphasis
on right attitude and motivation is uplifting."
—*Los Angeles Times Book Review*

THE DEFINITIVE GUIDE TO

SCREEN WRITING

SYD FIELD

Acclaimed as "The guru of all screen writers" (*CNN*), Syd Field is regarded by many Hollywood professionals as the leading authority in the art and craft of screenwriting in the world today. His internationally acclaimed best-selling books *Screenplay, The Screenwriter's Workbook,* and *The Screenwriter's Problem Solver* have established themselves as the "bibles" of the film industry. They are used in more than 395 colleges and universities and have been translated into 19 languages.

Field is currently on faculty at the USC Masters of Professional Writing Program. He chaired the Academic Liaison Committee at The Writer's Guild of America, West, has taught at Harvard, Stanford, UC Berkeley, UCLA, the AFI and many other noted institutions. He has been a special script consultant to 20th Century Fox, the Disney Studios, Universal and Tristar Pictures and has collaborated with such noted filmmakers as Alphonso Cuaron *(Y Tu Mama Tambien)*, James L. Brooks *(Broadcast News, As Good As It* Gets), Luis Mandoki *(When A Man Loves A Woman),* Roland Joffe *(The Killing Fields, The Mission),* and Tony Kaye *(American History X).*

Field has taught screenwriting workshops in South America, Mexico, Europe, and South Africa, and has conducted workshops for the Canadian Film Industry. He was chosen as the President of the International Film Jury at the 1999 Flanders International Film Festival, Ghent, Belgium.

Syd Field was the first inductee into the prestigious *Screenwriting Hall of Fame* of the American Screenwriting Association in 2001. Some of his former students include Anna Hamilton Phelan *(Mask, Gorillas in the Mist)*, John Singleton *(Boys In the Hood, Poetic Justice),* Randi Mayem Singer *(Mrs. Doubtfire)*, Laura Esquival *(Like Water For Chocalate*), Michael Kane *(The Color of Money),* and Kevin Williamson *(Scream, Scream 2* and *3).*

THE DEFINITIVE GUIDE TO
SCREEN WRITING

SYD FIELD

EBURY
PRESS

The Definitive Guide to Screenwriting
first published by Ebury Press in Great Britain in 2003

Screenplay, the Foundations of Screenwriting
first published by Dell Publishing in 1979

The Screenwriter's Problem Solver
first published by Dell Publishing in 1998

1 3 5 7 9 10 8 6 4 2

Text © 2003 Syd Field

Ebury Press, an imprint of Ebury Press.
Random House, 20 Vauxhall Bridge Road, London SW1V 2SA

The Random House Group Limited Reg. No. 954009

www.randomhouse.co.uk

A CIP catalogue record for this book is available from the British Library

ISBN 0091890276

Cover Design by Perfect Bound, London
Interior by seagulls

*Papers used by Ebury Press are natural, recyclable
products made from wood grown in sustainable forests*

Printed in Great Britain by Clays Ltd, St Ives plc

To all the Siddha Saints and Masters

who walked the path and keep the flame burning ...

and, of course, to Aviva, who helped show me the way ...

contents

INTRODUCTION

THE ORIGINS OF THIS BOOK

"My task…is to make you hear, to make you feel – and above all to make you see. That is all, and it is everything."

—Joseph Conrad

It seems like I've spent most of my life sitting in a darkened theater, popcorn in hand, gazing in rapt wonder at the images projected on a river of light reflected on that monster screen.

I was one of those kids who grew up in Hollywood surrounded by the film industry. While playing the trumpet in the Sheriff's Boys Band, like my brother before me, I was cast as one of the band members of Frank Capra's *The State of the Union* starring Spencer Tracy and Katharine Hepburn. I don't remember much about the experience except Van Johnson taught me how to play checkers.

Yes, I can truly say I was a child of Hollywood.

For the past thirty-five years, I've watched movies as they've become an integral part of our culture, part of our heritage, watched as they have become an international way of life. Once an audience

1

is joined together in the darkness of the movie theater, they become one being, one entity, connected in a community of emotion, an unspoken, deep-seated connection to the human spirit that exists beyond time, place and circumstance.

Going to the movies is both an individual and collective experience, a collection of singular moments standing out against the landscape of time. Watching those flickering images flutter across the screen can bear witness to the entire range of human experience: a moment of wonder and poetry, like the opening sequence of *Close Encounters of the Third Kind*, or capturing the full scope of human history as a wooden club thrown into the air merges into a spacecraft in Stanley Kubrick's *2001*. Thousands of years and the evolution of humankind condensed into two pieces of film; it is a moment of magic and mystery, wonder and awe. Such is the power of film.

As a writer-producer for David L. Wolper Productions, a freelance screenwriter, and head of the story department at Cinemobile Systems, I spent several years writing and reading screenplays. At Cinemobile alone, I read and synopsized more than 2,000 screenplays in a little more than two years. And of those 2,000 screenplays, I selected only forty to present to our financial partners for possible film production.

Why so few? Because 99 out of 100 screenplays I read weren't good enough to invest a million or more dollars in. Or, put another way, only one out of 100 screenplays I read was good enough to consider for film production. And, at Cinemobile, our job was making movies. In one year alone, we were directly involved in the production of some 119 motion pictures, ranging from *The Godfather* to *Jeremiah Johnson* to *Deliverance*.

When my boss, Fouad Said, the creator of the Cinemobile, decided to make his own movies, he went out and raised some $10 million in a few weeks. Pretty soon everybody in Hollywood was sending him screenplays. Thousands of scripts came in, from stars and directors, studios and producers, from the known and the unknown.

That's when I was fortunate enough to be given the opportunity of reading the submitted screenplays, and evaluating them in terms of quality, cost, and probable budget. My job, as I was constantly reminded, was to "find material" for our three financial partners: the United Artists Theatre Group, the Hemdale Film Distribution Company, headquartered in London, and the Taft Broadcasting Company, parent company of Cinemobile.

So I began reading screenplays. As a former screenwriter taking a much-needed vacation from more than seven years of free-lance writing, my job at Cinemobile gave me a totally new perspective on writing screenplays. It was a tremendous opportunity, a formidable challenge, and a dynamic learning experience.

What made the forty screenplays I recommended "better" than the others? I didn't have any answers for that, but I thought about it for a long time.

My reading experience gave me the opportunity to make a judgment and evaluation, to formulate an opinion: this is a *good* screenplay, this is *not a good* screenplay. As a screenwriter, I wanted to find out what made the forty scripts I recommended better than the other 1,960 scripts submitted.

Just about this time I was given the opportunity of teaching a screenwriting class at the Sherwood Oaks Experimental College in Hollywood. At that time, in the seventies, Sherwood Oaks was a professional school taught by professionals. It was the kind of school where Paul Newman, Dustin Hoffman, and Lucille Ball gave acting seminars; where Tony Bill would teach a producing seminar; where Martin Scorsese, Robert Altman, or Alan Pakula gave directing seminars; where William Fraker and John Alonzo, two of the finest cinematographers in the world, taught a class in cinematography. It was a school where professional production managers, cameramen, film editors, writers, directors, and producers all came to teach their specialties. It was the most unique film school in the country.

I had never taught a screenwriting class before, so I had to delve into my writing experience and reading experience to evolve my basic material.

What is a good screenplay? I kept asking myself. And, pretty soon, I started getting some answers. When you read a good screenplay, you know it – it's evident from page one. The style, the way the words are laid out on the page, the way the story is set up, the grasp of dramatic situation, the introduction of the main character, the basic premise or problem of the screenplay – it's all set up in the first few pages of the script. *Chinatown*, *American Beauty*, *Lord of the Rings*, *The Hours*, *All the President's Men*, are perfect examples.

A screenplay, I soon realized, is a story told with pictures. It's like a *noun*: that is, a screenplay is about a *person*, or persons, in a *place*, or places, doing his, or her, *"thing."* I saw that the screenplay has certain basic conceptual components common to the form.

These elements are expressed dramatically within a definite structure with a beginning, middle, and end. When I re-examined the forty screenplays submitted to our partners – including *The Wind and the Lion*, *Alice Doesn't Live Here Anymore*, and others – I realized they all contained these basic concepts, regardless of how they were cinematically executed. They are in every screenplay.

I began teaching this conceptual approach to writing the screenplay. If the student knows what a model screenplay is, I reasoned, it can be used as a guide or blueprint.

I have been teaching this screenwriting class for several years now. It's an effective and experimental approach to writing the screenplay. My material has evolved and been formulated by thousands and thousands of students all over the world. They are the ones who prepared me to write this book.

Many of my students have been very successful: Anna Hamilton Phelan wrote *Mask* in my workshop, then went on to write *Gorillas in the Mist*; Laura Esquival wrote *Like Water for Chocolate*; Carmen Culver wrote *The Thornbirds*; Janus Cercone wrote *Leap of Faith*; Linda Elsted won the prestigious Humanitas award for *The Divorce Wars*; and prestigious filmmakers such as James Cameron (*Terminator* and *Terminator 2*; *Judgment Day*, *Titanic*) used the material when they started their careers.

Screenwriting is a process. What you write one day is out of date the day after. What you write the day after is out of date the day after that. And what you write the day after the day after is out of date the day after that. That's just the way the writing process works; it is larger than you are. It has its own life, its own needs, its own requirements.

Others have not been so successful. Some people have the talent, and some don't. Talent is God's gift; either you've got it or you don't.

Many people have already formed a writing style prior to enrolling in the class. Some of them have to *unlearn* their writing habits, just as a tennis pro coaches someone to correct an incorrect swing, or a swimming instructor improves a swimming stroke. Writing, like tennis, or learning to swim, is an experiential process; for that reason, I begin with general concepts and then move into specific aspects of screenwriting.

The material is designed for everyone; for those who have no previous writing experience, as well as those who have not had much success with their writing efforts and need to rethink their basic approach to writing. Novelists, playwrights, magazine editors, housewives, businessmen, doctors, actors, film editors, commercial directors, secretaries, advertising executives, and university professors – all have taken the class and benefited from it.

The purpose of this book is to enable the reader to sit down and write a screenplay from the position of choice, confidence, and security; completely secure within himself that he knows what he's doing. Because the hardest thing about writing is *knowing what to write*.

When you complete this book, you will know exactly *what* to do to write a screenplay. Whether you do it or not is up to you.

Writing is a personal responsibility – either you do it, or you don't.

PROBLEM SOLVING

Additionally, while writing this guide, I felt a responsibility to address the variety of problems that can confront a writer at any time and I wanted to find some kind of tool that the screenwriter could use in order to recognize and define various problems of screenwriting. But I gradually became aware that I was really writing about the *solutions* to the problems and not really identifying them. It just didn't work. So I began to rethink my approach. To solve any kind of a problem means you have to be able to recognize it, identify it, and then define it; only in that way can any problem really be solved.

The more I began thinking about the "problem," the more it became clear that most screenwriters don't know exactly what the problem really is. There's a vague and somewhat tenuous feeling somewhere that something is not working; either the plot is too thin or too thick; or the character is too strong or too weak; or there's not enough action, or the character disappears off the page, or the story is told all in dialogue.

So I began analyzing the Problem-Solving process. The only way I could make this book work, I realized, was to recognize and define the various *symptoms* of the problem, very much the way a medical doctor isolates the various symptoms of his patients before he can treat the disease.

When I approached the Problem-Solving process from this point of view (and it *is* a process), I began to see that there's usually not just *one* symptom, but *many* symptoms. It soon became clear that many of the problems in screenwriting share the same symptoms, but the problems themselves are different in kind; only when you analyze the *context of the problem* can a distinction be made, and it is those distinctions that lead us on the path of recognizing, defining, and solving. For the truth is that you can't solve a problem until you know what it is.

With that in mind I began to understand that there are only three distinct categories of The Problem; when you're writing a screenplay, all problems spring either from *Plot*, *Character*, or *Structure*.

The art of Problem Solving is really the art of recognition.

You can look at any problem in two ways; the first is to accept the fact that a problem is *something that doesn't work*. If that's the case, you can avoid it, deny it, and pretend it doesn't exist. That's the easy way.

But there's another way of approaching the problem, and that's to look at any creative problem as a challenge, an *opportunity* for you to expand your screenwriting skills.

They are really both sides of the same coin. How you look at it is up to you.

"The World is as you see it..." (from Yoga Vasistha)

THE PROBLEM SHEET

At certain points in this book, I have provided *Problem Sheets*.

The *Problem Sheet* is an abbreviated guide that is meant to be used as an interactive tool. It lists a number of screenwriting *symptoms* that can help you identify and define various problems. If you have a problem, and you match it with some of the symptoms listed, the information in the pages that follow the *Problem Sheet* can help you find an answer. Some *symptoms* listed will be the same for several chapters. That's because the same symptoms are relevant for different kinds of problems; it really doesn't matter whether it's a problem of *Plot*, *Character*, or *Structure*. A problem is a problem, no matter how you label it.

THE SCREENPLAY

1

What is a screenplay? A guide, or an outline for a movie? A blueprint, or a diagram? A series of images, scenes, and sequences that are strung together with dialogue and description, like pearls on a strand? The landscape of a dream? A collection of ideas?

What *is* a screenplay?

Well, for one thing it's not a novel, and it's certainly not a play.

If you look at a novel and try to define its essential nature, you see that the dramatic action, the story line, usually takes place inside the head of the main character. We are privy to the character's thoughts, feelings, words, actions, memories, dreams, hopes, ambitions, opinions, and more. If other characters are brought into the action, then the story line embraces their point of view as well, but the action always returns to the main character. In a novel the action takes place inside the character's head, within the *mindscape* of dramatic action.

In a play, the action, or story line, occurs on stage, under the proscenium arch, and the audience becomes the fourth wall, eavesdropping on the lives of the characters. They talk about their hopes and dreams, past and future plans, discuss their needs and desires, fears and conflicts. In this case, the action of the play occurs within the *language* of dramatic action; it is spoken, in *words*.

Movies are different. Film is a visual medium that dramatizes a basic story line; it deals in pictures, images, bits and pieces of film: a clock ticking, a window opening, someone watching, two people laughing, a car pulling away from the curb, a phone ringing. A screenplay is a story told with pictures, in dialogue and description, and placed with the context of dramatic structure.

A screenplay is like a noun – it's about a *person*, or persons, in a *place* or places, doing his or her or their "*thing*." All screenplays execute this basic premise. The person is the character, and doing his or her thing is the action.

If a screenplay is a story told with pictures, what then do all stories have in common? A beginning, a middle and an end, though not always in that order. If we were to take a screenplay and hang it on a wall like a painting and look at it, it would look like the diagram on page 9.

This basic linear structure is the *form* of the screenplay; it holds all the elements of the story line in place.

To understand the dynamics of structure, it's important to start with the word itself. The root of structure, *struct*, means "to build" or "to put something together" like a building or a car. But there is another definition of the word structure, and that is "the relationship between the parts and the whole."

The parts and the whole. Chess, for example, is a *whole* composed of four parts; the *pieces*, queen, king, bishop, pawns, knights, etc., the *player or players* because someone has to play the game of chess; *the board*, because you can't play chess without it; and the last thing you need to play chess is the *rules*, because they make chess the game it is. Those four things – pieces, player or players, board, and rules, the parts – are integrated into a whole, and the result is the game of chess. It is the relationship between the parts and the whole that determines the game.

A story is a whole, and the parts that make it – the action, characters, scenes, sequences, Acts I, II, III, incidents, episodes, events, music, locations, etc. – are what make up the story. It is a whole.

Structure is what holds the story in place. It is the relationship between these parts that holds the entire screenplay, the whole, together.

It is the paradigm of dramatic structure.

A paradigm is a model, example, or conceptual scheme.

The paradigm of a table, for example, is a top with four legs. Within the paradigm, we can have a low table, a high table, a narrow table, a wide table; or a circular table, a square table, a rectangular table; or a glass table, a wood table, a plastic table, wrought-iron table, whatever, and the paradigm doesn't change – it remains firm, a top with four legs.

If a screenplay were a painting hanging on a wall, this is what it would look like:

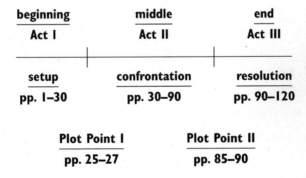

beginning	middle	end
Act I	Act II	Act III

setup	confrontation	resolution
pp. 1–30	pp. 30–90	pp. 90–120

Plot Point I	Plot Point II
pp. 25–27	pp. 85–90

This is the paradigm of a screenplay. Here's how it's broken down.

ACT I, OR THE SETUP

Aristotle talks about the three unities of dramatic action: time, place, and action. The normal Hollywood film is approximately two hours long, or 120 minutes, while the European, or foreign film, is approximately

90 minutes. The way it works is that a page of screenplay equals approximately a minute of screen time. It doesn't matter whether the script is all action, all dialogue, or any combination of the two; generally speaking, a page of screenplay equals a minute of screen time.

Act I, the beginning, is a unit of dramatic action that is approximately thirty pages long and is held together with the dramatic context known as the *setup*. Context is the space that holds the content of the story in place. (The space inside a glass, for example, is a context; it "holds" the content in place – water, beer, milk, coffee, tea, juice; the space inside a glass can even hold raisins, trail mix, nuts, grapes, etc.)

The screenwriter has approximately thirty pages to *set up* the story, the characters, the dramatic premise, the situation (the circumstances surrounding the action) and to establish the relationships between the main character and the other people who inhabit the landscape of his or her world. When you go to a movie, you can usually determine – consciously or unconsciously – whether you "like" the movie or "do not like" the movie within the first ten minutes. The next time you go to a movie, find out how long it takes you to make that decision.

Ten minutes is ten pages of screenplay. This first ten-page unit of dramatic action is the most important part of the screenplay because you have to show the reader who your main character is, what the dramatic premise of the story (what it's about) is, and what the dramatic situation (the circumstances surrounding the action) is. In *Chinatown*, for example, we learn on the first page that Jake Gittes (Jack Nicholson), the main character, is a sleazy private detective specializing in "discreet investigation." And he has a certain flair for it. On page 5 we are introduced to a certain Mrs. Mulwray (Diane Ladd), who wants to hire Jake Gittes to find out "who my husband is having an affair with." That is the dramatic premise of the film, because the answer to that question is what leads us into the story. The dramatic premise is what the screenplay is about; it provides the dramatic thrust that drives the story to its conclusion.

In *Witness* (Earl Wallace and William Kelley), the first ten pages reveal the world of the Amish in Lancaster County, Pennsylvania, and the death of Rachel's husband takes her and her young child to Philadelphia, where the boy happens to witness the murder of an undercover cop, and that leads to the relationship with the main character, John Book, played by Harrison Ford. The entire first act is designed to reveal the dramatic premise and situation, and the relationship between an Amish woman and a tough Philadelphia cop.

ACT II, OR THE CONFRONTATION

Act II is a unit of dramatic action that is approximately sixty pages long, goes from page 30 to page 90, and is held together with the dramatic context known as confrontation. During the second act the main character encounters obstacle after obstacle after obstacle that keeps him from achieving his or her dramatic need. Just look at *The Fugitive*. The entire story is driven by the main character's dramatic need to bring his wife's killer to justice. Dramatic need is defined as what your main character wants to win, gain, get, or achieve during the screenplay. What drives him or her forward through the action? What does your main character want: What is his or her need? If you know the character's dramatic need, you can create obstacles to that need, and the story becomes the main character overcoming obstacle after obstacle after obstacle to achieve (or not achieve) his or her dramatic need.

In *Chinatown*, a detective story, Act II deals with Jack Nicholson colliding with people who try to keep him from finding out who's responsible for the murder of Hollis Mulwray, and who's behind the water scandal. The obstacles that Jake Gittes encounters and overcomes dictate the dramatic action of the story.

All drama is conflict. Without conflict, you have no character; without character, you have no action; without action, you have no story; and without story, you have no screenplay.

ACT III, OR THE RESOLUTION

Act III is a unit of dramatic action that goes from the end of Act II, approximately page 90, to the end of the screenplay, and is held together with the dramatic context known as resolution. Resolution does not mean ending; resolution means solution. What is the solution of the screenplay? Does your main character live or die? Succeed or fail? Marry the man or woman, or not? Win the race or not? Win the election or not? Leave her husband or not? Act III *resolves* the story; it is not the ending. The ending is that specific scene, shot, or sequence that ends the script; it is not the solution of the story.

Beginning, middle, and end; Act I, Act II, and Act III. Setup, confrontation, resolution – the parts that make up the whole.

But this brings up another question: if these are some of the parts that make up the screenplay, how do you get from Act I, the setup, into Act II, the confrontation? And how do you get from Act II into Act III, the resolution? The answer is simple: create a plot point at the end of Act I and Act II.

A plot point is any incident, episode, or event that "hooks" into the action and spins it around into another direction – in this case, Act II and Act III. A plot point occurs at the end of Act I, at about pages 20 to 25. It is a function of the main character. In *Chinatown*, after the newspaper story is released claiming Mr. Mulwray has been caught in a "love nest," the *real* Mrs. Mulwray (Faye Dunaway) arrives with her attorney and threatens to sue Jake Gittes and have his license revoked. (This is the dramatic situation: without his detective license, he can't function.) But if she is the real Mrs. Mulwray, who was the woman who hired Jake Gittes? And *why*? And who hired the phony Mrs. Mulwray? And *why*? The arrival of the real Mrs. Mulwray is what "hooks" into the action and spins it around into Act II. Jake Gittes must find out who set him up, and why. It happens at about page 23.

In *Witness*, after John Book has gone through all the lineups and mug shots trying to identify the killer, he is talking on the phone, and we follow Samuel, the young boy, as he wanders around the police station. He stops at the trophy case and examines the trophies lined up inside, and catches sight of a newspaper story pinned up inside. He looks closer at the picture in the article and identifies the man pictured as the killer of the undercover cop on page 10 of the screenplay. Book sees him, puts down the phone's receiver, and walks to the boy in slow motion, then kneels down beside him. Samuel points at the picture, and Book nods his head in understanding. He knows who the murderer is. Now he has to bring him to justice. It is Plot Point I. It occurs on page 25 of the screenplay.

The plot point at the end of the second act is also an incident, episode, or event that "hooks" into the action, and spins it around into Act III. It usually occurs at about page 85 or 90 of the screenplay. In *Chinatown*, Plot Point II is when Jack Nicholson finds a pair of horn-rim glasses in the pond where Hollis Mulwray was murdered, and knows they belong to Mulwray, or to the person who killed him. This leads to the resolution of the story.

In *Witness*, after Book learns that his partner has been killed, he knows it's time to go back to Philadelphia and bring the guilty policemen to justice. But before he can leave, he must complete his relationship with Rachel.

When Rachel (Kelly McGillis) learns that Book is leaving, she carefully puts her hat on the floor, then runs to him, and they kiss and embrace and at last give in to their real feelings. This incident completes the action of Act II and sets the stage for Act III, when the killers appear to kill Book before he can tell anyone. The entire action of Act III deals with the shoot-out between Book and the three policemen. It is the resolution of the screenplay. The ending is when Book drives down the dirt road and the final end credits come up.

Do all good screenplays fit the paradigm? Yes. But that doesn't make them good screenplays, or good movies. The paradigm is a form, not a formula. Form is what holds something together; its structure, its configuration. The form of a coat or jacket, for example, is two arms, a front and a back. And within that form of two arms, front and back, you can have any variation of style, fabric, and color, but the form remains intact.

A formula, however, is totally different. In a formula, certain elements are put together so they come out *exactly the same* every time. If you put that coat on an assembly line, every coat will be exactly the same, with the same pattern, the same fabric, the same color, the same cut, the same material. It will not change, except for size.

The paradigm is a form, not a formula; it's what holds the story together. The spine, the skeleton, and the story are what determine structure; structure doesn't determine story.

Dramatic structure of the screenplay may be defined as a linear arrangement of related incidents, episodes, or events leading to a dramatic resolution.

How you utilize these structural components determines the form of your film. *Annie Hall*, for example, is a story told in flashback, but it has a definite beginning, middle, and end. *Last Year at Marienbad* does, too, though not in that order. So do *Citizen Kane*; *Hiroshima, Mon Amour*; *Dances With Wolves*; *The Silence of the Lambs*, and *The Fugitive*.

There is only form, not formula. The paradigm is a model, an example, or conceptual scheme; it is what a well-structured screenplay looks like, an overview of the story line as it unfolds from beginning to end.

Do all good screenplays fit the paradigm?

Screenplays that work follow the paradigm. But don't take my word for it. Go to any movie and see whether you can determine its structure.

Some of you may not believe that. You may not believe in beginnings, middles, and ends, either. You may say that art, like life, is nothing more than several individual "moments" suspended in some giant middle, with no beginning and no end, what Kurt Vonnegut calls "a series of random moments" strung together in a haphazard fashion.

I disagree.

Birth? Life? Death? Isn't that a beginning, middle, and end?

Think about the rise and fall of great civilizations – of Egypt, Greece, the Roman Empire, rising from the seed of a small community to the apex of power, then disintegrating and dying.

Think about the birth and death of a star, or the beginning of the Universe, according to the "Big Bang" theory that most scientists now agree on. If there's a beginning to the Universe, is there going to be an end?

Think about the cells in our bodies. How often are they replenished, restored, and recreated? Every seven years – within a seven-year cycle, the cells in our bodies are born, function, die, and are reborn again.

Think about the first day of a new job, meeting new people, assuming new responsibilities; you stay there until you decide to leave, retire, or are fired.

Screenplays are no different. They have a definite beginning, middle, and end.

It is the *foundation of dramatic structure*.

If you don't believe the paradigm, check it out. Prove me wrong. Go to a movie – go see several movies – see whether it fits the paradigm or not.

If you're interested in writing screenplays, you should be doing this all the time. Every movie you see then becomes a learning process, expanding your awareness and comprehension of what a movie is, or is not.

You should also read as many screenplays as possible in order to expand your awareness of the form and structure. Many screenplays have been reprinted in book form and most bookstores have them, or can order them. Several are already out of print, but check your library or local university theater arts library to see whether or not they have screenplays available.

I have my students read and study scripts like *Chinatown*, *Network*, *American Beauty*, *The Shawshank Redemption*, *Three Days of the Condor*, *The Hustler* (in paperback, *Three Screenplays* by Robert Rossen, now out of print), *Annie Hall*, and *Harold and Maude*.

These scripts are excellent teaching aids. If they aren't available, read any screenplay you can find. The more the better.

The *paradigm* works.

It is the *foundation* of a good screenplay.

Go to a movie. After the lights dim and the credits begin, ask yourself how long it takes you to make a decision about whether you "like" or "dislike" the movie. Be aware of your decision, then look at your watch.

If you find a movie you really enjoy, go back and see it again. See if the movie falls into the paradigm. See if you can determine the breakdown of each act. Find the beginning, middle, and end. Note how the story is set up, how long it takes you to find out what is going on in the movie, and whether or not you're hooked into the film, or dragged into it. Find the plot points at the end of Act I, and Act II, and how they lead to the resolution.

TALKING HEADS

Some years ago I saw a short film by a French filmmaker. It was about a man who walks into a McDonald's restaurant on the Champs-Elysées and buys a huge order of french fries. He finds a strategic spot in the restaurant and suddenly begins throwing french fries all over; at the people, against the walls, on the floors, on the ceiling, everywhere. The people are furious. (It's a serious comedy.) Many of the patrons challenge him but the man pays no attention and continues throwing the fries. The police arrive. They warn the man.

But as soon as they leave, the man goes right back to throwing french fries. Soon, the entire restaurant is in an uproar. At the peak of their frenzy the man whips out a camera and starts taking pictures. Photograph after photograph is taken, and then in a blazing cut we see these same people as the subject of huge photographs now on display in a prestigious art gallery in Paris. It is only then that we understand that this man is a renowned artist, and the same people who were cursing him at McDonald's are now spending huge bucks to buy these so-called works of art.

Art is freedom of expression. That's the idea behind the film; the idea is dramatized.

The European screenwriter takes an idea and dramatizes it. The American screenwriter takes an idea and builds it into a story to dramatize it. If we took the idea that art is the freedom of expression, we would create a story. So we would search for a visual metaphor, a visual arena, to show our character, the artist, struggling for some kind of new art form, a new expression.

Who is this artist? What is his life like? What are the relationships in his life? Where is he in his career? What is his relationship to art? What about his friends, his family? Is he successful or not?

These questions all have to be answered to create a story. We take this information, the answers to these questions (*writing is really the ability to ask the right questions*) so we can structure this idea into a story line; we set up the artist's life in Act I, show who he is and what he does. The Plot Point at the end of Act I will be the particular incident or event which finally shows him that, in order to survive, he must change his artistic expression and seek out a new form, maybe even a new medium. We set up a crisis period in his life.

Act II would focus on his struggle to create a new form, and all the conflicts and hardships he has to endure in his professional, personal, and private lives. Gradually, we see him forging his first new form of expression, and then, at Plot Point II, he finds out what he has to do to generate a fusion of environmental and performance art.

Act III would show him executing his new "art form" in the McDonald's restaurant. Which is the entire French film.

Art is the freedom of expression – as seen from the European point of view and an American perspective.

The point to be made is that whether it's a European or American film, the problems of screenwriting are the same; it doesn't matter in what language or culture the script is being written.

A screenplay is a story told in pictures, and there will always be some kind of problem when you *tell the story through words*, and not pictures.

It seems obvious, but I have had this experience over and over again: some of the writers I've worked with forget that a screenplay is a story told in pictures. They feel that if the characters can explain their particular thoughts, feelings, or emotions, the story line will somehow move forward through the character's dialogue, not the action. Through words, not pictures. They think because the character talks a lot there will be insight and dimension; but the truth is that we must see the character in a situation that *reveals* his/her personality, no matter what the conflict or obstacle, whether it is an internal, emotional one, or an external, physical one.

Why is this significant?

Because at this period in our history, we are in a major communications revolution, and the screenplay is a form that is constantly evolving, for film is a combination of both art and science. It is a craft that drifts upon the growth of scientific technology. There are times when the screenwriter writes something and science has to create a technology to make it happen. Like *Terminator 2: Judgment Day*; the special effects had not been created when the script was completed. They hoped the special effects would work, and they did, and because of the science, film took a giant leap forward to making the art of film "more real."

Without the computer graphics created for *Terminator 2: Judgment Day*, we would not have been so affected by the dinosaurs in *Jurassic Park* (David Koepp) or the oddity of *Forrest Gump* (Eric Roth). Or all those morphing commercials that have flooded the television screens.

The computer technology of the nineties literally exploded, creating a global revolution. The Internet, websites, all the on-line systems connect the world. Everywhere people are using the Internet as part of their daily news-gathering ritual, and it is changing the ways we communicate with each other on a global scale. And this revolution is gradually changing the way we see things. We have become a visual society, and are no longer a literate one; the last fifty years have changed all that. No longer do we get our news and opinions from the written word; we get it from CNN, or the local news and the Internet. Our children are computer literate by the age of six, and most of the time they are the ones who are teaching us to use the computer.

This evolution of science and art is creating a new language of film, a more visual way of telling stories for the screen. The language of film is becoming more visual; scripts filled with pages and pages of great dialogue are now considered "too talky." Two people talking in an office or restautant, explaining things to each other, rarely works any more.

This seems to be one of the most common problems in screenwriting. Over and over again, in country after country, most of the stories unfold through dialogue, not action. The characters talk and talk, and this only leads to a story that is dull and boring, developing through events that need to be explained.

Talking heads.

That's not screenwriting, that's stage writing. An essential part of all screenwriting is finding places where silence works better than words, finding the right visual arena, or image, to tell the story. Today's films are much more visual, the character's emotional arc expressed through the character's actions and reactions. "What is character but the determination of incident?" says Henry James. "And what is incident but the illumination of character?"

How people react to the incidents and situations of the story tells us something about who they are: in other words, what they do is who they are.

When I first saw *Forrest Gump*, I thought it was a very, very talky film. Most of the story is told through dialogue along with the voice-over narration. Act I reveals who Forrest is, and his voice-over tells us things we need to know, but the dialogue and images don't contradict each other, they *complement* each other. Forrest tells us he has to wear leg braces because he has "a curved spine," and wearing them will make him "straight as an arrow." At first glance Forrest is dumb, maybe even stupid, as his IQ test states, but "stupid is as stupid does," he says, quoting his mother. And on the surface most people think he's some kind of retard, a "cripple," physically challenged, and this image is shattered when he is chased by the bullies and forced to run for his life. Voice-over and dialogue complement each other, and this technique keeps the story from becoming talky, or dull and sentimental. Forrest is a man who follows his dreams, then makes them come true.

Later, his behavior shows us something else: Forrest Gump is anything *but* a cripple. Though the words, pictures, and actions are different, they complement each other and move the story forward.

The same with *How to Make an American Quilt* (Jane Anderson). Before the story can truly begin, we need to know who this character is. So Finn's narration opens the film when she's a little girl, and tells us about the relationship with her mother, grandmother, and quilting friends, and then, in a beautiful cut to present time, visually tells us what her problem is: her relationship to Sam and how anxious she is about getting married. She tells us that she has trouble completing things; she's working on her third master's thesis because every time she's getting ready to complete it, she moves on to another subject and starts all over again. That, of course, is what her mother did with the men in her life. For Finn it is this fear of commitment that drives the story forward. In the end, however, she learns to follow her heart as the crow leads her to her understanding and final acceptance that Sam is truly her soul mate.

Both these screenplays are studies in character, but in order to reveal who the characters are, and what the obstacles are that confront them, we must see who they are, through their actions *and* their words.

Not through talking heads.

So if you have a problem in that you think your story is being told in words, look for places to illustrate your character's behavior. In *Thelma & Louise* (Callie Khouri) the title characters are packing for a two-day holiday to the mountains. Here's the way Thelma packs: she grabs everything in sight, then throws and stuffs it into the suitcase.

She pulls open her cosmetics drawer and empties the contents into the suitcase. Pulls open another drawer of clothes, dumps it into the already bulging suitcase. And that, we see, is the way she lives.

Contrast this visually to the way Louise packs. They're going away for two days, so she takes two pairs of pants, two blouses, two bras, one bathrobe, two sweaters, two pairs of socks, throws in another pair just for good measure, closes her suitcase, wipes clean the single glass in her spotless kitchen sink, and leaves.

The difference between Thelma and Louise is the difference between night and day, an apple and an orange. The simple illustration of packing the suitcase reveals more about them than dialogue ever could.

Instead of having your characters talk about their situation, let their behavior make the story line unfold in a more visual manner. Action is character; what a person does is who he is. Film is behavior.

It's easy to let your characters' dialogue explain your characters and move the story forward. But a good screenplay is much more than talking heads. It is a story told with pictures, in dialogue, and description, and placed within the context of dramatic structure.

It is the visual arena of action.

THE SUBJECT 2

What is the SUBJECT of your screenplay?

What is it about?

Remember that a screenplay is like a noun – a person in a place, doing his/her "thing." The person is the *main character* and doing his/her "thing" is the *action*. When we talk about the subject of a screenplay, we're talking about *action* and *character*.

Action is *what happens*; character, *who* it happens to. Every screenplay dramatizes action and character. You must know who your movie is about and what happens to him or her. It is a primary concept in writing.

If you have an idea about three guys holding up the Chase Manhattan Bank, you've got to express it dramatically. And that means focusing on your *characters*, the three guys, and the *action*, holding up the Chase Manhattan Bank.

Every screenplay has a subject. *Bonnie and Clyde*, for example, is a story about the Clyde Barrow Gang holding up banks in the Midwest during the Depression, and their eventual downfall. Action and character. It is essential to isolate your generalized idea into a specific dramatic premise. And that becomes the starting point of your screenplay.

Every story has a definite beginning, middle, and end. In *Bonnie and Clyde*, the beginning dramatizes the meetings of Bonnie and Clyde and the forming of their gang. In the middle they hold up several banks and the law goes after them. In the end, they are caught by the forces of society and killed. Setup, confrontation, and resolution.

When you can articulate your subject in a few sentences, in terms of action and character, you begin expanding the elements of form and structure. It may take several pages of writing about your story before you can begin to grasp the essentials and reduce a complex story into a simple sentence or two. Don't worry about it. Just keep doing it, and you will be able to articulate your story idea clearly and concisely.

That is your responsibility. If you don't know what your story is about, who does? The reader? The viewer? If you don't know what you're writing about, how do you expect someone else to know? The writer always exercises *choice* and *responsibility* in determining the dramatic execution of the story. Choice and responsibility – these words will be a familiar refrain throughout this book. Every creative decision must be made by *choice*, not necessity. If your character *walks* out of a bank, that's one story. If he *runs* out of a bank, that's another story.

Many people already have ideas they want to write into a screenplay. Others don't. How do you go about finding a subject?

An idea in a newspaper, or on the TV news, or an incident that might have happened to a friend or relative can be the subject of a movie. *Dog Day Afternoon* was a newspaper article before it became a movie. When you're looking for a subject, your subject is looking for you. You'll find it someplace, at some time, probably when you're least expecting it. It will be yours to do or not do, as you choose. *Chinatown* grew out of a Los Angeles water scandal found in an old newspaper of that period. *Shampoo* grew out of several incidents that happened to a celebrated Hollywood hair stylist. *Taxi Driver* is a story about the loneliness of driving a cab in New York City. *Bonnie and Clyde*, *Butch Cassidy and the Sundance Kid*, *All the President's Men*, grew out of real people in real situations. Your subject will find you. Just give yourself the opportunity to find it. It's very simple. Trust yourself. Just start looking for an action and a character.

When you can express your idea succinctly in terms of action and character, when you can express it like a noun – my story is about this person, in this place, doing his/her "thing" – you're beginning the preparation of your screenplay.

The next step is expanding your subject. Fleshing out the action and focusing on the character broadens the story line and accentuates the details. Gather your material any way you can. It will always be to your advantage.

A lot of people wonder about the value, or necessity, of doing research. As far as I'm concerned, research is absolutely essential. All writing entails research, and research means gathering information. Remember, the hardest part of writing is knowing what to write.

By doing research – whether in written sources such as books, magazines, or newspapers or through personal interviews – you acquire information. The information you collect allows you to operate from the position of choice and responsibility. You can either choose to use some, or all, or none of the material you've gathered; that's your choice, dictated by the terms of the story. Not using it because you don't have it offers you no choice at all, and will always work against you and your story.

Too many people start writing with only a vague, half-formed idea in their heads. It works for about thirty pages, then falls apart. You don't know what to do next, or where to go, and you get angry and confused and frustrated, and just give up.

If it is necessary or possible to conduct personal interviews, you'll be surprised to find that most people are willing to help you any way they can, and they'll often go out of their way to assist you in your search for accurate information. Personal interviews have another advantage: they can give you a more immediate and spontaneous slant than any book, newspaper, or magazine story. It's the next best thing to having experienced something yourself. Remember: the more you know, the more you can communicate. And be in a position of choice and responsibility when making creative decisions.

I recently had the opportunity of working on a story with Craig Breedlove, onetime holder of the World Land Speed Record, and the first man to go 400, 500, and 600 miles per hour on land. Craig created a rocket car that traveled at a speed of 400 miles per hour for a quarter mile. The rocket system was the same system used to land a man on the moon.

The story is about a man breaking the World Water Speed Record in a rocket boat. But a rocket boat doesn't exist, at least not yet. I had to do all kinds of research to find out about my subject matter. What is the Water Speed Record? Where do you go to break the record? Is it possible for a rocket boat to beat the record? How do the officials time the boats? Is a speed of over 400 miles per hour on water possible? Out of our conversations I learned about rocket systems, the Water Speed Record, and designing and building a racing boat. And out of those conversations came an action and a character. And a way to fuse fact and fiction into a dramatic story line.

The rule bears repetition: the more you know, the more you can communicate.

Research is essential in writing the screenplay. Once you choose a subject, and can state it briefly in a sentence or two, you can begin preliminary research. Determine where you can go to increase your knowledge of the subject. Paul Schrader, who wrote *Taxi Driver*, wanted to write a movie that took place on a train. So he took a train from Los Angeles to New York, and when he stepped off the train he realized he didn't have a story. He hadn't found one. That's okay. Choose another subject. Schrader went on to write *Obsession*, and Colin Higgins, who wrote *Harold and Maude*, went on to write the train story, *Silver Streak*. Richard Brooks spent eight months researching *Bite the Bullet* before he put one word on paper. He did the same thing with *The Professionals* and *In Cold Blood*, even though the latter was based on a very well researched book by Truman Capote. Waldo Salt, who wrote *Midnight Cowboy*, worked on a screenplay for Jane Fonda, entitled *Coming Home*. His research included speaking to more than twenty-six paralyzed Vietnam veterans, which resulted in some 200 hours of taped interviews.

If you're writing a story about a bicycle racer, for example, what kind of racer is he? A sprinter or a long-distance racer? Where do bicycle races take place? Where do you want to set your story? In what city? Are there different types of races, or racing circuits? Associations and clubs? How many races are held throughout the year? What about international competition? Does it affect your story? The character? What kind of bikes do they use? How do you become a bicycle racer? These questions must be answered before you start putting words on paper.

Research gives you ideas, a sense of people, situation, and locale. It allows you to gain a degree of confidence so you are always on top of your subject, operating from choice, not necessity or ignorance.

Start with your subject. When you think subject, think action and character. If we draw a diagram, it looks like this:

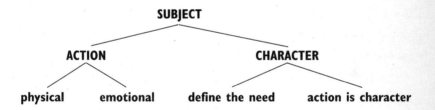

There are two kinds of action – *physical* action and *emotional* action. Physical action is holding up a bank, as in *Dog Day Afternoon*; a car chase, as in *Bullitt* or *The French Connection*; a race, or competition, or game, as in *Rollerball*. Emotional action is what happens inside your characters during the story. Emotional action is the center of the drama in *Love Story*, *Alice Doesn't Live Here Anymore*, and *La Notte*, Antonioni's masterpiece about a disintegrating marriage. Most films contain both kinds of action.

Chinatown creates a delicate balance of physical and emotional action. What happens to Jack Nicholson when he uncovers the water scandal is related to his own feelings about Faye Dunaway.

In *Taxi Driver* Paul Schrader wanted to dramatize the experience of loneliness. So he chose as his image a cab-driver. A cab, like a ship at sea, goes from port to port, fare to fare. The cabbie in his screenplay, as dramatic metaphor, cruises around the city with no emotional ties, no roots, no connection, a lonely, solitary existence.

Ask yourself what kind of story you are writing. Is it an outdoor action-adventure movie, or is it a story about a relationship, an emotional story? Once you determine what kind of action you're dealing with, you can move into your character.

First, *define the need* of your character. What does your character want? What is his need? What drives him to the resolution of your story? In *Chinatown* Jack Nicholson's need is finding out who set him up, and why. In *Three Days of the Condor*, Robert Redford needs to know *who* wants to kill him, and *why*. You must define the need of your character. What does he want?

Al Pacino holds up the bank in *Dog Day Afternoon* to get money for a sex-change operation for his male lover. That is his need. If your character creates a system to beat the tables in Las Vegas, how much does he need to win before he knows if the system works or doesn't? The need of your character gives you a goal, a destination, an ending to your story. How your character achieves or does not achieve that goal becomes the action of your story.

All drama is conflict. If you know the *need* of your character, you can create obstacles to fulfill that need. How he overcomes those obstacles is your story. Conflict, struggle, overcoming obstacles, are the primary ingredients in all drama. In comedy, too. It is the writer's responsibility to generate enough conflict to keep the audience, or reader, interested. The story always has to move forward, toward its resolution.

And it all comes down to knowing your subject. If you know the action and character of your screenplay, you can define the need of the character and then create obstacles to realizing that need.

The dramatic need of three guys holding up the Chase Manhattan Bank is directly related to the action of holding up the bank. The obstacles to that need create the conflict – the various alarm systems, the vault, the locks, the security measures that must be overcome for them to get away. (No one robs a bank to get caught!) The characters must plan what they do, and that means extensive observation and research, and preparing a well-coordinated plan of action before they can even attempt the robbery. The days of Bonnie and Clyde simply "dropping by" and robbing a bank are over.

In *Midnight Cowboy*, Jon Voight comes to New York to hustle women. That is his need. It is also his dream. And, as far as he's concerned, he's going to make a lot of money and satisfy a lot of women in the process.

What are the obstacles he immediately confronts? He gets hustled by Dustin Hoffman, loses his money, doesn't have any friends or a job, and the women of New York don't even acknowledge his existence. Some dream! His need collides head-on with the harsh reality of New York City. That's conflict.

Without conflict there is no drama. Without need, there is no character. Without character, there is no action. "Action is Character," F. Scott Fitzgerald wrote in *The Last Tycoon*. What a person does is what he *is*, not what he *says*!

When you begin to explore your subject, you will see that all things are related in your screenplay. Nothing is thrown in by chance, or just because it's cute or clever. "There's a special Providence in the fall of a sparrow," Shakespeare observed. "For every action there is an equal and opposite reaction" is a natural law of the Universe. The same principle applies to your story. It is the subject of your screenplay. KNOW YOUR SUBJECT!

Find a subject you want to treat in screenplay form. Reduce it to a few sentences in terms of action and character, and write it out.

THE PROBLEM SHEET

The Need to Explain

✎ Visual arena is too static

✎ Story seems too confusing, too complex

✎ Events are contrived, predictable

✎ The stakes are not high enough

✎ Not enough visual action

✎ The story builds too slowly, and wanders off in too many directions

✎ Characters are not defined

✎ Characters are too internal

✎ Everything has to be explained

✎ The minor characters seem to take over the action

Recently, I read a screenplay about a boat builder on the coast of the Yucatán who is forced out of business by an unscrupulous politician demanding bribes and he reacts by floundering in a lifestyle of drunkenness and bankruptcy. He becomes his own victim. Since the story is about his redemption, we see him go through his transformation by joining a rebel action to help bring about the fall of a Central American dictator.

It is a good action piece, has great visual locations, and has the potential to be a good vehicle for the character's growth, change, and development. But the screenplay didn't read that way and the story's potential was never realized. And here's why.

The writer opens the screenplay with a scene where the main character delivers a boat, which he has been commissioned to build for the politician. Everything seems fine; there are nice visuals but no real conflict as the scene is meant to reveal the extraordinary design abilities of the main character, the builder. The boat he has built is a piece of art. And, the way the scene is written, both characters seem satisfied with the transaction.

Cut to five years later. The main character is now struggling for work, has the reputation of being unreliable, an alcoholic, and we see him lose several jobs. And his design abilities are never again mentioned or play any significant part in the rest of the screenplay.

At Plot Point I, needing money he accepts a job as a crew member on a large fishing boat, and during a severe storm the boat is shipwrecked further up the coast. Forced to remain in this thinly populated area while they repair the boat, they discover a band of guerrillas who enlist them in their cause to overthrow the local political dictator, a man groomed and supported by the same unscrupulous politician that ran the main character out of business. He joins them and takes the first steps along his journey of repentance that leads to recognizing his own self-worth and regaining his dignity as a person.

That's the story. During the first part of my read things seemed OK, but around page 30 I began to notice that my attention was wandering, and the more I read the more aware I became of it. So I knew something was wrong; something was not working as well as it should. I started looking for the source of the problem. What I began to see was that the main character was constantly reacting to the situation, and somehow he seemed to be lost on the page in relationship to the other characters. He was involved in every scene, yes, but he seemed bland and uninteresting, and just seemed to disappear off the page.

The first symptom.

I went back to the very beginning of the screenplay, and started looking. When I examined the opening scene between the builder and the politician, I saw there was no conflict at all between the two men, either internal or external. And in the next scene, when the writer cuts into the story five years later, we see the *reaction* to the man's plight. What I saw immediately is the main character was always explaining his actions, his situation, his life, to the other characters. That stopped the forward flow of the story as the character has to justify why he is here, what he is feeling, what his dramatic need is. Because the reader isn't shown the character falling into the pit of hard times during those five years, he or she has to be informed what happened. If you don't show it, you have to say it; you have to explain it for the story to move forward. And when that happens your character is lost on the page, caught in the web of talking heads.

We don't have to explain everything in a screenplay; we just have to know what happens. It's not a question of not explaining anything, it's a question of how the explanation is written. In *Apollo 13* the very first shot under the credits is the actual newsreel footage of the first Apollo astronauts caught in the fire in the space capsule. Three lives were lost, and if we didn't see this, we would have to explain it, because it is the spark that ignites the whole story, moving Jim Lovell's crew up to the Apollo 13 slot in the NASA schedule.

Many times during the screenplay the screenwriter will have the urge, or the need, to explain things – things about the character, things about the situation, things about the story – because if something is not clear, it has to be explained. It is one of the most common problems screenwriters encounter. The process of screenwriting always remains the same, but the creative problems are always different. If there is an action scene, and we don't know what's happening, it has to be explained at some point in order to keep the story moving forward. That's the only way to hold the reader or audience's interest.

Exposition is a key element in the craft of screenwriting. The word itself is defined as the "information necessary to move the story forward."

There are two ways to write exposition; set it up through dialogue, or dramatize it through pictures. Exposition is the easiest, yet the hardest, dialogue to write. It states the obvious, which makes it easy, because the screenwriter simply puts down what needs to be said in order to move the story forward; hard, because the dialogue is usually so obvious, it's embarrassing.

How do you solve this? By finding ways to dramatize the exposition. By finding the right visual image, or metaphor, to serve the story line.

Broken Arrow opens with a fight scene in which Deke (John Travolta) is boxing with his air force copilot, Hale (Christian Slater). Who these characters are, and the forces working upon them, are revealed by their actions. Deke doesn't hesitate to use any maneuver he can to defeat Hale. Hale believes in the rules, fighting hard to win, but never sacrificing his humanity. There is a dialogue between the two men within the riveting action of this scene, and it reveals everything we need to know about the characters throughout the film. And, in the end, the motivation, or purpose, behind Deke's plan to steal two nuclear weapons only needs to be explained in a few lines of dialogue.

In *Jurassic Park* we create the explanation of the story, the premise, in the little interactive presentation that the Sir Richard Attenborough character puts on for his visitors. In his demonstration that is part animation and interactive live action, he explains that mosquitoes in the Jurassic Park era would feed off the dinosaur's blood, then get trapped in tree sap, which would fossilize to amber. Now, millions of years later, the amber is pierced and the mosquito fossil's blood siphoned off. And through the advancement of genetic technology we have been able to create dinosaur clones.

That's the entire premise of the movie. If we don't believe that, then "there is no willing suspension of disbelief" and the story becomes a joke.

So how do they set this up? They explain it, sure, with both pictures and images. But first you have to grab the reader or the audience's attention, so the script opens with an action sequence that reeks of mystery and suspense. That's Spielberg's great gift as a filmmaker. We don't yet know what's going on, but we know something really big and mean is inside that cage of steel and it's very, very dangerous.

Take a look at this sequence again. Nothing is explained. All we can do is watch as one of the technicians is yanked and hurled around like a piece of lettuce in a tossed salad. And at the end of the sequence we still don't know what's going on. But we're hooked; that's why in action-oriented films, or certain types of mysteries or thrillers, the writer opens with an action sequence that needs to be explained at some point during the story. It's called the *"inciting incident."* A primary rule in screenwriting is that we discover what's going on at the same time the character does. The main character and the reader or audience are connected by the mutual effort of trying to figure out what's going on.

Things have to be explained; sometimes through words, sometimes through pictures. It all depends on the type of screenplay you're writing.

The premise established, we meet the main characters, Sam Neill and Laura Dern, in the Badlands of South Dakota, working the dinosaur digs, using the latest computer technology to isolate the fossil remains of some prehistoric animal. A helicopter lands, bringing the Attenborough character, who convinces the two scientists that if they come with him and "sign off" on his project, he will fund their research digs for the next three years. They can't say no to that. They do need funds to continue their research project.

That's the first ten pages of the screenplay; nothing is explained, but it's all been set up, the situation demonstrated.

Now the second ten pages of dramatic action begin, and here it becomes necessary to establish exposition; there is the need to explain. As the characters drive through the open landscape, they see their first dinosaurs, living and breathing and roaming as they were during the Jurassic Period. It's like being lost on an island in time. Again, as we see the explanation, we don't need to explain it through dialogue.

And this is where the questions of "how they do it" and "why they do it" become important and do need to be explained. That's when we have the little interactive presentation explaining the science and technology, set amid the activity of the high-tech laboratory. The other characters are introduced and now we're ready to begin the "true" story.

At Plot Point I they enter Jurassic Park and the massive gates swing shut. Everything has been set up and explained, the characters introduced. Some explanations are part of the visual arena; for example, when they enter the park they see a cow being hoisted into a compound. The young girl is appalled as we hear a vicious roar then witness a lot of activity within the trees and then we see the empty harness, broken and bloody, being lifted out. Nothing needs to be said; no words are necessary. It's feeding time. We see the same thing with a goat chained to a post. Sitting. Waiting. A short time later, after the storm hits, we see only the chain swinging back and forth, empty. Then the T-rex is upon them.

A screenplay is a story told with pictures, so we have to create the pictures that reveal the story and keep it moving forward; then exposition and the need to explain are kept at a minimum.

The problem with so many screenwriters is that they rely too heavily on dialogue to move the story forward. In some screenplays, like the one mentioned at the front of this chapter, scene after scene deals with some kind of explanation about something that's already happened.

The result: the story moves too slowly, and seems to wander in several different directions. And despite the characters constantly seeming to explain themselves, the impression is that they are not well-defined, are passive instead of active. Washed out on the page. In the story about the boat builder in the Caribbean, it became necessary for the screenwriter to explain everything because *certain scenes had been omitted in the story line*. That makes it a problem of *Plot*.

In *Jurassic Park* the exposition is presented with a combination of visual elements in order to move the story forward; the introduction of the Sam Neill and Laura Dern characters on the fossil dig in the South Dakota Badlands shows us who these characters are, so the story doesn't become bogged down in explanations, as the writers weave the threads of the story line.

When you're writing a screenplay you have to explain things, that's part of the nature of the medium, but the real question is in *how you do it*. Whether through dialogue or pictures.

Think about it. If you feel there's something not quite working in your script, take a look at the *Problem Sheet* and see whether you're explaining too much. Here's what you can do.

First, you're dealing with an action and a character, and then you're creating conflict, so we have to know what your character is thinking and feeling in this particular situation. If you start explaining too many things, your story line becomes *confused* or *complex*, because you always have to explain what's happening to your main character. To fix it you have to add elements to the story line (*Plot*) and many times these dramatic events seem *contrived* and *predictable*. And if your story is moving forward mainly through dialogue, it becomes *talking heads*, and when that happens some of the *lesser characters start taking over the action*.

To solve this kind of problem you need to rethink your story from two points of view, from the visual as well as the character aspect. Do your scenes have enough of a visual dynamic? Or, do they take place in offices, rooms, and restaurants? In other words, does your screenplay go from INTERIOR to INTERIOR to INTERIOR to INTERIOR with hardly any EXTERIORS anywhere? If you are explaining things too much, one of the first symptoms you look for is whether the story is too closed or too narrow, and if it is, then you have to open it up visually.

Here's an example from a script that one of my students wrote. The story, a period piece set in the forties, is about a woman pilot who wants to compete in an aerial race flying a World War II fighter plane that has only been flown by men. During the story she has to battle the prejudice against her, her own fear that she may not be able to do it, as well as other obstacles. And because there is a lot of information that has to be given about the main character, the writer started to explain too many things.

First, I have to say that this entire exercise is taken out of context and is totally speculative. The scene I am going to excerpt is between the main character, Kate, and her boyfriend Holt, also a pilot, who reluctantly supports her in her quest to be the first woman to fly this plane in competition.

KATE

I'm a little nervous, that's all. Whatever possessed me to think I could do this?

HOLT

This … meaning the race? How is this different from mounting an exhibit at the museum?

(where she works)
You plot, plan, research, study, talk to a
lot of people, and the day the thing
opens, you're a wreck.

KATE

Do you think of Chris? Ever?
  (a friend who died flying the same plane)

HOLT

Sure. He was my best friend. I think of
him a lot. Especially today. He'd be real
proud of you.

KATE

You think so?

HOLT

I know it.
  (He hugs her.)
You scared?

KATE

A little.

HOLT

Good. A little scared is good. It keeps
you alert … Hey, if you're not good
enough, you won't qualify here either.
But if you do qualify, you're as good as
any man up there.

KATE

  (grinning)

Maybe better.

HOLT

Maybe. You'll enjoy it, once it starts.
You'll see. I love you, Kate, I don't want
you to do anything you don't want to do.
We can quit now. Just tell me what you
want to do.
    (She looks at him)
That's what I thought.

He lifts her from her perch and carries her to the bed.

HOLT

We have plenty of time before your briefing.

And then we cut to the next scene at the airport.

Words and phrases like *nervous, scared, Do you think about Chris? I love you*, all explain feelings, they don't show them. When that happens, the dialogue becomes too direct and tells us what the characters are thinking and feeling. That seems to empty the lines of conflict, and the scene becomes bland and somewhat dull. There is no subtext in the scene; the subtext is what is not said during the scene, all those hidden thoughts or feelings that are the core of what the scene is really all about.

What's the best way to fix this?

I think to really be effective, this particular scene has to be structured from the very beginning of the scene. It should be mentioned that this kind of problem can be solved either through *Plot* or *Character*. I'm approaching it through *Plot* because we have to *see* Kate in her environment to know that she can actually compete and hold her own in the flying race. That means we have to see her flying the plane more, so we can learn how she handles it, and the ideal way to do that would be to show her flying the plane and being unable to control it on some level; maybe she finds it difficult to land, or she loses control of the plane and finds it very difficult to regain control in the air. We need to create some conflict with her, something that might put her in jeopardy. This is missing in the screenplay. To show that also means showing her in various stages of her professional, personal, and private life. (That's why this solution is approached from the category of *Plot*.)

For example, Holt says that in an exhibit at the museum (Kate is assistant director), "You plot, plan, research, study, talk to a lot of people, and the day the thing opens, you're a wreck." All true, but we've not seen this side of her character yet in the screenplay. We've only seen bits and pieces of her at the museum, and never under any kind of stress or pressure. In order to really open up the script, we have to show her in some kind of emergency situation, which she handles. All drama is conflict. As I like to say, without conflict there is no action; without action there is no character; without character there is no story. And without story there is no screenplay.

What makes *The Silence of the Lambs* so effective is that Clarice Starling (Jodie Foster) is a student at the FBI Academy and over and over again we see her in the training environment. We see her skill with a gun, in hostagelike situations, on the firing range, in the library, and she discovers the severed head of a murder victim, so we know that when she comes face to face with the serial killer in the basement, she can hold her own. We know that she can take care of herself and this has carefully been structured into the story line from the very beginning. The first time we see her she's running the obstacle course, and we learn in the next scene that she ranks in the upper quarter of her class, comprised of both men and women.

If we had not seen that she could take care of herself in dangerous situations, then the ending of the film would have been totally unsatisfying; there would be no "willing suspension of disbelief" and we wouldn't buy it at all.

In the story about the woman pilot, a possible way to approach the scene and make it more visually effective without explaining things is to *add new scenes* to set up this scene. Then you can use the emotional currents to make it more potent and energetic. That's why the problem can be solved through *Plot*.

We can also approach it from *Character*, and that means going deeper into the relationship between Kate and Holt. In this particular draft of the script Kate and Holt have been together a little over two years. We don't know much about this relationship, other than what has been explained through the dialogue. He's there for her, supportive in her need, but there's no *past* to this relationship. It has to be created by the writer, with written essays about how they met, their past relationships; who they were with, how long it lasted, what happened that led to their breakup. These things have to be known, otherwise they will not be defined and will have to be explained.

There's another part of the scene that can be explored, and that's the relationship with "Chris," the friend of Holt's who died in the plane crash before the story begins. So far, he's only been talked about, never shown. That's the kind of scene that would affect the present scene directly; Chris's crash was not included in the script, but if we had seen it, and its effect on the characters, we might have been able to set up the relationship between Holt and Chris as well as between Kate and Chris. If we knew this relationship, we could get deeper into the emotional context of the scene at hand. Both characters could be struggling with their feelings in this scene; Holt with his memory of Chris, and his fear for Kate, and Kate in her relationship with Chris, her own fear she must confront, and her relationship with Holt, the man she loves. Remember *Top Gun*; it's this element of the Tom Cruise character conquering his own fear that drives the entire screenplay. It would add a much deeper dimension to the scene.

Instead, all the emotional nuances of the scene are approached through dialogue, explained rather than seen or felt. Because the emotional forces working on the scene were not prepared deeply enough, the presentation seems confined to the surface, lacking in depth. We don't know what Kate's thoughts and feelings are except what she says.

It's true that this is only one scene in the entire screenplay. But look how indicative it is; the whole screenplay is written in this tone, and it lacks a force and an energy that should be driving a story like this. Film is a visual medium and it must be approached both through its action and its character.

Otherwise, you just have to explain everything.

THE CREATION OF CHARACTER 3

How do you go about creating character?

What is character? How do you determine whether your character will drive a car, or ride a bicycle? How do you establish a relationship between your character, his action, and the story you're telling?

Character is the essential foundaton of your screenplay. It is the heart and soul and nervous system of your story. Before you put a word on paper, you must know your character.

KNOW YOUR CHARACTER.

Who is your main character? Who is your story about? If your story is about three guys holding up the Chase Manhattan Bank, which one of the three characters is the *main character*? You must select one person as the main character.

Who is the main character in *Butch Cassidy and the Sundance Kid*? Butch is. He is the man making the decisions. Butch has a great line where he broaches one of his usual wild schemes to Sundance, and Robert Redford just looks at Paul Newman, doesn't say a word, and turns away. And Newman mutters to himself: "I got vision and the rest of the world wears bifocals." And, it's true. Within the context of that screenplay, Butch Cassidy *is* the main character – he is the character who *plans* things, who *acts*. Butch leads and Sundance follows. It is Butch's idea to leave for South America; he knows their outlaw days are numbered, and to escape the law, death, or both, they must leave. He convinces Sundance and Etta Place to go with him. Sundance is a *major* character, not the *main* character. Once you establish the main character, you can explore ways to create a full-bodied dimensional character portrait.

There are several ways to approach characterization, all valid, but you must choose the best way for you. The method outlined below will give you the opportunity to choose what you want to use, or not use, in developing your characters.

First, establish your main character. Then separate the components of his/her life into two basic categories: *interior* and *exterior*. The interior life of your character takes place from birth until the moment your film begins. It is a process that *forms* character. The exterior life of your character takes place from the moment your film begins to the conclusion of the story. It is a process that *reveals* character.

Film is a visual medium. You must find ways to reveal your character's conflicts *visually*. You cannot reveal what you don't know.

Thus, the distinction between *knowing* your character and revealing him or her on paper.

Diagrammed, it looks like this:

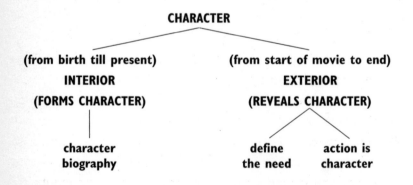

CHARACTER

(from birth till present)	(from start of movie to end)
INTERIOR	**EXTERIOR**
(FORMS CHARACTER)	**(REVEALS CHARACTER)**
character biography	define the need action is character

Start with the *interior* life. Is your character male or female? If male, how old is he when the story begins? Where does he live? What city or country? Then – where was he born? Was he an only child, or did he have any brothers or sisters? What kind of childhood did he have? Happy? Sad? What was his relationship to his parents? What kind of child was he? Outgoing, an extrovert; or studious, an introvert?

When you start formulating your character from birth, you see your character build in body and form. Pursue this through his school years, then into college. Is he married, single, widowed, separated, or divorced? If married, for how long and to whom? Childhood sweetheart; blind date; long courtship or none?

Writing is the ability to ask yourself questions and get the answers. That's why I call developing your character creative research. You're asking questions and getting answers.

Once you've established the interior aspect of your character in a character biography, move into the *exterior* portion of your story.

The *exterior* aspect of your character takes place from the moment your screenplay begins to the final fade-out. It is important to examine the relationships within the lives of your characters.

Who are they and what do they do? Are they sad or happy with their life, or life-style? Do they wish their lives were different, with another job, or another wife, or possibly wish they were someone else?

How do you reveal your characters on paper?

First, isolate the elements or components of their life. You must create your people in relationship to other people, or things. All dramatic characters interact in three ways:

1) *They experience conflict in achieving their dramatic need.* They need money, for example, to buy the necessary equipment to rob the Chase Manhattan Bank. How do they get it? Steal it? Rob a person, or store?

2) *They interact with other characters*, either in an antagonistic, friendly, or indifferent way. Drama is conflict, remember. Jean Renoir, the famous French film director, once told me it's more effective dramatically to portray a son of a bitch than a nice guy. It's worth thinking about.

3) *They interact with themselves*. Our main character might have to overcome his fear of prison to pull off the robbery successfully. Fear is an emotional element that must be confronted and defined in order to be overcome. All of us who have been "victims" at one time or another know that.

How do you make your characters real, multidimensional people?

First, separate your character's life into three basic components – *professional*, *personal*, and *private*.

Professional: What does your character do for a living? Where does he work? Is he the vice-president of a bank? A construction worker? A doctor? A scientist? A professor? What does he or she do?

If your character works in an office, what does he do in the office? What is his relationship with his coworkers? Do they get along? Help each other? Confide in each other? Socialize with each other during off-hours? How does he get along with his boss? Is it a good relationship, or is there some resentment because of the way things are going, or inadequate salary? When you can define and explore the relationships of your main character to the other people in his life, you're creating a personality and a point of view. And that is the starting point of characterization.

Personal: Is your main character single? Widowed, married, separated, or divorced? If married, whom did he marry? When? What is their relationship like? Social or isolated? Many friends and social functions, or few friends? Is the marriage solid, or is your character thinking about, or participating in, extramarital affairs? If single, what is his single life like? Is he divorced? There are a lot of dramatic possibilities in a divorced person. When you have doubts about your character, go into your own life. Ask yourself – if you were in that situation, what would you do in your character's place? Define the personal relationships of your character.

Private: What does your character do when he or she is by himself? Watch TV? Exercise – jogging or bicycling, for example? Does he have any pets? What kind? Does he collect stamps or participate in some interesting hobbies? In short, this covers the area of your character's life when he or she is alone.

What is the *need* of your character? What does he or she want in your screenplay? *Define the need of your character*. If your story is about a racecar driver racing in the Indianapolis 500, he wants to win the race. That is his need. Warren Beatty's need in *Shampoo* is to open up his own shop. That need propels him through the action of the screenplay. In *Rocky*, Rocky's need is to be on his feet at the end of 15 rounds with Apollo Creed.

Once you define the need of your character, you can create obstacles to that need. Drama is conflict. You must be clear on your character's need so you can create obstacles to that need. This gives your story a *dramatic tension* often missing from a novice's screenplay.

If we diagram the concept of character, it would look like the example below.

The essence of character is *action*. Your character is what he does. Film is a visual medium, and the writer's responsibility is to choose an image, or picture, that cinematically dramatizes his character. You can create a dialogue scene in a small and stuffy hotel room, or have the scene occur at the beach. One is visually closed; the other is visually open and dynamic. It's your story, your choice.

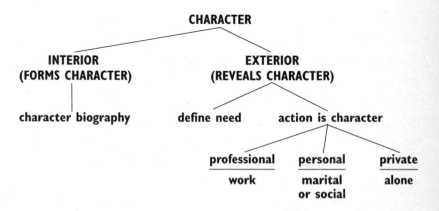

A screenplay, remember, is a story told with pictures. And "every picture tells a story," sings Rod Stewart. Pictures, or images, reveal aspects of character. In Robert Rossen's classic film *The Hustler*, a physical defect symbolizes an aspect of character. The girl played by Piper Laurie is a cripple; she walks with a limp. She is also an emotional cripple. She drinks too much, has no sense of aim or purpose in life. The physical limp underscores her emotional qualities – *visually*.

Sam Peckinpah does this in *The Wild Bunch*. A character played by William Holden walks with a limp, the result of an aborted hold-up some years before. It represents an aspect of Holden's character, revealing him to be an "unchanged man in a changing land," one of Peckinpah's favorite themes; a man born ten years too late, a man out of time. In *Chinatown* Nicholson gets his nose slit because, as a detective, he's "nosy."

Physical handicap – as an aspect of characterization – is a theatrical convention that extends far back into the past. One thinks of *Richard III*, or the use of consumption or VD that strike the characters in the dramas of O'Neill and Ibsen, respectively.

Form your characters by creating a character biography, then reveal them by their actions and possible physical traits.

ACTION IS CHARACTER.

WHAT ABOUT DIALOGUE?

DIALOGUE is a function of character. If you know your character, your dialogue should flow easily in line with the unfolding of your story. But many people worry about their dialogue; it might be awkward and stilted. It probably is. So what? Writing dialogue is a learning process, an act of coordination. It gets easier the more you do. It's OK for the first sixty pages of your first draft to be filled with awkward dialogue. Don't worry about it. The last sixty pages will be smooth and functional. The more you do it, the easier it gets. Then you can go back and smooth out the dialogue in the first part of the screenplay.

What is the function of dialogue?

Dialogue is related to your character's need, his hopes and dreams.

What should dialogue do?

Dialogue must communicate information or the facts of your story to the audience. It serves two basic functions: either it moves the story forward, or reveals information about the character. Dialogue moves the story forward. Dialogue reveals character. Dialogue must reveal conflicts between and within characters, and emotional states and personality quirks of character; dialogue comes out of character. If the dialogue does not serve either one of these two functions, then take it out.

KNOW YOUR CHARACTER.

Take your subject idea of action and character. Choose your main character and select two or three major characters. Write character biographies or three to ten pages, or longer if necessary. Start from birth and carry it into the present, until the story starts. This applies to past lives as well, if you like.

Isolate the three Ps to create your main character's relationships during the screenplay. Think about your people.

THE PROBLEM SHEET

What Is Character?

- The main character explains too much about himself/herself
- Main character is not very sympathetic
- The main character is too reactive, too internal, seems to disappear off the page
- I am the main character
- All the characters sound the same
- Minor characters are more interesting, stronger than the main character
- Relationships are too vague, not clearly defined
- Dialogue is too literary, too flowery, too obvious

The problem of creating real people in real situations can be so varied and so challenging that trying to define them is like trying to capture infinity in a glass. Generations of noted writers, from Aristotle to Ibsen, Eugene O'Neill to Arthur Miller, have struggled valiantly to articulate the art and the craft of creating good characters.

It is difficult to capture a "true human being" on paper, and more difficult in screenwriting, because we're dealing in pictures, not words. Great writers have always had this need to explain how they create character. One of the most profound literary theorists was Henry James, the great nineteenth-century American novelist. James was fascinated with the art and craft of writing, and approached it like a scientist, the same way his brother, William James, the famous psychologist, was occupied with the dynamics of the human mind. Henry James wrote several essays trying to document and capture the intricacies of creating character. In one of those essays mentioned earlier, James posed a literary question: "*What is* character *but the determination of incident? And what is* incident *but the illumination of character?*"

It's a profound statement.

Does that mean the character determines the incident? Or the incident creates character? This is something that should be analyzed and understood, especially when dealing with character. If you're trying to solve a problem relating to character, whether an action, reaction, or dialogue, it is essential to understand the dynamics of *Character*. If you examine the *Problem Sheet*, most of the symptoms described could apply to any number of problems or situations found within the characters. Most of the problems listed deal with defining and articulating the actions and dimension of character by relating to his thoughts, feelings, and emotions.

Waldo Salt, the great screenwriter of *Coming Home* and *Midnight Cowboy*, among others, when asked about how he went about creating characters, replied that first he chose a simple dramatic need and then added on to it, and colored it until it became a universal chord common to Everyman.

What is the dramatic need of your character? Do you know it? Can you articulate it? Can you trace it through the events of the story so it reflects a depth, and a change in the character? First of all, how do you determine whether you have a problem? Look at the *Problem Sheet*: do you feel your character is talking too much, or explaining too much about the story or characters? Do the characters sound the same? Do you think that you're the main character? Does your character seem to disappear off the page? Do other characters seem to overshadow your main character? This is a common problem and applicable to all sorts of situations. Remember, there's no *one way* to approach the problem of creating better character; there are many ways. The only rule you have to follow is whether it works or not.

The first thing you need to do in solving a problem of *Character* is determining what the problem is. Identify it. Define it. As you read through the material looking for any tell-tale signs or symptoms, you have to trust yourself and your instincts; if you feel this little "tug" of discomfort, that's usually an indicator that something is not working as well as it should.

What's the best way to approach solving the problem of *Character*? Start at the beginning; ask yourself the question *What is Character?*

That's the question Henry James explored when he began his inquiries into the nature of character. In a screenplay the story always has to move forward, from beginning to end, whether in a linear or a nonlinear fashion. The way you drive your story forward is by focusing on *the actions* of the *character*. As mentioned before, every scene in a screenplay should fulfill one or two functions: either it moves the story forward, or it reveals information about the character.

So what is *Character*? *Action is character; what a person does is who he is, not necessarily what he says.* Film is behavior. Because we're telling a story in pictures, we must show how the character acts and reacts to the incidents and events that he or she must confront and overcome. If you read your script again through the eyes of your character, and you begin to sense and feel that your characters are not as sharp or defined as you think they ought to be, and you want to make them stronger, more dimensional, and universal, the first thing you must determine is whether they're an *active force* in the screenplay; do they *cause* things to happen, or do things *happen to* them? It's one of the more prevalent problems of *Character*.

Take another look at the *Problem Sheet*; you'll see several symptoms common to main characters who seem to react to the events of the story. It's so important to remember that when you're writing the screenplay, the main character must always *cause things to happen*; not that she doesn't react to incidents or events some of the time, but if she is *always* reacting to events, she becomes passive, weak, and that's when she seems to disappear off the page. Lesser characters appear more interesting than the main character, and seem to have more life and flamboyance.

James's observations that character is determined by incident and that the incident determines character is really at the heart of the writing of screenplays.

Character is character. When executed properly, James's comment is an epiphany; just look at *Thelma & Louise*. The script sets up these two people by showing who they are. Louise, unmarried, a waitress, has a boyfriend, Jimmy, a musician, who's playing a gig on the road and hasn't called her once in three weeks. She's upset and resolves that she's not going to be home when he returns. So she decides to go to a friend's cabin in the mountains without telling him where she is. When he does arrive home, she just won't be there. That's the back story.

Thelma, on the other hand, appears to be a "ditzy" housewife; her kitchen is a mess, and her "breakfast," a little nibble from a frozen candy bar, which she puts back in the freezer only to whip it out for another bite, reveals an aspect of character; we *see* who she is by what she does, her actions.

Her husband, Darryl, an arrogant, egotistical fool, is a high-school hero whose best years are behind him. He treats her with so little respect that she has to lie to him just so she can go away for the weekend with her friend. "You get what you settle for," Louise remarks to her on the road.

Her personality is revealed by the way she packs her suitcase. She's going away for the weekend, and this will be the first time she's been away from her husband, but she doesn't know what she needs to take with her, so she takes everything. In contrast Louise only takes two each of the things she needs. Film is behavior.

Act I sets up their relationship, so when they pull into the parking lot of the Silver Bullet, the "dramatic hook," we get to learn more about their relationship with the men in their lives. By the time Harlan tries to rape Thelma, their characters have already been established. When Louise interferes, Harlan, using the foulest language, tells her to leave them alone, and Louise totally loses it; she pulls the trigger, kills Harlan, and in that one second their lives and destiny have changed. Plot Point I. It is this *incident* of being two fugitives on the run that will alter and define their character. The impulse to pull that trigger came out of an experience in Louise's past. This past event and how it affects present time will be covered in more depth in Chapter 13.

That change is what the whole script is about; it is the incident that really determines their character. Their flight to Mexico becomes a journey of self-discovery that eventually leads to their death; and this awareness of only a few choices left reveals that they have nothing in their "past life" to go back to; they have burned their bridges and have literally "run out of world," as writer Callie Khouri says. Their destiny has been determined by their actions, and those actions have revealed who they really are. It is a journey of self-discovery. They now understand there is no way back. You can't step into the same river twice.

"What is character but the determination of incident? And what is incident but the illumination of character?"

What is the particular incident or event that triggers the action of your screenplay? Once you know this key incident, then you can measure and evaluate how your character acts or reacts. In *Twister* the situation is set up in a back story situation where the two main characters (Helen Hunt and Bill Paxton) have filed for divorce, and when the script opens the papers are ready to be signed. The little opening sequence, in which a family races to the storm cellar to outrun a twister, shows us the dramatic need of the Helen Hunt character. Because she has lost her father to a twister, she has grown up and become a noted storm chaser. The Bill Paxton character wants to be free so he can marry his girlfriend, Melissa (Jami Gertz), and get on with his life and become a TV weatherman. From that point there really is no story; it's simply the storm chasers racing after the four twisters that becomes the subject and structure of the screenplay. These four encounters are the glue that holds everything together.

In *American Beauty*, Lester (Kevin Spacey) sees the young girl Angela (Mena Suvari). Seeing her literally changes his life. Remember the first few lines of voice over in the film: "My name is Lester Burnam, I'm 42 years old, and in a year, I'll be dead... In a way, I'm dead already." The whole screenplay revolves around that incident.

So what kind of problem do you see with your character? Is he or she too talky, too passive, or does the dialogue all sound the same, or do the other characters stand out more? Find out what it is. Locate and define it on the *Problem Sheet*. Can you define what you think the problem is? Imagine how it would look to you if the problem were already solved. Are your relationships clear, the emotional dynamics planted, and the character's arc charted? It doesn't matter whether you're writing an action, thriller, love story, or comedy. Character is character.

What makes good character? Four things: *dramatic need*, *point of view*, *attitude*, and *change*. In order to really solve the problem of *Character*, it's essential to go back into your character and rebuild the foundations of his or her life.

What is your character's *dramatic need*? That is, *what does your main character(s) want to win, gain, get, or achieve during the course of your screenplay*? Can you define it? Articulate it?

The *dramatic need* is what drives your character through the story line. In most cases you can express the dynamic need in a sentence or two. The dramatic need of *Twister*, for example, is to find a way to release all those little weather balls into the heart of the twister. In *Thelma & Louise* the dramatic need is to escape safely to Mexico, and that's what drives the two characters. Or, in *Apollo 13*, the dramatic need is to return the astronauts safely to earth.

But it didn't start out that way. When the story began, the dramatic need was to walk on the moon, and that changed when the oxygen tank blew. The dramatic question then being not whether they were going to land on the moon but whether they'd be able to survive and return to earth safely.

Many times the dramatic need will change during the course of the story. If your character's dramatic need does change, it will usually occur at Plot Point I, which is the true beginning of your story. Louise killing Harlan at Plot Point I forces the action in a new direction; instead of spending a weekend in the mountains, Thelma and Louise have become fugitives from the law. They must escape safely. Or, in *Dances With Wolves*, John Dunbar's dramatic need is to go to the farthermost point of the frontier. But when he finally reaches Fort Sedgewick, Plot Point I, his dramatic need is now to learn how to adapt to the land and create a relationship with the Sioux.

What about your character's *point of view – the way he or she views the world*? This is usually a belief system, and as the psychologists say, "What we believe to be true, is true."

There's an ancient Hindu scripture titled *Yoga Vasistha*, which states that "*the World is as you see it.*" That means what's inside your head – your thoughts, feelings, emotions, memories – are reflected outside, in your everyday experience. It is our mind, how we *see* the world, that determines our experience.

In *The Shawshank Redemption*, after almost twenty years in the Shawshank Prison, Red has acquired a cynical point of view because, through his eyes, *hope* is simply a four-letter word. His spirit has been so crushed by the prison system that he declares to Andy, "Hope is a dangerous thing. Drive a man insane. It's got no place here. Better get used to the idea." And it is his emotional journey that leads him to the right understanding, which is that "hope is a good thing," as Andy tells him.

Andy, of course, has a different point of view; he believes that "there are things in this world not carved out of gray stone. That there's a small place inside of us they can never lock away. Hope." And that's what keeps Andy going in prison, that's what made him sacrifice a week of his life in "the hole," just so he could hear the two opera singers singing an aria from Mozart.

The third thing that makes good character is *Attitude*. *Attitude* is defined as a "manner or opinion," and is usually an intellectual pose or decision. Being "macho" is really an attitude. I'm tough, see, I'm better than you are, it's all attitude. Have you ever gone into a store to buy something and found yourself dealing with a person who does not want to be there at all, or a person who looks down on you? Have you ever walked into a fancy restaurant not wearing the "right" clothes? It's that kind of judgment where someone is convinced "they're right" and "you're wrong"; judgments, opinions, evaluations, all stem from attitude. Understanding your character's attitude is allowing him to reach out and touch his humanity.

The Truth About Cats and Dogs (Audrey Wells) is a delightful romantic comedy that is entirely based on the character's attitude. Abby, the character played by Janeane Garofalo, is a woman who lives *by her opinion, her attitude*; the decision she's made is that all men really want in a woman is a pretty face and a great body. This attitude governs her behavior through the entire film. And Nora, the Uma Thurman character, just takes it for granted that she's not very bright. You know, the "dumb blond" with the heart of gold. Marilyn Monroe is a legend because of her attitude expressed through the parts she played. Both Abby and Nora have to learn that their attitude is "not who they really are." Their journey through the film is to accept themselves for who they really are.

An *attitude*, as differentiated from point of view, can be right or wrong, good or bad, positive or negative, angry or happy, cynical or naive, superior or inferior, liberal or conservative. Do you know anybody who "thinks they're better than anyone else"? Or people who feel the world owes them a living; or "it's really who you know" that determines your success factor in this world.

Sometimes it's difficult to separate the *point of view* from the *attitude*. Many of my students struggle to define these two qualities, but I tell them it really doesn't matter; when you're creating the basic core of your character, you're taking one large ball of wax and in this case, pulling it into four separate pieces. The parts and the whole, right? Who cares whether one part is the *point of view* and another the *attitude*? It doesn't make any difference; the parts and the whole are really the same thing. So if you're unsure about whether a particular character trait is a *point of view* or an *attitude*, don't worry about it. Just separate the concepts in your own mind.

The fourth element that makes up good character is *change*. Does your character change during the course of the screenplay? If so, what is the change? Can you define it? Articulate it? Can you trace the emotional arc of the character from the beginning to the end? In *The Truth About Cats and Dogs* all three characters undergo a change that brings about a new awareness of who they really are. Abby's final acceptance that Brian really loves her *for who she is* completes the character arc of the change.

In *The Shawshank Redemption* Andy endured prison life only until he learned that it could be proven someone else had committed the murder of his wife and her lover. Only when the warden refuses to help him get a new trial and Tommy, the witness, is killed does he refuse to serve any longer. When he entered the prison he considered himself guilty, even though he hadn't pulled the trigger, but now he has served "his time" and realizes the moment has come for him to escape. As we learn later, he has been preparing this for years.

Having a character change during the course of the screenplay is not a requirement if it doesn't fit your story. But since change is a universal constant of life, if you can impel a change within your character, it creates an arc of behavior and adds another dimension to the material.

These ingredients are what make up the foundation of good character; if you know these four elements, *dramatic need*, *point of view*, *attitude*, and *change*, you can approach any problem that deals with character.

BUILDING A CHARACTER

We've touched upon the foundations of character creation through the character biography and isolating his relationships.

Now what?

How do you take the *idea* of a person, as it exists in scrambled, fragmented form, and make him or her into a living, flesh-and-blood person? A person you can relate to and identify with?

How do you go about "putting life" into your characters? How do you build character?

It's a question that poets, philosophers, writers, artists, scientists, and the Church have pondered since the beginning of recorded time. There is no definite answer – it's part and parcel of the mystery and magic of the creative process.

The key word is "process." There is a way to do it.

First, create the *context* of character. Then fill the context with *content*. *Context* and *content*. These are abstract principles that offer you an invaluable tool in the creative process. They comprise a concept that will be used often in the book.

This is *context*:

Imagine an empty coffee cup. Look inside it. There is a space inside that cup. The *space* inside *holds* the coffee, tea, milk, water, hot chocolate, beer, or whatever liquid is the *content* of that cup.

The cup *holds* the coffee. The space inside the cup that holds the coffee is *context*.

Hold that image and the concept will become clear as we progress.

Let's explore the process of building a character in terms of context.

First, define the NEED of your character.

What does your character want to achieve, or get, during the course of your screenplay?

Is it a million dollars? To rob the Chase Manhattan Bank? To break the Water Speed Record? To go to New York and become a "midnight cowboy," like Jon Voight? To sustain the relationship with "Annie Hall"? To realize a life-long dream to become a singer in Monterey, California, like Alice in *Alice Doesn't Live Here Anymore*? To find out "what's going on?" like Richard Dreyfuss in *Close Encounters of the Third Kind*? These are all character needs.

Ask yourself – what is the NEED of your character?

Then, do the character biography. As suggested, write anywhere from three to ten pages, or more if you like. Find out who your character is. You may want to start with your character's grandparents to obtain a clear picture for yourself. Don't worry about how many pages you write. You are beginning a process that will continue to grow and expand during the creative preparation of your screenplay. The biography is for you and does not have to be included in the screenplay at all. It is only a tool for you to use in creating your character.

When your character biography is completed, move into the *exterior* portion of your characters. Isolate the *professional*, *personal*, and *private* elements of your character's life.

That's the start point. *Context*.

Now, let's explore the question WHAT IS CHARACTER?

What *is* character?

What do all people have in common? We're the same, you and I; we have the same needs, the same wants, the same fears and insecurities; we want to be loved, to have people like us, to succeed, be happy and healthy. We're all the same under the skin. Certain things unite us.

What separates us?

What separates us from everyone else is our POINT OF VIEW – how we view the world. Every person has a point of view.

CHARACTER IS A POINT OF VIEW – it is the way we look at the world. It is a *context*.

Your character could be a parent, and thus represent a "parent's" point of view. He or she could be a student and would view the world from a "student's" point of view. Your character could be a political activist, like Vanessa Redgrave in *Julia*. That is her point of view, and she gives her life for it. A housewife has a specific point of view. A criminal, a terrorist, a cop, a doctor, lawyer, rich man, poor man, a woman, liberated or otherwise – all present individual and specific *points of view*.

What is your character's point of view?

Is your character liberal or conservative? Is he or she an environmentalist? A humanist? A racist? Someone who believes in fate, destiny, or astrology? Someone who puts their faith in doctors, lawyers, the *Wall Street Journal*, and the *New York Times*? A believer in *Time*, *People* and *Newsweek*?

What is your character's point of view about his work? About his marriage? Does your character like music? If so, what kind? These elements become specific and integral parts of your character.

We all have a point of view – make sure your characters have specific and individual points of view. Create the *context*, and the *content* follows.

For example, your character's point of view may be that the indiscriminate of whales and dolphins is morally wrong, and he supports that point of view by giving donation, volunteering his services, attending meetings, participating in demonstrations, wearing a T-shirt with SAVE THE WHALES AND DOLPHINS on it. Dolphins and whales are two of the most intelligent species on the planet. Some scientists speculate they may be "smarter than man." Scientific data supports the fact that the dolphin has never hurt or attacked a member of the human species. There are numerous tales of dolphins protecting downed World War II flyers and navy men against the vicious onslaught of sharks. There must be a way to save these intelligent life-forms. Your character, for example, may boycott tuna as a means of protesting the senseless slaughter of whales and dolphins by commercial fishermen.

Look for ways your characters can support and dramatize their points of view.

What else is character?

Character is also an ATTITUDE – a *context* – a way of acting or feeling that reveals a person's opinion. Is your character superior in attitude? Inferior? A positive person, or a negative? Optimistic or pessimistic? Enthusiastic about life or job, or unhappy?

Drama is conflict, remember – the most clearly you can define your character's need, the easier it becomes to create obstacles to that need, thus generating conflict. This supports you in creating a tense, dramatic story line.

It's an effective rule in comedy as well. Neil Simon's characters usually have a simple need that sparks conflict. In *The Goodbye Girl*, Richard Dreyfuss plays an actor from Chicago who sublets a New York apartment from a friend, and when he arrives he finds the apartment "occupied" by his friend's former roommate (Marsha Mason) and her young daughter (Quinn Cummings). He wants in, and she won't leave – the apartment is hers, she claims, and possession *is* nine-tenths of the law. This conflict is the beginning of their relationship, based on the attitude that each is "right."

Adam's Rib is another case in point. Written by Garson Kanin and Ruth Gordon, it stars Spencer Tracy and Katharine Hepburn as two attorneys – husband and wife – pitted against each other in the courtroom. Tracy is prosecuting a woman (Judy Holliday) charged with shooting her husband, and Hepburn is defending her! It is a magnificent comedic situation dealing with basic questions of "equal rights" for men and women. Made in 1949, it anticipated the struggle for women's rights, and remains a classic American film comedy.

Define your character's need, then create obstacles to that need.

The more you know about your character the easier it is to create dimension within the fabric of your story.

What else is character?

Character is PERSONALITY. Every character visually manifests a personality. Is your character cheerful? Happy, bright, witty or outgoing? Serious? Shy? Retiring? Charming in manner, or uncouth? Sloppy, surly, without wit or humor?

What kind of personality does your character have?

Is she nonchalant, devilish, or mischievous? These are all personality traits – they all reflect character.

Character is also BEHAVIOR. The essence of character is action – what a person does is what he is.

Behavior is action. Suppose a character in a Rolls-Royce steps out of the car, locks it, then crosses the street. He sees a dime in the gutter – what does he do? If he looks around to see if anyone is watching, sees no one, then bends down and picks up the coin, that tells you something about his character. If he looks around, sees someone watching him, and *does not* pick up the dime, that, too, tells you something about his character, dramatized by his behavior.

If you establish your character's behavior within a dramatic situation, you may give the reader or audience insight into their own lives.

Behavior tells you a lot. A friend of mine had the opportunity of flying to New York for a business interview. She had mixed feelings about going. The interview was for a prestigious and high-salaried job she wanted; but she didn't know whether she was willing to move to New York. She wrestled with the problem for more than a week, then finally decided to go, packed her bags and drove to the airport. But when she parked her car at the airport, she "accidentally" locked her keys inside the car – with the motor running! It's a perfect example of a behavioral action revealing character; it told her what she knew all along – she didn't want to go to New York!

A scene like that illustrates a lot about character.

Does your character get angry easily, and react by throwing things as Marlon Brando did in *A Streetcar Named Desire*? Or, does he get intensely *angry*, like Marlon Brando in *The Godfather*, and smile grimly and not show it? Is your character late, or early, or on time for appointments? Does your character react to authority the way Woody Allen does in *Annie Hall* when he tears up his driver's license in front of a policeman? Every action and speech based on individual character traits expands our knowledge and comprehension of your characters.

If you reach a point in your screenplay where you don't know what your characters will do in a certain situation, go into your own life and find out what you would do in a similar situation. You're the best source material you have. Exercise it. If you created the problem, you can solve it.

It's the same in our everyday lives.

It all comes out of knowing your character. What does your character want to achieve during the course of a screenplay? What is it that drives him or her forward to achieve that goal? Or not achieve it? What is his need, or purpose, in your story? Why is he or she there? What do they want to get? What should we, the reader or audience, feel about your people? That's your job as a writer – to create real people in real situations.

What else is character?

Character is also what I term REVELATION. During the story we learn something about your character. In *Three Days of the Condor*, Robert Redford orders lunch at a neighborhood restaurant. We learn he is intelligent, a writer "with the finest collection of rejection slips in the world," and later we dramatically accept the way he adapts to his new situation – someone is out to kill him and he doesn't know *who* or *why*. Something is revealed to us about the character of Robert Redford in the tightly written screenplay by Lorenzo Semple, Jr., and David Rayfiel.

The screenwriter's function is to reveal aspects of character to the reader and audience. We must learn something about your character. During the progression of your screenplay, your character usually learns something about his plight in terms of the story at the same time the audience does. In this way, character and audience share in the discovery of plot points that sustain the dramatic action.

IDENTIFICATION is also an aspect of character. The recognition factor of "I *know* someone like that" is the greatest compliment a writer can receive.

ACTION IS CHARACTER – what a person does is what he is, not what he says.

All the above-mentioned character traits – point of view, personality, attitude, and behavior – are related and will overlap each other during the process of building your character. This puts you in a position of choice; you can choose to use some, or all, of these character traits, or none of them. Knowing what they are, though, expands your command of the process of building a character.

It all springs from character biography; out of your character's past comes a point of view, a personality, an attitude, behavior, a need and purpose.

When you are in the writing process you will find it will take you anywhere from twenty to fifty pages before your character starts talking to you, telling you what *they* want to *do* and *say*. Once you've made contact, and established a connection with your people, they'll take over. Let them do what they want to do. Trust your ability to exercise the choice of action and direction during the "word on paper" stage.

Sometimes your characters might alter the story line and you may not know whether to let them do it, or not. Let them do it. See what happens. The worst that can happen is you'll spend a few days realizing you made a mistake. It's important to make mistakes; out of accidents, and mistakes, springs creative spontaneity. If you've made a mistake, simply rewrite that section and it will all fall into place.

One of my students came to me and told me he was writing a drama, complete with unhappy or "tragic" ending. But at the beginning of the third act, his characters started acting "funny." Gag lines started coming out, and the resolution became funny, not serious. Every time he sat down to write, the humor just poured out; he couldn't stop it. He became frustrated, and finally gave up in despair.

He came to me almost apologetic. In all honesty, he explained, he didn't know what to do. I suggested that he sit down and start writing. Let the words and dialogue come out as they wanted to. If it's funny, let it be funny. Just write and complete the third act. Then he could see what he had. If it was funny all the way through and he didn't like it, all he had to do was put it in a drawer somewhere and file it away, and then go back and write the third act the way he wanted to in the first place.

He did it, and it worked. He threw out the comedy version of the third act, then wrote it serious, the way he wanted to. The comedy was something he *had* to do, something he *had* to get out. It was his way of avoiding "completing" the screenplay. Many times, writers on the verge of completing a project will hold on to it and not finish it. What are you going to do after it's complete? Do you ever read a book and hate to finish it? We all do it. Just recognize it as a natural phenomenon, and don't worry about it.

If it ever happens to you, simply write the material the way it comes out. See what happens. Writing is always an adventure; you never really *know* what's going to come out. The worst that can happen if you make a mistake is that you spend a few days rewriting something that didn't work!

Just don't expect your characters to start talking to you from page 1. It doesn't work that way. If you've done your creative research and KNOW YOUR CHARACTER, you're going to experience some resistance before you break through and get in touch with your people.

The end result of all your work and research and preparation and thinking time will be characters who are real and alive and believable; real people in real situations.

That's what we all aim for.

Go into your character biographies and establish a specific *point of view* for your main character and three major ones. Create an *attitude*, and think about some *behavioral* or *personality* traits that will reveal your characters. Think about *context* and *content*. You're going to run into them again.

THE PROBLEM SHEET

Circle of Being

- The main character is dull, boring
- The characters lack depth, dimension
- The character's emotional arc is too thin and undefined
- There's not enough conflict
- The emotional stakes are not high enough
- The dialogue is stilted, awkward
- All the characters sound the same
- The main character explains too much
- The dramatic need of the main character is vague, undefined
- There seems to be a lack of tension
- Story goes off in too many directions

There are times during the screenwriter's journey when the story works well, with a tense and dramatic plot, and all the characters seem to have interesting backgrounds, but there's a nagging sense that the dialogue is thin, maybe "tinny," filled with clichés, and doesn't seem to go anywhere. Something seems not to be working, and you really can't put your finger on what it is; maybe you've had the script read by a few friends or associates, and they tell you they "like it." When you press them further, more often than not they point to the dialogue and say it may need polishing.

Dialogue is a *function of character*. It's true that some writers have a better ear for writing dialogue than others; they're just born with a natural talent and ability, and it's really a gift. But if you know your character well enough, if you feel comfortable inside his or her skin, the dialogue will be individual and appropriate and capture the "essence" of that character. The dialogue may not be that great but it'll still work. The function of dialogue, remember, is simple; dialogue either moves the story forward or reveals information about the character. You can say things, explain things, or show things in order to reveal character.

If you look at the *Problem Sheet*, most of the symptoms listed there deal with dialogue. After all, dialogue is one of the most striking qualities about your character. It tells us who he or she is, sets up the exposition, moves the story forward, adds humor, and can be one of the elements used in transition. If you think your dialogue is too thin, or your characters all sound alike, or if you explain too much, the best way to solve the problem is to go back to the beginning and rethink your character.

One of the ways to accomplish this is by doing an exercise I call the *"Circle of Being."* It's a process, really, a process that allows you to uncover some kind of an incident or event in your character's life that emotionally parallels and impacts the story line; it's an event that happens to your main character when he or she is between the ages of ten and sixteen. This is an age period where some kind of traumatic event could conceivably occur that would affect the entire course of your character's life. It might be the death of a parent, or of a loved one; it could be physical abuse that results in a deep emotional scar, it could be a physical event or injury, and quite possibly a move to a new city or country.

Thelma & Louise is a very good example. As Louise was growing up in Texas she was raped and discovered she was unable to get justice. It was this incident that "formed" her behavior and ultimately led to the incident that powers the entire story line, the shooting of the rapist Harlan in the parking lot. It explains why she pulled the trigger in the first place, and why she couldn't set one foot inside the state of Texas. If you think about it, the *Circle of Being* is a valuable exercise, or a tool, that you can use in crafting, enriching, and enhancing your character. If you go into your character's life and ask yourself what traumatic incident might have occurred to him or her between the ages of ten and sixteen, see what happens.

Why ten and sixteen? Because it happens to be a very important age in the person's life. The noted behaviorist Joseph Chilton Pierce states that there are four major growths, or spurts, of human intelligence in our lives. The first occurs when the child is about a year old, when he or she learns to walk. The second spurt occurs about age four, when the child learns that he or she has an identity, as a boy or girl, and has a given name. At this age, the child is able to communicate his or her needs.

The third stage, or spurt, in the growth of human intelligence occurs when the child is about nine or ten; that's the age when he or she understands that he has a definite personality, a singular and individual voice. The young person is learning to question authority, forming his or her own opinions, and starting "speaking his mind." This is a very vital time in the life of the child.

The fourth stage, and the most important developmental spurt, according to Pierce, occurs when the person is about fifteen or sixteen. The teenager. That's the age when the teenager rebels against everything and tries to find his/her own voice, suddenly understands that his parents are no longer the center of the universe, and looks outward into the world for role models, seeking forms of behavior, like clothes or hair, that are acceptable to his peers and express who he is. He has an identity. It's a period of life that is so influential that it will form a subconscious identity, or impression, for the rest of his life.

The *Circle of Being* is a wonderful tool that lets you dig into the emotional substance and dimension of your character. Just look how it affected Louise; when Callie Khouri wrote the screenplay, she did not refer to the incident at all except to state that Louise had no intention whatsoever of stepping one foot inside Texas, no matter what the reason. But the director, Ridley Scott, thought the audience should know about this event and how it triggered Louise's actions, so he had Khouri make a few references to the incident; Hal, the Harvey Keitel character, even told her, "I know what happened in Texas," and Thelma guesses that "it happened to you, didn't it?" referring to the rape attempt. To the very end Louise never responds to this.

This incident is the reason for Louise to stubbornly insist that they're not going to cross the Texas state line. Because the only way to get to Mexico without going through Texas is to go through

Oklahoma, the decision ultimately costs them their lives. This *Circle-of-Being* incident is relived in the parking lot when she sees Harlan attempting to rape Thelma, and she totally loses it.

Thelma & Louise is an extraordinary film, but many writers I've talked to didn't like it for this very reason; they say Louise "over-reacted" by shooting Harlan, and could not "willingly suspend their disbelief" enough to get into the story after that. But I think they didn't get that it was really the sixteen- or eighteen-year-old rape victim Louise who pulled that trigger, not Louise in present time.

If you can go back into your character's life and create an incident or event that becomes an influence or a force working on your character, you can enhance the texture of any character you're writing. By creating the *Circle of Being* you can generate a plot complication that will expand the depth and dimension of your character and literally drive the story forward.

I call this process the *Circle of Being* because if you picture your character as a circle and then section him/her off, as you would divide a piece of pie, you section off the physical, emotional, mental, and intellectual incidents or events that make up the fabric of your character. In this way you can create a well-rounded portrait of your character, and then everything you do – all the emotions, thoughts, and feelings you dramatize – works to expand your characterization.

One of the most powerful examples of *Circle of Being* and the way it can be used is the incident that powers the action in Arthur Miller's play *Death of a Salesman*. Now, even though it's a play, and it's explained through dialogue, it is this *Circle of Being* that makes the character of Willy Loman so powerful. The story, about an ageing salesman forced to come to grips with the loss of his dream, is a masterpiece and one of the greatest American plays of our time.

Sometimes, depending on your story line, you might want to verbally express the *Circle-of-Being* incident, that in other stories, like *Thelma & Louise*, is stronger because it's not explained. You, as writer, don't necessarily have to explain it, but – and it's a very big *but* – you have to know it. Because if you don't know it, who does?

In this particular scene from *Death of a Salesman*, Willy Loman has come to see his "boss" – actually, the son of the man he worked for for over thirty-four years – with his dreams and the American dream shattered to pieces. Now, with the last vestige of his dignity, he has come to ask the son of his boss if he can give up the road, literally his way of life, and work at the main office. Willy Loman is a salesman, and he doesn't know anything else.

Willy is asking Howard, the son, for a job on the floor, and first he asks for $65 a week, then drops his request to $50 a week, and then, in his final humiliation, he is literally forced to beg for $40 a week. But this "is a business, kid, and everybody's gotta pull his own weight," and Willy Loman's sales figures have not been the best lately. Willy responds by retreating into his memory and tells Howard what drew him to becoming a salesman: "When I was a boy – eighteen, nineteen," he says, " I was already on the road. And there was a question in my mind as to whether selling had a future for me ..."

He pauses for a long moment, then continues on. "[That's when] I met a *salesman* in the Parker House. His name was Dave Singleman. And he was eighty-four years old, and he'd drummed merchandise in thirty-one states. And old Dave, he'd go up to his room, y'understand, put on his green velvet slippers – I'll never forget – and pick up his phone and call the buyers, and without ever leaving his room, at the age of eighty-four, he made his living. And when I saw that, I realized that selling was the greatest career a man could want. 'Cause what could be more satisfying than to be able to go, at the age of eighty-four, into twenty or thirty different cities, and pick up a phone, and be remembered and loved and helped by so many different people? Do you know when he died – and by the way he died the *death of a salesman*, in his green velvet slippers in the smoker of the New York, New Haven and Hartford, going into Boston – hundreds of salesmen and buyers were at his funeral."

That's Willy Loman's dream; that's what drives him to get up every morning and hit the road, and when that dries up, the dream is dead and life is not worth living. That's the *Circle-of-Being* experience in

Willy's life. Remember Andy Dufresne's line in *The Shawshank Redemption*. "Hope is a good thing, maybe the best of things, and no good thing ever dies." But if the dream collides with reality, as in the case of Willy Loman, and all hope is lost, then what's left? The death of a salesman.

That's the force of the power of the *Circle of Being*. Once you've created an experience or an incident that affects the life of your character, then you can base the emotional arc on that incident and have the character confront and resolve (or not resolve) the experience. It becomes a way of embellishing the depth and dimension of character, to create a strong and defined point of view and attitude, and contains within it the spark of conflict.

In *The Silence of the Lambs* the *Circle of Being* plays a prominent role in generating the transformation of the character Clarice Starling, played by Jodie Foster. *The Silence of the Lambs* is the story of a young FBI trainee tracking down a serial killer, but before she can accomplish that she must come to grips with an incident that occurred in her own life when she was about ten years old. That incident was the death of her father, a small-town policeman killed during an attempted robbery. But if you dig deeper into this extraordinary script (from the extraordinary novel by Thomas Harris), you'll find that this is really a story of Clarice's relationship with "three fathers." Jack Crawford (Scott Glenn) is the director of the Behavioral Science Division at the FBI Academy, and gives her the break to interview Hannibal Lecter that directly leads to her becoming involved in hunting and capturing the serial killer, Buffalo Bill. Hannibal Lecter (Anthony Hopkins) is her mentor, guiding and teaching her what to look for when pursuing a serial killer. It is through their relationship and his relentless psychological prodding and insight that she is forced to confront the death of her father, something she had buried deep in her unconscious.

It is a *Circle-of-Being* event. Because of her father's death she was sent away to live with an uncle in Montana. One night she was awakened by the screaming of lambs being slaughtered. She tried to rescue one of the baby lambs, but was caught and sent away to live in an orphanage. It is Hannibal Lecter's forcing her to look at this emotional issue that ultimately frees her of it, and at the end of the film she can build a new life, both in a committed relationship as well as in her job as a top-notch FBI agent. But only when she can confront this incident of the past, the *Circle of Being*, can she be free. It's exactly the same with Louise in *Thelma & Louise*, except Louise never gave up holding on to the rape and it literally cost her her life. But Clarice, under the tutelage of Lecter, was strong enough to be able to surrender to it, deal with it, and let it go.

The Silence of the Lambs ends with Clarice receiving a diploma, and at the reception following her graduation she receives a phone call from Hannibal Lecter asking "if the lambs have stopped screaming ..." And then he shares his "admiration" for her by telling her that "I have no plans to call on you, Clarice, the world being more interesting with you in it. Be sure you extend me the same courtesy." He is the first to acknowledge Clarice's transformation from the trainee with an incomplete childhood into a trained professional, ready to fly.

So if you feel that your character is too thin and one-dimensional, too passive or too reactive, or speaks in dialogue that is too direct or explanatory, one way to solve the problem is to go back and explore his or her life in terms of the *Circle of Being*.

THE PROBLEM SHEET

Dull, Thin, and Boring

- The characters are too talky and explain too much
- Dialogue is too direct, too specific
- Characters are flat, one-dimensional
- There is no Circle of Being
- All the characters sound the same
- Characters' actions are predictable
- The material is flat and boring

✎ Relationships between the characters are weak and undefined

✎ I am saying the same thing over and over again

✎ There is no subtext; the story is too thin

How often have you read something you've written and, much to your chagrin, found that the writing seems to be flat, the characters thin and one-dimensional, and as much as you want to deny it, or as much as you defend it, you cannot escape the cold, hard fact that everything you've written seems to be dull, thin, and boring? When you think about all the time and effort you've spent and all the sacrifice and denial you've had to ensure to end up with pages like *this* – oh, Lord!

Believe it or not, this is a pretty common refrain among screenwriters. And of course, as little as you want to admit it, it's true most of the time; the writing *is* dull, *is* thin, and *is* boring. Once you've recovered from the shock of your discovery, then you can rack your brains trying to figure out what you can do to make it work, or make it better; you might think about adding some action scenes, or adding a subplot, or creating a new character, like a love interest, perhaps, simply to liven up the action.

That's one solution, and it may work in some screenplays, at least for a little while. So you decide to add some new scenes and a new character to liven up the action, but when you sit down to reread the material, you suddenly notice something else isn't working and you get that sinking feeling in the gut that you really haven't fixed the material, you've just put a Band-Aid over it. Given it a paint job.

The real problem, *the source* of what makes the material dull, thin, and boring, persists. In despair, though hoping for the best, you have friends read it, but all they can tell you is that this or that needs to be strengthened, and when you try to fix this or that the material still doesn't seem to work. You're more confused than ever.

What usually happens when you're trapped in this scenario is that your confusion gives rise to frustration, which then funnels up into anger, then smothers you in a blanket of despair and depression, and the ultimate result is that you just give up. It's all part of the writer's journey.

The problem is still there. What can you do about it?

Let's take it step by step. The first thing you need to do is simply stop writing, sit back, and try to gain some kind of objective overview of your screenplay. And just because you're not writing does not mean *you're not writing*; it just means you're rethinking a creative problem. A script that's "dull, thin, and boring" is best approached from the perspective of *Character*.

In one of his literary essays, Henry James suggested that the main character of a story occupies the center of a circle, and all the other characters surround him in an outer circle. James felt that each time the main character comes in contact with one of the other characters, some light or knowledge or insight should be revealed about the main character. And he used the image of someone entering a dark room and turning on the lamps in each corner, illuminating a specific part of the room.

James called this the *"Theory of Illumination."* It's a wonderful tool to use when you want to expand the dimensions of character. In *Witness*, for example, a young Amish boy witnesses the murder of an undercover policeman. John Book (Harrison Ford) attempts to have the boy identify the killer in a series of mug photos and lineups, but they are unsuccessful. So, for lunch, Book takes the boy and his mother for a hot dog. The scene opens with Book picking up the food and setting it on the table. Without looking at the boy and his mother, he heaps some mustard on the dog and takes a big bite. As he's chewing, he notices that Rachel and her son are saying a short prayer over the food. Immediately, Book becomes embarrassed and self-conscious. With a silly little grin on his face he waits until they've finished their prayer before he finishes chewing.

As they eat, she launches into a conversation about what Book's sister (Patti LuPone) had told her about him; she told Rachel that "you [Book] should get married and have children of your own. Instead of trying to be a father to hers. Except she thinks you're afraid of the responsibility." "Oh," Book replies. "Anything else?" "Oh, yes," Rachel continues, getting into it. "She thinks you like policing because you think you're right about everything. And you're the only one who can do anything. And that when you drink a lot of beer you say things like none of the other police would know a crook from a ... um ... bag of elbows. Yes, I think that's what she said."

It's a wonderful little scene. In just a few lines (the scene is less than a page long), we know everything we need to know about John Book. Rachel sheds light on, and illuminates, what kind of person he really is. First, look at his name. It's no accident – he is a policeman who "lives by the book." He thinks he's "right" about everything – this is his *attitude* – and he constantly complains about the policemen he works with. He's unmarried, but he likes kids and "tries to be a father" to his sister's children.

This little scene reveals so much about Book's character. What makes it work so well is that within the body of the scene they're doing something, eating, putting mustard and ketchup on the dogs, not just sitting around talking. Even this little action of eating reveals the different points of view between these two characters. And two different points of view is the first step in generating a substantial source of conflict. In this case it represents a different way of life. As the boy and his mother bless their food, Book just wolfs it down, and so illuminates visually the difference between them.

James's *Theory of Illumination* is a good way to give your character a lot more richness and texture, which, in turn, makes him or her more interesting, full, not thin. In *Witness* the business of preparing the hot dogs for their meal gives the characters something to do during their dialogue scene, which keeps the action moving. And it's all written into the screenplay.

There are many different ways to use the *Theory of Illumination* to reveal information about a character: you can have the main character reveal something about himself or herself to another character (do this only if you can't find another way to reveal the information); or another character might say something about the main character, as in the *Witness* scene. Or maybe a voice-over narration would be appropriate, as in *The Shawshank Redemption*, or *Dances With Wolves*, or *How to Make an American Quilt*, but just make sure this narrative device is appropriate to your story. Don't use a voice-over narration just once or twice during the screenplay, though, it's true, in *Apollo 13* it is used only once, at the very end of the script when Jim Lovell sums up the results of the mission. You can achieve the same purpose using some kind of subtitle, or crawl, or newspaper head-lines. In *Stand By Me* (Raynold Gideon and Bruce Evans), the script ends with the Richard Dreyfuss character sitting at the computer writing the story we've just seen; you might also use some kind of magazine headline or partial story text on a computer screen. Occasionally something about the main character may be revealed in a dream sequence or in a flashback, like Andy's escape in *The Shawshank Redemption*, or maybe a flash-forward (which is basically what *Apollo 13* accomplished with the voice-over at the end).

All of these various tools or devices are effective ways of illuminating some of the visual and emotional aspects of the main character. But you have to be consistent with whatever device you use, because *the integrity of the screenplay must be maintained*. That's what makes *Pulp Fiction* work so well; the humor, along with the nonlinear structure, are woven throughout the film. All the characters are introduced in the beginning and then the three separate stories are played out in their entirety.

Before you decide to use any of these various techniques, however, you must go back to the drawing board of your character. How do you do this? First, make an inventory about the relationships between your main character and the other characters in the story. Can you define these relationships clearly and succinctly? Are they deep enough, or interesting enough? In *Independence Day* (Dean Devlin and Roland Emmerich) the Jeff Goldblum character is very thin in his portrayal; all we know about him is that he still wears his wedding ring even though he's been divorced for three years. The only reason his wife left him, at least that we know of, is because she wanted to advance her career. What about their relationship? Was it working? Harmonious? What about children? What was their marriage like? Although this is a back story, and not necessary to state in the body of the film, it's imperative that the writer knows this in order to achieve the full dimension of character. It's pretty thin in the script; the only reason it works is because this is an "event" film, and, as in *Twister* and *Mission: Impossible*, the special effects are really the star; the main character only leads us to the effects. Most of the time these "event" films are really dull, thin, and boring.

Once you've examined the relationships of your main character, decide which ones need to be expanded, given more texture and dimension. One of the ways to do this is by writing a one- or two-page, free-association (*automatic writing*) essay that redefines the relationship. In this exercise you want to recreate the relationship from the beginning. Where did these characters meet? How long ago? What kind of incidents or events can you create that will help define and clarify and strengthen their relationship?

Creative research means you enter the world of the character in order to define and redefine their lives and relationships. The more you know about your characters and the events of their lives, the more options you have to choose from in order to make them visually interesting and exciting.

Explore their first meeting. What were their thoughts and feelings about each other? What was it that made their friendship ripen or grow, or what was it that caused the relationship to turn sour? How long has this relationship endured? That could mean any relationship between man and woman, boyfriend, girlfriend, boss or associate; it could mean a rivalry on the tennis court or in the courtroom. In films like *Seven* we don't actually know why the Brad Pitt and Gwyneth Paltrow characters left the place they were living and moved to the big city. We really don't need to know, but you better bet that Andrew

Kevin Walker, the screenwriter, knows. Their decision to leave the community they were living in and come to the city is what leads to the powerful conclusion of the film. So if you don't know things about your characters, about the important decisions and events that happened in their lives, who does?

If you feel the characters are talking too much, or the dialogue is too specific or direct, or the characters are flat and one-dimensional, and the material is simply dull and boring, there are several ways to approach the problem.

Let's break it down into three distinct categories: What can you do if the screenplay seems *Dull*? Does the script plod along with excessive dialogue, or do the incidents and events take too long to develop? Or are your descriptions too thick and dense, and do you have a hard time following the narrative line? All these are symptoms of dull writing. What can you do?

First, change the style of your writing. Don't try to write complete, literary sentences. Focus on short, descriptive passages, maybe one-word sentences, where the words are used to accentuate color and humor to the reader.

If you're writing more of a character piece, go back and redefine your characters by writing short, two- or three-page essays dealing with the character relationships. Look for ways to strengthen your characters to make them more interesting. Go into their professional life, their personal life, and their private life, what they do when they're alone. That means hobbies, gardening, exercise classes, raising pets. In *Crimson Tide* the little dog the Gene Hackman character takes everywhere adds to and expands the characterization.

Then, of course, you have to look for conflict; to find ways of going deeper into the scenes in order to achieve maximum dramatic value (MDV) in your character relationships. That means possibly redefining your character's *point of view*, the way he or she looks at the world. Conflict is one sure way to avoid dull writing, but you have to go into your character's life in order to effectively portray this. Conflict, remember, can be internal, like an emotional problem, or external, a threatening force working on the characters, as that induced by the hunt for the aliens in *ID4* or the storms in *Twister*. It's up to you to design and integrate these conflicts into the story line.

You might possibly want to change your character's *point of view*. Look for the opposing points of view during your scenes; what are your characters thinking or feeling about the situation? When your character enters the scene, do you know where he or she has come from? What happened to him or her before the scene occurs? Do you know what the purpose or motivation of this character is in the scene? Does the scene reflect your character's dramatic need? Look within the context of the scene for ways to generate conflict; do the characters have a different point of view in terms of what's at stake in the scene? Is the problem external to them, like a physical or emotional threat? The film *Seven* is a good example of this. The tension between the serial killer, the Kevin Spacey character, and the Brad Pitt and Morgan Freeman characters, is taut and tense because we don't know what's going to happen, though we know something must happen for the story to resolve itself. Remember, in good writing, we discover what's happening at the same time the character does. Reading a screenplay should always be an *act of discovery*. That's why the ending of *Seven* is so memorable.

What do you do if your material is too *Thin*?

Add something to fill it out; either create another character so you can add more scenes, and give more detail to the character, or think about adding an action sequence, and if that's not enough and you need to go deeper into the story line to give it more body and texture, you might think about adding a subplot.

Before you can make any decisions about what to do, go back into each scene and check out the action point of where you entered it. Many times a writer will enter a scene too late and leave it too early, and that results in cutting away from the action before it's fully realized. It dilutes the narrative line and is one of the causes of a script's being too thin. If you go back into the basic construction of each one of your scenes, you can always structure it into beginning, middle, and end. Set up scenes beginning in the preceding scene if possible, then determine what's going to happen in the middle of the scene, and finally the end of the scene, where you pay it off before you segue into your transition for the next scene. It might be a good exercise to list the components that make up the beginning of the scene, the elements that make up the middle of the scene, and what happens at the end; so, you have lists of actions for the beginning, middle, and end of the scene. Then you can take whatever elements you need and structure them into a new scene.

Now, what if it seems *Boring*? You're reading your script and your eyes hurt, your attention wanders, and it's hard to understand what's going on, it's hard to sit still, and you have to fight off the urge to get up to find something to eat, and reluctantly you have to admit to yourself that you're bored to tears. Your worst fears seem to have come true. How do you deal with that?

First, some practical pointers. Nothing turns a reader off more than having to read thick and dense single-line paragraphs that fill up half to three-quarters of a page. To support the reader, make sure your descriptive paragraphs are not longer that four or five sentences. If you've laced your script with long descriptive paragraphs, break them up into shorter paragraphs. Make sure the descriptive prose is not too "thick," or "dense"; a good screenplay should have a lot of white space on the page. You don't have to cut the material, just break it up into new paragraphs every four or five sentences. So many times a screenwriter will write a thick descriptive paragraph that fills up most of the page and it just stops the reading process cold. Lean, clean, and tight. That's what you want in your screenplay.

What else can you do to remove the element of "boring"?

Check your writing style. You want to write in an active, present-tense style, so make your descriptive sentences shorter, tighter. Check the dialogue; is it too wordy, too long, and too explanatory?

Cut it down. Be ruthless. Either dialogue moves the story forward or it reveals character. If it doesn't satisfy these two requirements, cut it.

After you've done this, see if there are places in the text where you can add some kind of action, either a car chase or a kiss; just know that whatever action you choose has to *fit within the fabric of your story line*. Obviously, you can't add something without reason, or something that doesn't fit, or something that's completely out of context. If you check your material carefully you might find a few places where an action sequence, or some humor, might help to relieve the heaviness or density of the reading experience.

After you've made that assessment, move into individual scenes. Are there places where your characters are just talking heads, sitting in a restaurant, driving a car, or walking through the park? What are they doing during the scene? What's happening around them? For example, if they're sitting in a restaurant having an intense conversation, give them something to do. Let them be eating shrimp, for example, or corn on the cob, or let a tooth chip or break; or let the character be coming down with a cold; try to add something to the detail in the scene that the characters have to deal with. If your characters are driving in a car let another driver cut them off and maybe the driver over-reacts, so you've now got two things going on at the same time; the conversation as well as the reaction to the other driver. This adds depth and tension to the action.

In *The Shawshank Redemption*, when Andy Dufresne has locked himself in the warden's office and is playing the operatic aria, the guards and warden are banging on the door. Two different things are going on simultaneously. So look for ways to incorporate any kind of secondary action into your scenes.

When Andy makes contact with Red for the first time, Red is playing catch with a baseball and this action continues through the entire scene. Give your characters something to do during the scene. You don't have to explain anything, just show it.

There will be times when a dialogue scene isn't working. No matter what you do, or how many times you change the character's lines, the scene just doesn't seem to gel. If this is the case, there are a few things you can do: number one, go into the scene and clarify its elements. Define the purpose of the scene. What is the dramatic need of the main character? What does he or she want during the scene; what is he or she doing there? Where did the character come from before the scene began? Where is he or she going after the scene is over? You don't have to write this information into the scene, or explain it, but you, the writer, must know it. Don't assume anything; clarify and define the character's dramatic need until there's no question in your mind about what happened before the scene began and what's going to happen after it's over.

If the scene or sequence still isn't working there's something else you can do: switch the lines of the characters. If Bill's the main character and he's in the scene with his ex-girlfriend, Sally, and he wants something from her, some information, or a package, whatever, simply switch the lines. Give Bill's lines to Sally and Sally's lines to Bill and see what happens. If that doesn't work, rewrite the scene and change the character's point of view. If Bill is the main character, and Sally is a major or minor character, write the scene from Sally's point of view and let Bill be the secondary character. That means you have to enter the scene from Sally's point of view and see the purpose of the scene through her eyes.

This is an amazing little exercise. It removes any resistance you might have to the scene, and somehow dissolves the blocks that keep it from working. Once you've written the scene this way, go back and rewrite it from Bill's point of view. See what happens.

These little things can change the tone and texture of your screenplay. They can add depth and dimension to the scenes so the reading experience does not end up being dull, thin, and boring.

WHICH COMES FIRST – THE CHARACTER OR THE SCREENPLAY?

4

There are two ways to approach a screenplay. One is to get an idea, then create your characters to fit that idea. "Three guys holding up the Chase Manhattan Bank" is an example of this. You take the idea, then "pour" your characters into it: a down-and-out fighter getting an opportunity to fight the Heavyweight Champion of the World, as in *Rocky*; a man holding up a bank to get money for a sex-change operation, as in *Dog Day Afternoon*; a man setting out to break the Water Speed Record, as in *The Run*. You create the characters to fit the idea.

The other way to approach a screenplay is by creating a character; out of that character will emerge a need, an action, and a story. Alice, in *Alice Doesn't Live Here Anymore*, is an example of this. Jane Fonda had an idea about a character in a situation, expressed it to her associates, and *Coming Home* was created. *The Turning Point* by Arthur Laurents emerged from the characters eventually played by Shirley MacLaine and Anne Bancroft. Create a character and you'll create a story.

One of my favorite screenwriting classes at Sherwood Oaks Experimental College was "creating a character." We built a character, male or female, and created an idea for a screenplay. Everyone participated, throwing out ideas and suggestions, and gradually a character began forming and we started shaping a story. It took a couple of hours, and we usually ended up with a solid character and sometimes a pretty good idea for a movie.

We had a good time, and it began a process that managed to parallel the symmetrical chaos of the creative experience. Creating a character *is* a process, and until you've done it, and experienced it, you're more than likely to stumble around awkwardly like a blind man in a fog.

How do you go about creating a character? We started from scratch. I asked a series of questions and the class responded with answers. I took the answers and shaped them into a character. And, out of that character, a story emerged.

Sometimes it worked beautifully; we came up with an interesting character and a good dramatic premise for a movie. Other times it didn't work. But considering the time we had and circumstances of the class, we didn't do badly at all.

The following is an updated, edited and abridged version of a class that worked well. The questions go from general to the specific, and from *context* to *content*. When you read it, you might want to substitute your own answers for the ones we selected and make the story your own.

"We're going to participate in an exercise and create a character," I explained to the class. "I'll be asking questions, and you'll supply the answers."

They agreed to that, amid some laughter.

"OK," I say, "how are we going to start?"

"Boston," Jo booms out from the back of the room.

"Boston?"

"Yeah," he says. "He's from Boston!"

"No," several women yell. "She's from Boston!"

"That's OK with me"; I ask if it's OK with everyone. They agree.

"OK." Our subject is a woman from Boston. That's our start point.

"How old is she?" I ask.

"Twenty-four." Several people agree.

"No," I say. When you write a screenplay, you're writing it *for* someone, for a *star*, someone who is "bankable." Faye Dunaway, Jane Fonda, Diane Keaton, Raquel Welch, Candice Bergen, Mia Farrow, Shirley MacLaine, Jill Clayburgh.

We move on. "What's her name?"

The name "Sarah" comes into my head and we go with it.

"Sarah what?"

Sarah Townsend, I decide. A name is a name.

Our start point becomes Sarah Townsend, a late twenties, early thirties woman from Boston. She is our subject.

Then we create the *context*.

Let's get her personal history. For the sake of simplicity, I'll only give one answer to each question I ask. In class there are several answers given and I select only one. Feel free to disagree with them if you want; make up your own answers, create your own character, your own story.

"What about her parents?" I ask. "Who's her father?"

A doctor, we decide.

Her mother?

A doctor's wife.

"What's her father's name?"

Lionel Townsend.

What's his background?

We toss a lot of ideas around and finally end up with this: Lionel Townsend belonged to the upper strata of Boston society. Wealthy, smart, conservative, he went to medical school at Boston University.

What about Sarah's mother? What was she before she became a doctor's wife?

A teacher. "Elizabeth's her name," someone remarks. Good. Elizabeth might have been teaching when she met Lionel, and she continues teaching grade school during the time he's completing medical school. When he begins his medical practice, she gives up her teaching to become a housewife.

"When did Sarah's parents get married?" I ask.

If Sarah's in her late twenties, her parents must have married in the seventies either during or after the Vietnam war. They've been married almost thirty years. "How'd you figure that out?" someone asks.

"Subtraction," I reply.

What's the relationship between mother and father?

Consistent, and possibly routine. For what it's worth, I add, Sarah's mother's a Capricorn, her father a Libra.

When was Sarah born?

Early seventies. April, an Aries. Does she have any brothers or sisters? No, she's an only child.

Remember, this is a process. For every question asked there are many answers. If you don't agree with them, change them, create your own character.

What kind of childhood did she have?

A lonely one. She wanted brothers and sisters. She was alone most of the time. She probably had a good relationship with her mother until she was in her teens. Then as always, things went haywire between parent and child.

What's the relationship between Sarah and her father?

Good, but strained. Possibly he wanted a son instead of a daughter; to please her father, Sarah became a tomboy.

This antagonizes her mother, of course. Possibly Sarah is always trying to find a way to please her father, to earn his love and affection. Being a tomboy solves this problem, but creates another one by antagonizing her mother. This will figure later in her relationship to men.

Sarah's family is like all other families, but we're sketching in as much detailed conflict as we can for dramatic purposes.

We're beginning to grasp the dynamics of the Townsend family. So far, there's not been too much disagreement, so we continue to explore the *context* of Sarah Townsend.

I remark that many young women search for their father or father figures throughout their lives. It's interesting to use this as a foundation of character, much in the way that many men search for their mothers in many of the women they meet. Not that it happens all the time. Only that it *does* happen; let's be aware of it so we can possibly use it to our advantage.

There's a lot of discussion about this. I explain when you're creating a character you have to compile nuances of character, so you can choose to use them, or choose not to use them. I tell the class this exercise is based on trial and error. We're going to use what works, and discard what doesn't.

Her mother probably educates Sarah in the ways of the world and, no doubt, cautions her about men. She might tell her daughter, "You can never trust a man. They're only after one thing – your body. They don't like a woman who's too smart." And so on and so on. What Sarah's mother tells her may be true for some of you, or it may not. Use your own experience in creating a character.

At an early age, perhaps Sarah expressed the desire to become a doctor, like her father, and her mother cautioned her against that, saying, "What about marriage, a family?" In her mother's experience, young women usually don't become doctors.

Let's move on. What kind of high school experience did Sarah have?

Active, social, mischievous. She made good grades without having to work very hard for them. She had many friends, and was the leader in rebelling against many of the school's restrictive policies.

Most young people rebel, and Sarah's no exception. She graduates, and decides to go to Radcliffe, which pleases her mother, but majors in political science, which upsets her mother. She's socially active, has an affair with a graduate student in political science. Her actions, based on her rebellious nature, become part of her character – a point of view, an attitude. She graduates from Radcliffe with a degree in political science.

Now what?

She moves to New York to get a job. Her father supports her and is in favor of the move. Her mother does not; she's upset. Sarah's not doing the things she wants her to do – get married and settle down, as befits a "proper young woman from Boston."

Remember, I add, drama is conflict. I explain the relationship between mother and daughter may be used during the screenplay. Or, it may not. Let's see whether it works or not before we make any decision. The writer always operates from the position of choice and responsibility.

Sarah's move to New York is a major crossroads in our creation of character. So far, we've focused on the *context* of Sarah Townsend. Now we're going to be creating *content*.

Let's define the *exterior* forces working on Sarah. Here's the diagram.

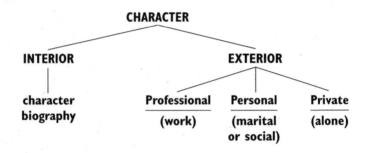

At this point, someone mentions the war in Iraq, and wants to create a story using the war as backdrop or as the context of the story. We discuss this and I feel there are a lot of positive things that we could use to create an effective screenplay. But then I bring up the fact that the war is still incomplete – we don't know what's going to happen in terms of stabilizing the country. And the war aspect, at least at this point, seems very limited. Someone asks if we could do this as a period piece, using the situation of the war as a force working on the character. It's a good idea, and I suggest that we could use the Vietnam War as the background of the story. All it means is changing some of the background events working on Sarah. We decide to do that and see what happens. The events we've created are still valid to some degree, and do not have to change radically. We do that, and decide that Sarah leaves college and moves to New York in the early seventies. So, we do a conversation of discovery and research the times.

Sarah arrives in New York City in the spring in the seventies. What does she do? Gets an apartment. Her father sends her some money each month, and does not tell her mother; Sarah's on her own and prefers it that way. Then what?

She gets a job. What kind of job does she get?

Let's discuss that. We know basically the *kind* of person Sarah is: upper-middle-class, independent, free-spirited, rebellious, on her own for the first time and loving it. Committed to herself and her life.

New York, 1972. What are the exterior forces working on her?

Nixon is in the White House. The Vietnam War still rages; the country is in a state of nervous exhaustion. Nixon goes to China. McGovern's gaining in the Presidential primaries and there's hope "he might be the one." George Wallace is gunned down in a shopping center. *The Godfather* is on release.

What kind of job would "fit" Sarah dramatically?

A job working at McGovern headquarters in New York. This is a point of discussion. We talk about it. Finally, I explain that for me the job satisfies her rebellious nature, it reflects her first independent step away from home. It satisfies her activist political stance and draws on her background as a political science major in college and it gives her parents something to disapprove of. Both of them. We're going after conflict, right?

From now on, through a process of trial and error, we're going to be searching for a theme, or dramatic premise; *something* that will move Sarah into a particular direction to generate a dramatic action. The SUBJECT of a screenplay, remember, is *action* and *character*. We've got the character, now we've got to find the action.

This is a hit-and-miss operation. Things are suggested, changed, rearranged, mistakes are made. I'll say one thing, then contradict myself in the next sentence. Don't worry about it. We're after a specific result – a story: we've got to let ourselves "find" it.

New York. 1972. An election year. Sarah Townsend is working for the McGovern campaign as a paid staff member. Who are her parents voting for?

What does Sarah discover about politics from her experience in the campaign?

That politics aren't necessarily clean or idealistic. Perhaps she discovers something illegal going on – would she do anything about it?

Maybe something happens, I suggest, that creates a major political issue. Perhaps a boyfriend of hers resists the draft and flees to Canada. She might become involved in the movement to bring home the draft resisters.

Remember, we're building a character, creating *context* and *content*, searching for a story that will soon appear. Create a character and a story will emerge.

Someone says Sarah's father has a different point of view from her – he feels draft resisters are traitors to their country and should be shot. Sarah would argue the opposite; the war is wrong, immoral and illegal; and the people responsible for it, the politicians, should be taken out and shot!

Suddenly, an amazing thing happens in the room. The air becomes tense, heavy with energy as the fifty or so people in the class polarize their *attitudes* and *points of view* about something that happened several years before. The wounds, I realize, are still not healed. We talk about the impact of Vietnam for several minutes. The war is over, we decide. Let's bury it.

Then someone yells out, "Watergate!" Of course! June 1972. Is that a dramatic event that would affect Sarah?

Yes. Sarah would be outraged; it is an event that will generate, or stimulate, a dramatic response. It is a potential "hook" in our, as yet, uncreated, untold, and undefined story. This *is* a creative process, remember, and confusion and contradiction are part of it.

Two and a half years later, Nixon is gone, the war is almost over, and the issue of amnesty becomes paramount. Sarah, by virtue of her political involvement, has seen and experienced an event firsthand which will guide her to a form of dramatic resolution, as yet unknown.

A student mentions Sarah might be involved in the movement to bring home draft resisters with complete amnesty. Sarah, we all realize, is a politically motivated person. "Does it work?" is my question. Yes.

Would Sarah be motivated enough to enter law school and become an attorney? I ask.

Everybody responds and we have a lot of discussion about it. Several members of the class don't think it works; they can't relate to it. It's OK. We're writing a screenplay. We need a character who is larger than life; I can see Jane Fonda, Faye Dunaway, Shirley MacLaine, Vanessa Redgrave, Marsha Mason, Jill Clayburgh, or Diane Keaton in the part of a woman attorney. As the cliché goes, "It's commercial," whatever that means.

At Cinemobile, the first question my boss, Fouad Said, asked me about a script was, "What's it about?" The second question was, "Who's going to star in it?" And I always answered the same thing: Paul Newman, Steve McQueen, Clint Eastwood, Jack Nicholson, Dustin Hoffman, Robert Redford, etc. That satisfied him. You're not writing a screenplay to paper your walls with. You're writing it, I hope, to sell it!

You may agree or not agree about a woman attorney from Boston as the main character in a movie. My only comment is that it works!

To me, Sarah goes to law school for a specific reason – to help change the political system!

A woman attorney is a good, dramatic choice. Does being a lawyer fit her character? Yes. Let's follow it out, see what happens.

If Sarah is practicing law, something *could* happen, an event or incident that would spark the germ of a story. People start throwing out suggestions. Sarah could be working in military law to aid the draft resisters, one person remarks. Another says she might be working in the area of poverty law. Or business law, or maritime law, or labor relations. An attorney offers a large range of dramatic possibilities.

A woman from Boston remarks that Sarah could be involved in the busing issue. It's a very good idea. We're looking for a dramatic premise, something that will trigger a creative response, a "hook."

That's when it happens – someone mentions he heard a news story about a nuclear power plant. That's it! I realize that's what we've been searching for, the "hook," the jackpot! At that time, Sarah could become involved with a nuclear power plant; perhaps the issue of safety precautions, or lack of them, or the building site, or the political power behind it. This *is* what we've been looking for, I say – an exciting, topical story issue; the "hook," or "gimmick," of our story line. I commit to the choice of Sarah becoming an attorney.

Everyone agrees. We now expand the exterior forces working on Sarah and begin to fashion our story.

Suppose we take the premise that Sarah Townsend becomes involved with a movement to oppose the construction of nuclear power plants. Perhaps she discovers through an investigation that a particular nuclear plant is unsafe. Politics being what they are, maybe a politician supports the plant despite the fact that it may be unsafe. Like the Karen Silkwood case, someone suggests. Right.

This becomes our story's "hook," or dramatic premise. (If you don't agree, find your own hook!) Now, we have to create the specifics, the details, the *content*, and we'll have the SUBJECT for a screenplay – an *action* and a *character*.

The screenplay would focus on the subject of the nuclear power plant, which is to be a major political issue in our country, perhaps the world, within the next decade.

What about the story?

Recently, the authorities closed a nuclear power plant in Pleasanton, California, when they discovered it was situated less than 200 feet from a major fault line, the epicenter of an earthquake. Can you imagine what would happen if an earthquake crumbled a nuclear power plant? Try to put your mind around that!

Let's create the opposite point of view. What would her father say about nuclear power plants? "Nuclear energy must work for us," he might say. "In our energy crisis we have to think ahead, develop an energy source for the future; that future is nuclear energy. We just have to insure their safety standards and create rules and guidelines determined by Congress and the Atomic Energy Commission." And, as we all know, those decisions are not always based on reality, but political necessity.

This might be something Sarah accidentally discovers – possibly a political favor that directly relates to an unsafe condition in a nuclear power plant. Now, something's got to happen that will create the dramatic situation.

Someone suggests a person at the nuclear plant could be contaminated and the case is brought to Sarah's law firm, and that's how she becomes involved in the case.

It's a very good suggestion! It becomes the dramatic story line we've been looking for; within the story, a worker becomes contaminated, the case is brought to Sarah's firm, and she's put on the case. The *plot point* at the end of Act I would be when Sarah discovers the worker's contamination, his fatal illness, is caused by unsafe safety procedures; despite threats and obstacles, she decides *to do* something about it. This is a period piece, remember, and could set the stage for re-examining various nuclear facilities.

Act I is the *setup* – we could open with the worker being contaminated. A visually dynamic sequence. The man collapses on the job, is carried out of the plant, an ambulance roars through the streets of Boston. Workers gather, protest; union officials meet and decide to file suit for action that will defend the workers from the unsafe conditions within the plant.

By circumstances, situation, and design, Sarah is chosen to handle the case. Union officials don't like it – she's a woman. The authorities deny her access but she manages to explore the plant anyway; learns about the unsafe conditions. A "brick" is thrown through her window. Threats are made. The law firm can't help her. She goes to the political representatives in charge, is given the runaround, told it's the worker's fault for getting contaminated.

The media start sniffing around. She learns there's a "political connection" between safety standards and plant management. Maybe, someone says, they discover some missing plutonium.

That's the *plot point* at the end of Act I.

Act II is *confrontation*. Sarah confronts obstacle after obstacle in her investigation, so many obstacles that she suspects some kind of political cover-up. She cannot ignore it any longer. We need a "love interest" – perhaps she's involved with a recent divorced attorney with two children. Their relationship becomes strained; he thinks she's "crazy," "paranoid," "hallucinating," and they may not be able to keep it together under the strain.

She will experience conflict and resistance from members of her law firm, she may be told she's going to be removed from the case if she persists in her investigation. Her parents will disagree with her, so she'll have conflict there. The only people who will support and help her are the people who work at the nuclear power plant; they want her to succeed, to publicly expose the unsafe working conditions. We can use the media, and possibly create a reporter who believes she should continue the investigation. He's going to get a story out of it. Possibly there's a romantic link between them.

What about the *plot point* at the end of Act II? It must be an incident or event, remember, that "hooks" into the action and "spins" it around into another direction.

Perhaps the reporter comes to her with definite "proof" that there's been some kind of political favoritism involving many officials. She has the facts in her hands – what is she going to do about it?

Act III is the *resolution*. Sarah, with the help of plant workers and the media, publicly exposes political favoritism in the government's unsafe regulation of safety standards.

The plant is closed until new safety standards are established. Sarah is congratulated on her persistent, courageous, and victorious stand.

There are different kinds of endings. In "up" endings, things work out. Think of *Erin Brockovitch*. In "sad," or "ambiguous," endings "it's up to the audience" to figure out what happens as in *The Hours* or *The Shawshank Redemption*. In a "down" ending, everybody dies:

American Beauty, *The Wild Bunch*, *Butch Cassidy and the Sundance Kid*, *Bonnie and Clyde*, *The Sugarland Express*.

If you're ever in doubt about how to end your story, think in terms of an "up" ending. There are better ways to end your screenplays than have your character caught, shot, captured, die, or be murdered. In the sixties we had "down" endings. The filmgoers of the seventies and eighties wanted "up" endings. Just look at *Star Wars*. It has made more money in a shorter period of time than any other movie in history. And, the two things that run Hollywood are fear and greed.

Resolve your stories any way you want, but if you can, put a positive spin on it.

We put a working title on it: *Precaution!*

Here's our story then: In the early seventies a young woman attorney in Boston discovers unsafe working conditions at a nuclear power plant, and despite political pressure and threats to her life, succeeds in publicly exposing it. The plant is shut down until repairs are made and a safe condition exists.

Not too bad – considering it took us less than an hour to create a character and a story with a strong dramatic premise!

We have an interesting *main character*, Sarah Townsend; an action, uncovering the scandal. We have a beginning, a *plot point* at the end of Act I, potential conflict in the second act, a *plot point* at the end of Act II, and a dramatic resolution.

You may not agree with it or like it – the purpose of the exercise is to set into motion a process, to show you how creating a character generates a dramatic action which uncovers a story.

As I've said, there are two ways to approach a screenplay: create an idea and "pour" your characters into it, or create a character and let the story emerge out of the character. The second approach is the one we've just used. It all came out of "a young woman from Boston." Try it! See what happens.

THE PASSIVE ACTIVE

THE PROBLEM SHEET

The Passive Active

- ✎ Main character is too passive, too reactive
- ✎ The main character is too internal, disappears off page
- ✎ The characters all sound alike
- ✎ Character conflicts are too thin
- ✎ The characters explain too much
- ✎ The dialogue is dull, uninteresting
- ✎ Minor characters are more interesting than the main character
- ✎ Conflict is expressed through dialogue, not action
- ✎ There is no subtext in scene
- ✎ The story is predictable and contrived

There are times during the screenwriting process when the main character seems to vanish, literally disappears off the page. No matter what the character does, either in terms of fulfilling the story's action or in revealing information about himself/herself, the personality, the behavior, or the dramatic need vanishes and the character is lost within the matrix of the action. And then, at other times, a minor character suddenly emerges, developing such a strong and vibrant personality that he or she totally overshadows the main character.

I call this phenomenon the *passive active*. It's where the main character seems to wander around looking for something to do, and, no matter what he or she does do, always reacts instead of acts, and is portrayed as passive instead of active.

It can be a real problem, if your story line is built around this particular character and he/she gets lost in the narrative story line or seems to disappear off the page. One of the best ways of becoming aware of this problem is to evaluate the material and determine whether the main character is *reacting* to the situation or is *actively creating* it.

You're writing for the visual medium. One of the strongest rules governing the craft is that your main character must be active, and be the catalyst of the action, the spark that *causes* things to happen. That doesn't mean you shouldn't let your character(s) react to a particular situation during the screenplay, just the opposite. Characters are always reacting to events or forces that affect them.

In *Three Days of the Condor* (Lorenzo Semple and David Rayfiel), the Robert Redford character is literally "out to lunch" when the entire cell of his CIA unit (they read books looking for information) is wiped out. When he discovers this, he understands it won't be too long before the assassin comes after him, and he enters the Second Act not knowing what to do or whom to trust. For the entire First Half of Act II the Redford character is only reacting. It is only at the Mid-Point, about sixty pages in, that he kidnaps the Faye Dunaway character and begins to be active again. And it works perfectly. If you haven't seen it in a while check it out.

Action and *reaction* are two sides of the same coin. As a matter of fact, Newton's Third Law of Motion states that "for every action there is an equal and opposite reaction." It's just something to be aware of, and it can be a good rule to follow. If something happens to a character, if he or she is affected by an incident or event, the reaction is a normal part of character revelation. It only becomes a problem when the character is reacting constantly, not only to an incident or event, but also to other characters. Things always seem *to happen* to him/ her; the character doesn't cause or trigger them. If you show your characters reacting too much of the time, they'll simply disappear off the page or, as sometimes happens, disappear off the movie screen.

I was watching television one evening and a Steven Seagal movie, *On Deadly Ground*, came on. I started watching. This was a film that Seagal starred in as well as directed. The film opens with some beautiful location shots of the Alaskan wilderness, and we cut to an oil well fire that's burning out of control. A helicopter wings its way over the rugged country, bringing the Seagal character to the fire. He lands, gets out, and approaches the team of firefighters. They can't handle it and they don't know what to do. So what does the Seagal character do? With only a few words he dons his fire suit and walks directly into the raging inferno. He stands there, surrounded by flames, casually plants some explosives, then just as casually walks out. The other characters scatter, looking for cover, but the Seagal character simply stands there as the oil well explodes, putting out the fire.

Pretty strong stuff, right? Strong action, a strong character, and some powerful visual images. What I saw during the thirty or forty minutes I watched the film was that it was a perfect example of the *passive active*. Why? Because the portrayal of the characters was so thin, the film became laughable. Michael Caine played the mean and totally corrupt oil baron, but his performance (I am sure it was written as it was played) was a one-dimensional, histrionic, over-the-top characterization of a man obsessed with carrying out his evil scheme.

Opposing him, of course, was the good guy, Seagal. The portrait of the Seagal character is the perfect expression of the passive active. As the main character he's the strong, silent type, a man who doesn't talk too much, a man who wants to avoid trouble, except when pushed too far, and only then will he react and take action – and as we see, he's a character who can literally do anything. Whether it's putting out the oil fire single-handed, or being a master of martial arts, or breaking into a computer and uncovering secret passwords, or protecting the rights of a drunken and downtrodden Eskimo. He is a man who is reacting to the situations caused by others, the bad guys. And all this is shown in the first fifteen minutes, by the way!

The unscrupulous oil baron, the bad guy, and the Seagal character, the good guy, quickly square up and it's pretty predictable who's going to come out on top.

It's easy to see what Seagal and the writer were striving for here; they wanted to portray the Seagal character as the strong, silent type, but because we are not privy to what he is thinking or feeling, he comes across as a character who only *reacts* to the events instigated by the Michael Caine character. That makes him a reactive character. Throughout the film the main character does not once instigate any actions, he only responds to actions initiated by someone else; so all we know about him is that he's reacting to what's happening to him and how it affects the tribal community of Eskimo.

His character, portrayed as the strong and silent type, is a man who seemingly knows everything, is right about everything, and lives according to a strict moral code that came out of the early westerns of Tom Mix. He was so busy being the "good guy" and reacting to the things the bad guys have done, that he becomes a boring character and literally disappears off the screen.

For example, here's a situation that is supposed to reveal an aspect of his character. It's a typical bar fight, and it could have been taken right out of a Tom Mix western. Seagal's sitting in the bar, drinking alone at a table. Three big tough guys, oil riggers, are hassling a drunken Eskimo who wants another drink. They taunt him, then begin pushing and shoving him around until he collapses into a corner. Seagal doesn't do anything, he simply stares at them. When they belligerently ask what he's looking at, Seagal at first does not reply. When they continue taunting him, he stands and the oil rig workers exchange words with him. Seagal walks towards them and, before they can continue talking, launches into them, throwing them all over the place, and in only a matter of minutes he reduces the oil workers, and there must be at least ten of them, into whimpering weaklings, begging and groveling for mercy.

It's pretty standard fare. We've seen it hundreds of times, for it's a predictable bar fight: the hero sits alone minding his own business when some tough guys pick on someone who can't take care of himself, usually a drunk, and the hero steps in and rescues him. What makes this interesting for our purposes is that the Seagal character is so passive, portraying an attitude rather than any emotion. And that's the way he is during the entire film. We don't know anything about him, and all we see about this character is a strong, silent, passive attitude. He becomes the passive active. It's not very interesting.

The screenwriter's job is to keep the reader interested enough to keep turning pages, or in this case, keep my fingers off the remote. The real lesson to be learned in this case is that at no time do we know enough about Seagal to see or understand his thoughts, feelings, or emotions; all he reflects is his attitude. His humanity, or believability, is all contained inside his head.

That being the case, the only thing this kind of a character can do is react to the situation. By placing a character in these types of situations, reacting to something someone else has initiated, the screenwriter causes his main character to vanish, to disappear off the page.

In many of Robert Redford's films he portrays this type of active/reactive character. Take a look at *The Horse Whisperer*, *Sneakers* (Larry Lasker and Walter Parkes), *Indecent Proposal* (Amy Holden Jones) or *Out of Africa* (Kurt Luedtke). In *Sneakers* he plays a character who doesn't show any thoughts or feelings, he simply states that he has a plan and then we see him implementing the plan and then he seems to disappear into the background. He is a passive yet active character.

So if you're writing, or rewriting, a screenplay and you sense that your character is washed out, or unseen on the page, or he or she is overshadowed by another character, or the story line seems contrived or predictable, or conflict seems to be missing, the chances are your character is too passive and is busy reacting to other characters or situations rather than creating or initiating the action.

One of the "rules" of screenwriting is that action is character. It must be remembered that film is behavior, and what a person does, his or her actions, reveals who he or she is. But there has to be a way for the reader to connect with the character; there must be a character-audience bond established for the script to be effective. If this bond is not formed, then there's a whole dimension missing in the illumination of character. And when that's the case, there is no "willing suspension of disbelief."

How do you go about solving the problem of the passive character? First, it has to be approached from the perspective of *Character*. A lot of writers try to solve the problem by approaching it through *Structure*; they seem to feel that if they can add enough action sequences, or tense dramatic moments, that will take care of the problem. All that does, however, is accentuate the passivity of the main character. Just like *On Deadly Ground*. It's not enough to pile on a number of action sequences, because it doesn't really solve the problem.

So, how do you recognize the problem of the *passive active*?

Take a look at the *Problem Sheet*, and see if you can recognize some of the symptoms. When you reread your material, does your main character seem to be lost in the background of the action? Do you find that one of the minor characters seems to leap off the page and draw attention away from the main character? Do your characters all sound alike, as if there is only one voice for all? What about conflict? Is there enough? Is your character's point of view clearly established and defined? Do you find your dialogue dull and boring? Or maybe your main character is constantly explaining things, and the story moves forward through dialogue rather than action? Are your scenes focused or flat and one-dimensional, with no color and texture?

All these symptoms could be indicative of the problem of a character who's too passive.

So what do you do? There are many ways to solve this kind of problem, but perhaps the easiest is to examine the character from the perspective of *conflict*. Do you know the character's *point of view*? Have you gone into the background of the main character and established a strong *Circle of Being*? What about the point of view within each scene? And what about your character's *dramatic need*? Is it clearly defined in your own mind? If not, go back and redefine your character's *dramatic need* and *point of view* in relation to the conflict of the story line. Go through and extract the elements of each scene and make sure you've got enough conflict, either on an emotional level in terms of the scene's *subtext*, i.e. what's not said during the scene; or on the level of direct confrontation or even physical conflict. Don't make things too easy for your character. If things happen too easily, the action becomes contrived and predictable.

Which brings up another point. Sometimes the screenwriter, wanting to avoid being too direct, or too "on target," in the dialogue, tries to be a little too subtle, a little too indirect. That creates a sense of confusion and a lack of understanding, so the needs of the character become lost in *what the character is not saying*. The dialogue seems vague and off center and the reader really doesn't know what's going on, and the story line seems to wander off in several directions. It's a symptom of the screenwriter's wanting to be too clever.

There are times in a screenplay when the dialogue has to be direct, for exposition purposes, in order to move the story forward, whether on a physical or an emotional level. And sometimes these scenes are the hardest to write just because they are so direct and on the mark. They're so easy, you think there's something wrong. This is where you don't need subtlety of action or dialogue, you need clarity and definition to keep your character active and interesting. The great American novelist F. Scott Fitzgerald always felt that the hardest thing a writer has to do is to "write down" to his readers; what he meant by that was that it's very hard to write material that is too specific and too direct, with no subtlety either in thought, action, or exposition. This happens all the time if you "try" to make your character alive and interesting. If you think you're really being smart and clever writing "indirect" dialogue, there's a good chance the motivation and need of your character will simply wash out and disappear off the page, lost in the twilight zone between clarity and confusion.

That's when another character will start to take over and become more interesting than the main character. If you get the feeling a minor character is dominating or overshadowing the main character, and is more lively and more interesting, it's a pretty good indication the main character might be too passive, and you're going to have to strengthen the characterization. It should be noted that there will be moments when your main character will be reacting to another character, action, or situation, and that's not bad – it's when reaction becomes his or her only response that it proves a detriment, and that's why you have to be careful walking the line between action and reaction.

Consider the character of Dr. Richard Kimble in *The Fugitive* (Andrew Davies), who is constantly reacting to a particular situation; in this case he's wanted for the murder of his wife, and is on the run, trying to elude capture by the law in the form of the Tommy Lee Jones character. His dramatic need, to prove his innocence and find out who actually committed the crime, is what drives him through the screenplay. It's the engine that keeps the story moving forward. So even though he's continually reacting, he's an active character because he causes things to happen, he's always *doing something* to try and prove his innocence. And he's not averse to helping a little child who's been misdiagnosed, by going back into the hospital and making a notation on the chart. The little side journey reveals his character through his behavior. Film, as I am so fond of saying, is behavior.

Even if you have a character confined in a physical location it does not mean that he or she has to be passive. Hannibal Lecter in *The Silence of the Lambs* (Ted Tally) is a good case in point. Locked inside a prison cell, he is far from being passive.

An effective way to make a character more active is to go back into your scenes and redefine the dramatic need, both in terms of overall story and in the context of each individual scene. If you determine the point of view of each character in each scene, then it's possible to rewrite the scene adding conflict to achieve the maximum dramatic value. Part of the reason a character seems to be passive and reactive is because there's a lack of conflict. Nine times out of ten if you feel your character is too passive, or is reacting too much to an external situation or character, it's due to a lack of conflict. So go back and redefine the internal and external forces working on the character.

If it's an internal, emotional reaction to a situation or event, try to create a visual metaphor and *let us see it*. For example, in *Dances With Wolves* after the John Dunbar character arrives at the fort at Plot Point I, the first thing he does is give himself the task of cleaning up the area; his behavior tells us that he's cleaning up his life and putting things back in order.

If you find it too difficult, then write a new character biography that will create a new *Circle of Being*, and in this way you can establish a strong and perceptive point of view that will generate more conflict.

That's the essence of transforming a character from passive to active.

ENDINGS AND BEGINNINGS

Question: What's the best way to open your screenplay?

Showing your character at work? In a relationship? Jogging? In bed, alone, or with someone? Driving? Playing golf? At the airport?

Up until now we've discussed abstract principles in writing the screenplay in terms of action and character. At this point, we leave those general concepts behind and move into specific and fundamental components of the screenplay.

Let's backtrack. We began with the idea that a screenplay is like a *noun* – about a *person*, or persons, in a *place*, or places, doing his or her "*thing*." All screenplays have a *subject* and the subject of a screenplay is defined as the *action*, what happens, and the *character*, to whom it happens. There are two kinds of action – *physical* action and *emotional* action; a car chase and a kiss. We discussed character in terms of *dramatic need*, and broke the concept of *character* down into two components – *interior* and *exterior*; your character's life from birth until the movie ends. We talked about *building* character and *creating* character and introduced the idea of *context* and *content*.

Now what? Where do we go from here? What happens next? Look at the *paradigm*:

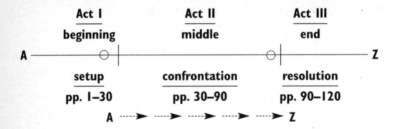

What do you see?

DIRECTION – that's what. Your story *moves forward* from A to Z; from *setup* to *resolution*. Remember the definition of screenplay *structure*: "a linear *progression* of *related* incidents, episodes, and events leading to a dramatic resolution."

That means your story *moves forward* from beginning to end. You've got ten pages (ten minutes) to establish three things to your reader or audience: (1) *who* is your main character? (2) *what* is the dramatic premise – that is, what's it about? and (3) what is the dramatic *situation* – the dramatic circumstances surrounding your story?

So – what's the best way to open your screenplay?

KNOW YOUR ENDING!

What *is* the ending of your story? How is it *resolved*? Does your main character live or die? Get married or divorced? Get away with the holdup, or get caught? Stay on his feet after 15 rounds with Apollo Creed, or not? What is the ending of your screenplay?

A lot of people don't believe you need an ending before you start writing. I hear argument after argument, discussion after discussion, debate after debate. "My characters," people say, "will determine the ending." Or, "My ending grows out of my story." Or, "I'll know my ending when I get to it."

Bullshit!

Those endings usually don't work and are not very effective when they do; often weak, neat, contrived, they are a let-down rather than an emotional shot-in-the-arm. Think of the endings of *Star Wars*, *Heaven Can Wait*, or *Three Days of the Condor*; strong and conclusive, definitely resolved.

The ending is the first thing you must know before you begin writing. Why?

It's obvious when you think about it. Your story always moves forward – it follows a path, a direction, a line of development from beginning to end. And *direction* is a *line of development*, the *path along which something lies*.

KNOW YOUR ENDING!

You don't have to know the specific details, but you have to know *what happens*.

I use an example out of my own life to illustrate this.

There was a moment in my life when I didn't know what I wanted to do or be. I had graduated from high school, my mother had just died, as my father had some years before, and I didn't want to get stuck in some job or go off to college. I didn't know what I wanted, so I decided to travel around the country. My older brother was in medical school in St. Louis at the time, and I knew I could stay with him or could visit friends in Colorado and New York. So, one morning, I simply got in my car and headed east on Highway 66.

I never knew where I was going till I got there. I preferred it that way. I had good times and bad times, and loved it; I was like a cloud on the wind, drifting without aim or purpose.

I did that for almost two years.

One day, driving through the Arizona desert, I realized I had traveled that same road before. Everything was the same, but different. It was the same mountain in the same barren desert but it was two years later. In reality, I was going nowhere. I spent two years trying to get my head straight, and I still had no purpose, no aim, no goal, no destination, no *direction*. I suddenly saw my future – it was nowhere.

I became aware of time slipping away, almost like an acid trip, and I knew I had to "do" something. So I stopped wandering and went back to school. At least I'd have a degree after four years, whatever that means! Of course, it didn't work out that way – it never does.

When you go on a trip, *you are going some place*; you have a destination. If I'm going to San Francisco, that's my destination. How

I get there is a matter of choice. I can fly, drive, take a bus, a train, ride a motorcycle, a bike, jog, hitchhike, or walk.

I can *choose* how to get there.

The same principle applies to your screenplay. What is the ending of your screenplay? How does your story resolve itself?

Good films are always resolved – one way or another. Think about it.

What's the ending of: *Close Encounters of the Third Kind*? *Bonnie and Clyde*? *An Unmarried Woman*? *Red River*? *Looking for Mr Goodbar*? *Saturday Night Fever*? *Three Days of the Condor*? *Alice Doesn't Live Here Anymore*? *Butch Cassidy and the Sundance Kid*? *The Treasure of the Sierra Madre*? *Casablanca*? *Annie Hall*? *The Goodbye Girl*? *Coming Home*? *Jaws*? *Heaven Can Wait*?

When you see a well-made film, you'll find a strong and directly stated ending, a definite resolution.

The days of ambiguous endings are over. Vanished. They went out in the 1960s. Today, the audience wants a clear-cut resolution. Do your characters get away or not? Do they make the relationship work, or don't they? Is the "Death Star" destroyed? The race won or lost?

What is the ending to your screenplay?

And, by ending, I mean resolution. How is it solved? A good illustration is *Chinatown*. There were three drafts of the screenplay, three different endings and two different resolutions.

The first draft of *Chinatown* is much more romantic than the others. Jake Gittes opens and closes the story with a voice-over narration, just the way Raymond Chandler does in most of his stories. When Evelyn Mulwray walks into Jake Gittes' life, he becomes involved with a woman from a different class; she is wealthy, sophisticated, and beautiful and he falls head over heels in love with her. Near the end of the story, when she learns her father, Noah Cross (John Huston), tried to hire Gittes to find her daughter/sister, she realizes he will stop at nothing to get the girl, so she sets out to kill her father. She knows it's the only solution. She phones Noah Cross and tells him to meet her along a deserted part of the coast near San Pedro. When Cross arrives, it is raining heavily, and as he walks up the dirt road looking for his daughter, she jams down her car's accelerator and tries to run him over. He narrowly escapes and races to a marshy area nearby. Evelyn leaves the car, pulls a gun and begins tracking him. Shots are fired. He hides behind a large wooden sign advertising "fresh bait." Evelyn sees him and fires again and again into the sign. Blood mingles with the falling rain and Noah Cross falls over backwards, dead.

A few moments later, Gittes and Lieutenant Escobar arrive at the scene and then we cut to various shots of modern-day Los Angeles and the San Fernando Valley. Gittes, in voice-over narration, tells us Evelyn Mulwray spent four years in prison for killing her father, that he manages to get her daughter/sister safely back to Mexico, and the land scheme Noah Cross so brilliantly conceived results in about 300 million dollars profit. The resolution of this first draft is that justice and order prevail; Noah Cross gets what he deserves, and the graft and corruption of the water scandal is responsible for Los Angeles being what it is today.

That was the first draft.

At that point, Robert Evans, the producer (the man also responsible for *Godfather* and *Love Story*), brought in Roman Polanski (*The Pianist*) as director. Polanski had his own ideas about *Chinatown*. Changes were discussed, then made, and relations between Polanski and Robert Towne, the screenwriter, became tense and strained. They disagreed about many things, mostly about the ending Polanski wanted, in which Noah Cross gets away with murder. The second draft is therefore altered considerably. It is less romantic, the action is trimmed and tightened, and the focus of the resolution changed substantially. The second draft is very close to the final one.

Noah Cross does get away with murder, graft and incest, and now Evelyn Mulwray becomes the innocent victim who pays for her father's crime. Towne's point of view in *Chinatown* is that those who commit certain types of crimes, like murder, robbery, rape or arson, are punished by being sent to prison, but those who commit crimes against an entire community are often rewarded by having streets named after them or plaques dedicated to them at City Hall. Los Angeles literally owes its survival to the water scandal known as The Rape of the Owens Valley; it is the backdrop of the film.

The ending of the second draft now has Gittes planning to meet Evelyn Mulwray in Chinatown; he has arranged for her to be taken to Mexico by Curly (Burt Young), the man in the opening scene, and her daughter/sister is waiting at the boat. Gittes has discovered that Cross is the man behind the murders and water scandal, and when he accuses him, Cross takes him prisoner; they leave for Chinatown. When they arrive, Cross tries to detail Evelyn, but Gittes manages to subdue the older man. Evelyn races to her car only to be blocked by Escobar. Gittes makes a drastic move and lunges at the policeman; during the scuffle, Evelyn drives away. Shots are fired and she is killed, shot in the head.

The last scene shows Noah Cross weeping over Evelyn's body while a stunned Gittes tells Escobar that Cross is the man "responsible" for everything.

The ending in the third draft is modified to accent Towne's point of view, but the resolution is the same as the second draft. Gittes is taken to Chinatown, but Escobar is already there, and arrests the private detective for withholding evidence and puts him in handcuffs. When Evelyn arrives with her daughter/sister, Cross approaches the young girl. Evelyn tells him to stay away, and when he doesn't, she pulls a gun and shoots him in the arm. She gets into her car and drives away. Loach, the cop, fires, and Evelyn is killed, shot through the eye. (Sophocles has Oedipus tear out his eyes when he realizes he committed incest with his mother.)

Horrified by Evelyn's death, Cross puts his arm protectively around his daughter/granddaughter and forcefully whisks her away into the darkness.

Noah Cross gets away with it all; murder, the water scandal, the girl. "You gotta be rich to kill somebody, anybody, and get away with it," Gittes tells Curly in the opening scene.

The *resolution* must be clear in your mind before you write one word on paper; it is a *context*, it *holds* the ending in place.

The same principle applies to a recipe. When you cook something, you don't throw things together and then see what you've got! You know what you're going to cook before you go into the kitchen; all you have to do is cook it!

Your story is like a journey, the ending its destination. Both are related.

Cat Stevens sums it up in his song *Sitting*:

Life is like a maze of doors,
and they open from the side you're on.
Just keep on pushin' hard, boy, try as you may,
you might wind up where you started from.

The Chinese say "the longest journey begins with the first step," and in many philosophical systems "endings and beginnings" are connected; as in the concept of Yin and Yang, two concentric circles joined together, forever united, forever opposed.

Endings and beginnings are related, and the principle can be applied to the screenplay. *Rocky* is a case in point. The film opens with Rocky fighting an opponent; it ends with him fighting Apollo Creed for the Heavyweight Championship of the World.

In life, the ending of one thing is usually the beginning of something else. If you're single and get married, you're ending one way of life and beginning another. If you're married, then get divorced or separated or become widowed, the same principle holds true; you're going from living with someone to living alone. An ending is always a beginning, and a beginning is really an ending. Everything is related in the screenplay, as in life.

If you can find a way to illustrate this in your screenplay, it is to your advantage. *The Sugarland Express*, written by Hal Barwood and Matthew Robbins, does this well.

The film opens at the crossroads of a two-lane highway. A Greyhound bus pulls to a stop and Goldie Hawn gets out and walks up the road as the credits begin.

The story progresses. She breaks her husband out of a detention center to kidnap their child from its foster parents; they take a highway patrolman hostage, then proceed to be hunted down by the law and ultimately, he is killed. (Beginning, middle, and end, right?)

A shootout ends the film. The camera pans and the last shot is a crossroads on a two-lane highway. An empty highway opens the film and an empty highway closes it.

The Hustler opens with Paul Newman arriving to play pool with Minnesota Fats; it ends with Newman leaving the pool hall after winning the game, a self-imposed exile from the world of pool. The film opens with a pool game and closes with a pool game.

In *Three Days of the Condor*, Robert Redford's first line raises the dramatic premise of the entire film: "Anything in the pouch for me, Dr. Lapp?" The answer to that question results in several people being brutally murdered, and Redford almost losing his life. He has uncovered a "CIA" within the CIA – and, he doesn't know it until the end of the movie. His discovery is the final key that resolves the movie.

The ending of *Condor*, by Lorenzo Semple, Jr., and David Rayfiel, from the novel *Six Days of the Condor* by James Grady, is an excellent example of story resolution. Ably directed by Sidney Pollack, it is a fast-moving, well-constructed thriller that works on all levels – the acting is excellent, the cinematography effective, the ending tight and lean; there is no "fat" in the film. It's one of my favorite teaching films, and fits the "paradigm" perfectly.

By the end of the movie, Redford has tracked down the mysterious Lionel Atwood – a high-level executive in the CIA – but he doesn't know *who* Atwood is or what his connection is, if any, to the murders committed. In the "resolution scene," Redford establishes that Atwood is the man who ordered the murders; that he is responsible for establishing a secret cell of the CIA within the CIA because of the world "oil fields." This established, Max von Sydow appears, the hired assassin of the intelligence underworld, and abruptly kills Atwood. He is now back in the employ of the "company," the CIA. Redford breathes easier; he's alive. "At least for now," von Sydow reminds him.

No loose ends. Everything is resolved dramatically, in terms of action and character; all questions raised are answered. The story is complete.

The filmmakers added a "tag" scene at the end. Robert Redford and Cliff Robertson are standing in front of the *New York Times* Building, and Redford states that if anything happens to him, the *Times* has the story. But "will they print it?" Robertson asks.

It's a good question.

Fade out. The end.

The "tag" scene is not the resolution of the film; it simply states a dramatic point of view. It's "our" government, the movie says: we the people have the right to know what goes on within the trappings of government.

We must exercise it.

Endings and beginnings; two sides of the same coin.

Choose and structure and dramatize your ending carefully. If you can relate your beginning and ending, it adds a nice cinematic touch. Open with a scene on a river and end it on the ocean; water to water. Or highway to highway, sunset to sunset. Sometimes you'll be able to do it, sometimes not. See if it works; if it does, use it; if not, junk it.

When you know your ending you can effectively choose your opening.

What *is* the opening of your screenplay? How does it begin? What do you write after FADE IN:?

If you've determined your ending you can choose an incident or event that leads you to the end. You might reveal your main character at work, at play, alone or with someone, either business or pleasure. What happens in the first scene of the film? Where does it take place?

There are several ways to open your screenplay. You can "grab" the audience with a visually exciting action sequence, as *Star Wars* does. Or, you can create an interesting character introduction as Robert Towne does in *Shampoo*: a darkened bedroom, moans and squeals of pleasurable delight – the phone rings, loud, insistent, shattering the mood. It's another woman – for Warren Beatty, who's in bed with Lee Grant. It shows us everything we need to know about his character.

Shakespeare is a master of openings. Either he opens with an *action* sequence, like the ghost walking the parapet in *Hamlet*, or the witches in *Macbeth*, or he uses a scene revealing something about the character: Richard III is hunch-backed and laments about the "winter of our discontent"; Lear demands to know how much his daughters love him, in terms of dollars and cents. Before *Romeo and Juliet* begins the chorus appears, bangs for silence, and synopsizes the story of the "star-crossed lovers."

Shakespeare knew his audience; the groundlings standing in the pit, the poor and oppressed, drinking freely, talking boisterously to the performers if they didn't like the action on stage. He had to "grab" their attention and focus it on the action.

An opening can be visually active and exciting, grabbing the audience immediately. Another kind of opening is expository, slower-paced in establishing character and situation.

Your story determines the type of opening you choose.

The Watergate break-in opens *All the President's Men*; it is a tense and exciting sequence. *Close Encounters of the Third Kind* opens with a dynamic, mysterious sequence because we don't know what's going on. *Julia* is moody, reflective, establishing character wound within the strands of memory. *An Unmarried Woman* opens with an argument, then *reveals* the life of the *married* woman, Jill Clayburgh.

Choose your opening well. You've got ten pages to grab the reader, or audience; if you open with an action sequence as in *Rocky*, keep it under eight pages and then set up your story.

Where to put the "credits" is a film decision, not a writing one. Determining the placement of credits is the last thing done on a film, and it's the decision of the film editor and director. Whether it's a dynamic credit montage or simply white cards superimposed on a black background, credits are not your decision. You can write "credits begin," or "credits end" if you want, but that's it. Write the screenplay, don't worry about the credits.

"THE FIRST TEN PAGES"

The first ten pages of your screenplay are absolutely the most crucial. Within the first ten pages a reader will know whether your story is working or not; whether it's been set up or not. That's the reader's job.

As the head of the story department at Cinemobile, I was always seventy scripts behind. The pile on my desk was rarely smaller. When I was almost caught up, a stack of scripts suddenly appeared from nowhere – from agents, producers, directors, actors, studios. I read so many screenplays that were boring and poorly written I could tell within the first ten pages whether the script was set up correctly. I gave the writer thirty pages to set up the story; if it wasn't done by then I reached for the next script on the pile. I had too many to read to waste my time reading a script that didn't work. I was reading three scripts a day. I didn't have time to *hope* the writer did his job; he either set up his story or he didn't. If he didn't, I threw the script into the large trash bin that served as the "return file."

"That's showbiz."

Nobody sells a script in Hollywood without the help of a reader. In Hollywood, "nobody reads"; producers don't read, readers read. There is an elaborate filtering system regarding screenplays in this town. Everybody says they're going to read your script over the weekend, and that means they're going to give it to somebody to read within the next few weeks; a reader, a secretary, a receptionist, a wife, girlfriend, assistant. If the "reader" says she "likes" the screenplay, the person will get another opinion or scan the first few pages himself, ten pages to be exact.

You've got ten pages to grab your reader. What are you going to do with them?

I tell everyone in my screenwriting class they should be seeing as many movies as possible. At least two movies a week. In movie theaters. If you can't afford that, at least one movie in a theater and one on TV.

It's very important for you to see movies. All kinds of movies; good films, bad films, foreign films, old films, new films. Every film you see becomes a learning experience; if you examine it, it will generate a process giving you an expanded awareness of the screenplay. A movie should be viewed as a working session; talk about it, discuss it, see whether it fits the *paradigm* or not.

When you go to a movie, for example, how long does it take you to make a decision about whether you like it or not? After the lights fade, and the movie begins, how long does it take you to make a decision, either consciously or unconsciously, about whether the movie is worth the price of the admission?

And you *do* make that decision, whether you're aware of it or not. You already know the answer.

Ten minutes. Within the first ten minutes you're going to make a decision about the film you're seeing. Check it out. The next time you go to a movie notice how long it takes you to decide whether you like it or not. Look at your watch.

Ten minutes is ten pages. Your reader or audience is either going to be with you, or not. How you build and structure your opening is going to influence the reaction of the reader and viewer.

You've got ten pages to establish three things: (1) *who* is your main character? (2) *what* is the dramatic premise – that is, what's your story about? and (3) what is the dramatic *situation* of your screenplay – the dramatic circumstances surrounding your story?

Citizen Kane illustrates this perfectly. The film opens with Charles Foster Kane (Orson Welles) dying alone in his large palace called Xanadu. He holds a toy paperweight in his hand. It rolls out of his hand onto the floor and the camera lingers on the paperweight showing a boy with a sled, and over this we hear Kane's dying words: "Rosebud ... Rosebud."

Who is Rosebud? *What* is Rosebud? The answer to that question is the subject of the movie. It could be called an "emotional detective story." The life of Charles Foster Kane is revealed by the reporter trying to find the meaning and significance of "Rosebud."

The last shot of the movie shows a sled burning in the giant incinerator; as the flames devour it we see the word "Rosebud" appear, symbolizing the lost childhood that Charles Foster Kane gave up to become what he was.

You've got ten pages to "grab" your reader and thirty pages to set up your story.

Endings and beginnings are essential to a well-constructed screenplay. What's the best way to open your screenplay?

KNOW YOUR ENDING!

Determine the ending of your screenplay, then design your opening. The primary rule for the opening is: Does it work? Does it set your story in motion? Does it establish your main character? Does it state the dramatic premise? Does it set up the situation? Does it set up a problem that your character must confront and overcome? Does it state your character's need?

THE PROBLEM SHEET

Endings
- Story's resolution is not paid off
- The ending does not work
- The ending is too soft, too weak, confusing
- The ending seems contrived, too predictable, unsatisfying
- Main character dies (the easy solution)
- The main character disappears at the end
- A surprise twist comes out of nowhere
- Everything happens too fast
- Ending is not big or commercial enough
- Ending is too big and expensive to make

If there's one problem that screenwriters have to deal with more than any other, it's the problem of *endings*. How to end the screenplay so it works effectively, so it's satisfying and fulfilling, so it makes an emotional impact on the reader, so it's not contrived or predictable, so it's real, believable, not forced or fabricated; an ending that resolves all the main story points; an ending, in short, that works.

What's so interesting about endings is that, most of the time, the ending is not really the problem, it's the fact that it *doesn't work effectively*. It's either too soft, or too slow, too wordy or too vague, too expensive or not expensive enough, too down, too up, too contrived, too predictable, or too unbelievable. Sometimes it's simply not dramatic enough to resolve the story line, or maybe a surprise twist in the story line comes out of nowhere, with no relationship to the story or characters; it just creates a solution to the script, is an easy way to end the story line. This happens a lot with young film students; the easiest way to end the screenplay is by having the main character die, or having everybody die.

Strong endings are an essential part of the screenplay. Whether it's a drama, comedy, or action thriller, or whatever, doesn't really matter; what's important is that the ending be a dynamic conclusion to the story line.

By itself the *ending* means the last part, or finish, or the conclusion. The best way to achieve the ending of the screenplay is to let it evolve, or be born, from the resolution of the story. Like a star evolving from the interstellar dust, a good and appropriate ending will always be born from the resolution. That's the start point, the beginning of a good ending.

Understanding the basic dynamics of a story's resolution is essential. By itself *resolution* means "a solution or explanation; to make clear." And that process begins at the very start of the screenwriting process. When building or constructing a story line, you must first determine the resolution. What is the resolution of your story? At the initial conception of your screenplay, when you were still working out the idea and shaping it into a dramatic story line, you made a creative choice, a decision, and determined what the resolution was going to be: does your character live or die? Succeed or fail? Escape from

Shawshank Prison and make it safely to Mexico? Re-enter the earth's atmosphere and survive the ordeal of the damaged spacecraft as in *Apollo 13*? Confront her fear of commitment and access her own inner courage and commit to marriage as in *How to Make an American Quilt*? Does Larry Flint win the court decision in the legal battle over the First Amendment or not, as in *The People vs. Larry Flint* (Scott Alexander and Larry Karaszewski)? Does the Emergency Action Message arrive in time to prevent the launching of the nuclear missile in *Crimson Tide*?

The resolutions of all these films contain the seeds of each particular ending. It's important to note that *resolution* and *ending* are not the same thing. They are connected, in the same way that an ice cube and water are connected, in terms of the relationship between the parts and the whole. The resolution is a whole whereas the ending is made up of parts. It is the resolution that contains the seed of the ending, and if planted and nurtured correctly, it can bloom into a full-fledged dramatic experience. And that's what we all strive for. Endings are manifested in the resolution and the resolution is conceived from the beginning. It's a natural law that endings and beginnings are related; the ending of one thing is always the beginning of something else. Be it a wedding, or a funeral, or a life change like a new job or career, the ending of a relationship or the beginning of a new one, or a move to a new city or country, or whether it's winning or losing in the lottery, it's all the same; the end of one thing is always the beginning of something else.

The surest way for your ending to work is to know the resolution. Then find the best way to show the specific scene or sequence so you can make it visually and dramatically effective.

What happens to the end of your story? If you don't know (and this ambivalence usually occurs when you're first evolving your story line), then ask yourself *what you would like the ending to be*, regardless of whether it's too simple, too trite, too happy, or too sad. And please don't get caught up in the game of "What kind of an ending would *they* like?" whoever *they* are. What ending do *you* want?

The ending of the screenplay is that point where the entire story line is paid off, so you have to design it carefully from Plot Point II. *Seven* has a great ending, and that's what makes the film so disturbing, so you carry it with you when you leave the theater. If necessary, retrace your steps from Plot Point II.

When you reach the Plot Point at the end of the Second Act, what elements are left unresolved? There will be one or two things that need to be resolved in Act III. What are they? Can you define them?

The ending cannot be a separate and isolated incident or event. Everything is connected in a screenplay, everything exists in relationship between the parts and the whole. So, if you feel your ending does not work, if it's too soft or subtle, or comes out of nowhere, or the main character seems to be lost, or you really don't know what to do to write an ending that works, then it's time to sit down at the drawing board and begin the ending from a specific point: Plot Point II.

First, set up what you have to pay off. Determine what elements of the story must be resolved at the end of the screenplay. If need be, write an essay about what happens in Act III so the story line can be resolved. Then you might want to go through the action and, in free association, in a page-or-two essay, begin to list the ways this film can end. Don't be attached to any one single shot, scene, or sequence. Just list the various ways the endings can be achieved. If that doesn't clarify the action, and you're still unclear about how the material should end, simply write down how you would like it to end, regardless of budget, believability, or anything else that gets in the way. Just throw down any thoughts, words, or ideas, without any regard as to how to do it. That's really the first step in the completion process. It's important to tie together all the loose ends of the narrative line so the screenplay becomes a complete reading experience that rings true and is integral to the action and the characters.

There are other ways to end your screenplay as well. There may be an instance where Act III becomes an entire sequence, a full and complete unit of action; *Apollo 13* is such a case; so is *Witness*, so is *Crimson Tide*. And if you look at *Pulp Fiction*, the end is really the "bookend" ending with the Tim Roth and Amanda Plummer robbery attempt in the restaurant, which, coincidentally, opens the movie. Endings and beginnings are connected, right? In each of these scripts the ending completes the action of Act III.

In *Apollo 13* the entire Third Act focuses on their re-entry back to earth and we follow the action from the moment the LEM separates from the spacecraft, cutting back and forth to the command center, to the anxious three minutes that turns out to be four, waiting for them to plunge through the atmosphere, not knowing whether the heat shield will protect them or not. When they finally do break through the cloud cover and safely land in the ocean and are rescued, that is the resolution; the ending is simply the voice-over of Jim Lovell telling us what happened to the three astronauts after their ordeal in space. It's played over shots of them on the aircraft carrier.

The Plot Point at the end of Act II in *Witness* has John Book (Harrison Ford) and Rachel (Kelly McGillis) completing their relationship as they embrace underneath the birdhouse that Book had broken when he first arrived, and has now restored. Act III opens when the three crooked cops pull over the ridge, park their car, pull out their weapons, and make their way down to the farmhouse. Once there, they break into the farmhouse and hold Rachel and the grandfather hostage while they hunt Book and young Samuel, trying to kill them. So the entire Third Act is really a shootout, and the end comes out of that action; John Book says goodbye to Rachel and young Samuel, and over the end credits, as he drives the car up the long dirt road leading back to Philadelphia, Daniel, Rachel's suitor, played by Alexander Godunov, walks towards the farmhouse. *Witness* is a great little film that works on all levels. The ending of one thing is always the beginning of something else.

It's different with *Crimson Tide*. At Plot Point II the emergency action message is interrupted and the Denzel Washington character takes over the command of the sub as the countdown to launch the nuclear missiles continues. Act III is the entire sequence, and ends when they finally receive the complete message telling them to cancel the nuclear strike. That's the resolution.

The ending is something else. There is a little tag added on after the action is complete; a naval enquiry is held, and it is decided that both men were right in their actions, because the naval regulations happen to be unclear in this particular situation and must be changed. The Gene Hackman character retires from active duty, the Denzel Washington character will be promoted to captain and receive command of his own ship.

Two different points of view, resolved, effective, complete. It's what a good ending is meant to do.

A good ending is only as strong as Act I; in other words, a good ending is set up from the very beginning of the screenplay. It will always come out of the integrity of the story. In many scripts the ending seems predictable; that is, we know what's going to happen, we just don't know *how*. *Jerry Maguire* (Cameron Crowe) is a script like that. We know from the very beginning what's going to happen, and the two people are going to get together, but the fun comes in watching how it happens.

So what makes a good ending? It has to work, first of all, by satisfying the story; so when we reach the final fadeout, or walk out of the movie experience, we want to feel full and satisfied, much as if we were leaving the table after a good meal. It's this feeling of satisfaction that must be fulfilled in order for the ending to work effectively. And of course, it's got to be believable.

Absolute Power (William Goldman) is slick and well done, and Clint Eastwood's direction is marvelous. The story moves along with tense sophistication and ease. Now, this is a case, at least for me, where I admired the film even though it did not engage the "willing suspension of disbelief." Not for one instant did I believe that the President of the United States, with only three people in the Secret Service, could bring this all about: the opening sequence, the inciting incident, shows a man and a woman, drunk, staggering into the bedroom of a large mansion, just as a burglar is cleaning out the vault. The thief can only watch as the sexual encounter turns violent and the woman, defending herself from the man, picks up the letter opener and prepares to stab him. The door bursts open and two Secret Service agents appear and kill the woman.

When the chief of staff and the two agents discover that the Clint Eastwood character, the burglar, has seen the whole thing, they go after him. Naturally, they find out who he is, but, of course, they must break all laws to kill him. In this case I don't buy it at all, but what's so interesting to me is the relationship between the father (Eastwood) and his estranged daughter. This relationship is a significant part of the film, and when the President orders the Secret Service agents to kill Eastwood's daughter, Plot Point II, the master thief decides to take on the President. And, in the end, justice is served, and the father and daughter are reconciled.

So, even though I did not "willingly suspend my disbelief," I bought the ending. It was a fulfilling and satisfying experience.

What you want to accomplish is the best possible ending that works. You want to be true to your story line, and not have to resort to any tricks, gimmicks, or contrived elements, in order to make it work. What's the best way to do this? First, and I think this goes without saying, you have to be clear on what kind of film you're writing; then you can begin to devise and execute an appropriate ending.

So, how would you like it to end? What is the resolution? Then, what do you have to do to achieve it? If the ending doesn't work the way it is, or how you think it should, feel free to go back and play with it a little. Think about the ending in terms of the reader or viewer's satisfaction, because the key to a successful ending is the feeling of satisfaction or fulfilment. Whether it's happy or sad makes no difference. Is the story line resolved? In *The English Patient*, the ending and the beginning are the same.

If I could sum up the concept of endings, and declare what is the one most important thing to remember, I would say that *the ending comes out of the beginning*. Someone, or something, initiates an action, and how that action is resolved becomes the story line of the film.

THE SETUP 7

Everything is related in a screenplay, so it becomes essential to introduce your story components from the beginning. You've got ten pages to grab or hook your reader, so you've got to set up your story immediately.

That means page one, word one. The reader must know what's going on immediately. Tricks or gimmicks don't work. You've got to set up the story information in a visual way. The reader must know *who* the main character is, *what* the dramatic *premise* is, that is, what it's about, and the dramatic *situation* – the circumstances surrounding the action.

These three elements must be introduced within the first ten pages, or immediately following an action sequence like the opening of *Raiders of the Lost Ark*. I tell students in my workshops and seminars that you must approach the first ten pages of your screenplay as a *unit*, or *block*, of dramatic action. It is the unit that sets up everything to follow, and therefore must be designed and executed with efficiency and good, solid dramatic value.

There is no better illustration of this than Robert Towne's screenplay of *Chinatown*. Towne is a master at setting up his story and characters. It is textured with skill and precision, layer by layer, and the more I read the script, the more I learn how good it really is.

As far as I'm concerned, *Chinatown* is one of the best classic American screenplays written during the 1970s, a virtual renaissance of American screenwriting. Not that it's better than *Godfather I* or *Apocalypse Now* or *All the President's Men* or *Close Encounters of the Third Kind*, or even the later *Shawshank Redemption* or *The Hours*, but as a reading experience the story, visual dynamics, backdrop, backstory, and subtext are woven together to create a solid dramatic unity of a story told with pictures.

The first time I saw the film, I was bored, tired, and dozed off during the screening. It seemed a very cold and distant film. I saw it again and felt it was a good film, but nothing spectacular. Then, in a class at Sherwood Oaks, I read the screenplay. It blew me away. The characterizations, the style of writing, the movement, the flow of the story are flawless.

Recently, I was invited by the Ministry of Dutch Culture and the Belgium Film Industry to teach a screenwriting workshop in Brussels, and I took *Chinatown* with me to use as a teaching example. The workshop was attended by film professionals and students from Belgium, France, Holland, and England; together we viewed, read, and analyzed the script in terms of structure and story. It was a profound learning experience. I thought I knew the script perfectly, but I learned I hardly knew it at all. What makes it so good is that it works on *all* levels – story, structure, characterization, visuals – yet everything we need to know is set up within the first ten pages. It is a *unit* or *block* of dramatic action.

Chinatown is about a private detective who is hired by the wife of a prominent man to find out who he's having an affair with, and in the process becomes involved in several murders and uncovers a major water scandal.

The first ten pages set up the entire screenplay. What follows are the first ten pages of *Chinatown* as they appear in the screenplay. Read it carefully. Notice how Towne sets up his *main character*, how he introduces the dramatic premise, reveals the dramatic situation.

(NOTE: All questions about screenplay form will be discussed in Chapter 13.)

(*page 1 of screenplay*)

CHINATOWN

by Robert Towne

FADE IN

FULL SCREEN PHOTOGRAPH

grainy but unmistakably a man and woman making love. Photograph shakes. SOUND of a man MOANING in anguish. The photograph is dropped, REVEALING another, more compromising one. Then another, and another. More moans.

> **CURLY'S VOICE**
> (*crying out*)
> Oh, no.

INT. GITTES' OFFICE

CURLY drops the photos on Gittes' desk. Curly towers over GITTES and sweats heavily through his workman's clothes, his breathing progressively more labored. A drop plunks on Gittes' shiny desktop.

Gittes notes it. A fan whirrs overhead. Gittes glances up at it. He looks cool and brisk in a white linen suit despite the heat. Never taking his eyes off Curly, he lights a cigarette using a lighter with a "nail" on his desk.

Curly, with another anguished sob, turns and rams

his fist into the wall, kicking the wastebasket as he
does. He starts to sob again, slides along the wall
where his fist has left a noticeable dent and its
impact has sent the signed photos of several
movie stars askew.

Curly slides on into the blinds and sinks to his knees.
He is weeping heavily now, and is in such pain that
he actually bites into the blinds.

Gittes doesn't move from his chair.

GITTES

All right, enough is enough – you can't
eat the Venetian blinds, Curly. I just had
'em installed on Wednesday.

Curly responds slowly, rising to his feet,
crying. Gittes reaches into his desk and pulls out
a shot glass, quickly selects a cheaper bottle of
bourbon from several fifths of more expensive
whiskeys.

Gittes pours a large shot. He shoves the glass across
his desk toward Curly.

(2)

GITTES

– Down the hatch.

Curly stares dumbly at it. Then picks it up, and drains
it. He sinks back into the chair opposite Gittes,
begins to cry quietly.

CURLY
(drinking, relaxing a little)
She's just no good.

GITTES
What can I tell you, kid? You're right.
When you're right, you're right, and
you're right.

CURLY
– Ain't worth thinking about.

Gittes leaves the bottle with Curly.

GITTES
You're absolutely right, I wouldn't give
her another thought.

CURLY
(pouring himself)
You know, you're okay, Mr. Gittes. I
know it's your job, but you're okay.

GITTES
(settling back, breathing a little easier)
Thanks, Curly. Call me Jake.

CURLY
Thanks. You know something, Jake?

GITTES
What's that, Curly?

CURLY

I think I'll kill her.

(3)

INT. DUFFY & WALSH'S OFFICE

noticeably less plush than Gittes'. A well-groomed,
dark-haired WOMAN sits nervously between their two
desks, fiddling with the veil on her pillbox hat.

WOMAN

– I was hoping Mr. Gittes could see to
this personally –

WALSH

*(almost the manner of someone
comforting the bereaved)*
– If you'll allow us to complete our
preliminary questioning, by then he'll
be free.

There is the SOUND of ANOTHER MOAN coming
from Gittes' office – something made of glass
shatters. The Woman grows more edgy.

INT. GITTES' OFFICE – GITTES & CURLY

Gittes and Curly stand in front of the desk, Gittes
staring contemptuously at the heavy breathing hulk
towering over him. Gittes takes a handkerchief and
wipes away the plunk of perspiration on his desk.

CURLY

(crying)
They don't kill a guy for that.

GITTES

Oh they don't?

CURLY

Not for your wife. That's the unwritten
law.

Gittes pounds the photos on the desk, shouting:

I'll tell you the unwritten law, you dumb
son of a bitch, you gotta be rich to kill
somebody, anybody, and get away with
it. You think you got that kind of dough,
you think you got that kind of class?

(4)

Curly shrinks back a little.

CURLY

… No …

GITTES

You bet your ass you don't. You can't
even pay me off.

This seems to upset Curly even more.

CURLY

I'll pay the rest next trip – we only
caught sixty ton of skipjack around San
Benedict. We hit a chubasco, they don't
pay you for skipjack the way they do
tuna or albacore –

GITTES
(easing him out of his office)
Forget it. I only mention it to illustrate a
point ...

INT. OFFICE RECEPTION

He's now walking him past SOPHIE, who pointedly
averts her gaze. He opens the door where on the
pebbled glass can be read: J.J. GITTES and
Associates – DISCREET INVESTIGATION.

GITTES
I don't want your last dime.
He throws an arm around Curly and flashes a
dazzling smile.

GITTES
(continuing)
What kind of a guy do you think I am?

CURLY
Thanks, Mr. Gittes.

GITTES
Call me Jake. Careful driving home,
Curly.

He shuts the door on him and the smile disappears.

(5)

He shakes his head, starting to swear under his
breath.

SOPHIE
– A Mrs. Mulwray is waiting for you, with
Mr. Walsh and Mr. Duffy.

Gittes nods, walks on in.

INT. DUFFY & WALSH'S OFFICE

Walsh rises when Gittes enters.

WALSH
Mrs. Mulwray, may I present Mr. Gittes?

Gittes walks over to her and again flashes a warm,
sympathetic smile.

GITTES
How do you do, Mrs. Mulwray?

MRS. MULWRAY
Mr. Gittes …

GITTES
Now, Mrs. Mulwray, what seems to be
the problem?

She holds her breath. The revelation isn't easy for her.

MRS. MULWRAY
My husband, I believe, is seeing
another woman.

Gittes looks mildly shocked. He turns for
confirmation to his two partners.

GITTES

(gravely)
No, really?

MRS. MULWRAY

I'm afraid so.

GITTES

I am sorry.

Gittes pulls up a chair, sitting next to Mrs. Mulwray – between Duffy and Walsh. Duffy cracks his gum.

(6)

Gittes gives him an irritated glance. Duffy stops chewing.

MRS. MULWRAY

Can't we talk about this alone, Mr. Gittes?

GITTES

I'm afraid not, Mrs. Mulwray. These men are my operatives and at some point they're going to assist me. I can't do everything myself.

MRS. MULWRAY

Of course not.

GITTES

Now – what makes you certain he is involved with someone?

Mrs. Mulwray hesitates. She seems uncommonly nervous at the question.

MRS. MULWRAY

– a wife can tell.

Gittes sighs.

GITTES

Mrs. Mulwray, do you love your
husband?

MRS. MULWRAY

(shocked)
… Yes, of course.

GITTES

(deliberately)
Then go home and forget about it.

MRS. MULWRAY

– but …

GITTES

(staring intently at her)
I am sure he loves you, too. You know
the expression, "let sleeping dogs lie"?
You're better off not knowing.

(7)

MRS. MULWRAY

(with some real anxiety)
But I have to know!

Her intensity is genuine. Gittes looks to his two
partners.

GITTES

All right, what's your husband's first
name?

MRS. MULWRAY

Hollis. Hollis Mulwray.

GITTES

(visibly surprised)
– Water and Power?

Mrs. Mulwray nods, almost shyly. Gittes is now
casually but carefully checking out the detailing of
Mrs. Mulwray's dress – her handbag, shoes, etc.

MRS. MULWRAY

– he's the Chief Engineer.

DUFFY

(a little eagerly)
– Chief Engineer?

Gittes' glance tells Duffy Gittes wants to do the
questioning. Mrs. Mulwray nods.

GITTES

(confidentially)
This type of investigation can be hard
on your pocketbook, Mrs. Mulwray.
It takes time.

MRS. MULWRAY

Money doesn't matter to me, Mr. Gittes.

Gittes sighs.

GITTES
Very well. We'll see what we can do.

EXT. CITY HALL – MORNING

already shimmering with heat.

(8)

A drunk blows his nose with his fingers into the fountain at the foot of the steps.

Gittes, impeccably dressed, passes the drunk on the way up the stairs.

INT. COUNCIL CHAMBERS

Former Mayor SAM BAGBY is speaking. Behind him is a huge map, with overleafs and bold lettering: "PROPOSED ALTO VALLEJO DAM AND RESERVOIR"
Some of the councilmen are reading funny papers and gossip columns while Bagby is speaking.

BAGBY
– Gentlemen, today you can walk out
that door, turn right, hop on a streetcar
and in twenty-five minutes end up
smack in the Pacific Ocean. Now you
can swim in it, you can fish in it, you can
sail in it – but you can't drink it, you
can't water your lawns with it, you can't
irrigate an orange grove with it.

Remember – we live next door to the
ocean but we also live on the edge of
the desert. Los Angeles is a desert
community. Beneath this building,
beneath every street, there's a desert.
Without water the dust will rise up and
cover us as though we'd never existed!
　　(pausing, letting the implication sink in)

CLOSE – GITTES

sitting next to some grubby farmers, bored. He
yawns – edges away from one of the dirtier farmers.

BAGBY (O.S.)
　　(continuing)
The Alto Vellajo can save us from that
and I respectfully suggest that eight and
a half million dollars is a fair price to pay
to keep the desert from our streets – and
not on top of them.

(9)

AUDIENCE – COUNCIL CHAMBERS

An amalgam of farmers, businessmen, and city
employees have been listening with keen interest.
A couple of the farmers applaud. Somebody
shooshes them.

COUNCIL COMMITTEE

in a whispered conference.

COUNCILMAN
(acknowledging Bagby)
– Mayor Bagby … let's hear from the
departments again – I suppose we better
take Water and Power first. Mr. Mulwray.

REACTION – GITTES

looking up with interest from his racing form.

MULWRAY
walks to the huge map with overleafs. He is a slender
man in his sixties who wears glasses and moves with
surprising fluidity. He turns to a smaller, younger man,
and nods. The man turns the overleaf on the map.

MULWRAY
In case you've forgotten, gentlemen,
over five hundred lives were lost when
the Van der Lip Dam gave way – core
samples have shown that beneath this
bedrock is shale similar to the permeable
shale in the Van der Lip disaster. It
couldn't withstand that kind of pressure
there.
(referring to a new overleaf)
Now you propose yet another dirt-
banked terminus dam with slopes of two
and one half to one, one hundred twelve
feet high and a twelve-thousand-acre
water surface. Well, it won't hold. I won't
build it. It's that simple – I am not
making that kind of mistake twice. Thank
you, gentlemen.

(10)

Mulwray leaves the overleaf board and sits down.
Suddenly there are some whoops and hollers from
the rear of the chambers and a red-faced FARMER
drives in several scrawny, bleating sheep. Naturally,
they cause a commotion.

> **COUNCIL PRESIDENT**
> *(shouting to farmer)*
> What in the hell do you think you're
> doing?
> *(as the sheep bleat down the aisle
> toward the Council)*
> Get those goddam things out of here!

> **FARMER**
> *(right back)*
> Tell me where to take them! You don't
> have an answer for that so quick, do
> you?

Bailiffs and sergeants-at-arms respond to the impre-
cations of the COUNCIL and attempt to capture the
sheep and the farmers, having to restrain one who
looks like he's going to bodily attack Mulwray.

> **FARMER**
> *(through above, to Mulwray)*
> – You steal the water from the Valley, ruin
> the grazing, starve my livestock – who's
> paying you to do that, Mr. Mulwray,
> that's what I want to know!

OMITTED

The scene ends and we cut to Los Angeles River bed where Gittes watches Mulwray through binoculars.

Let's take a look at the first ten pages:

The main character, Jake Gittes (Jack Nicholson) is introduced in his office, showing photographs of Curly's wife being unfaithful.

We learn things about Gittes. On page 1, for example, we find that he "looks cool and brisk in a white linen suit despite the heat." He is shown to be a meticulous man who uses his "handkerchief to wipe away the plunk of perspiration on his desk." When he walks up the steps of City Hall a few pages later, he is "impeccably dressed." These *visual* descriptions convey character traits that reflect his personality. Notice how Gittes is *not physically described* at all; he's not tall, thin, fat, short, or anything else. He seems like a nice guy. "I wouldn't take your last dime," he says. "What kind of a guy do you think I am?" Yet, he offers Curly a drink from a "cheaper bottle of bourbon from the several fifths of more expensive whiskeys." He's vulgar, yet exudes a certain amount of charm and sophistication. He's the kind of man who wears monogrammed shirts and silk handkerchiefs, and has his shoes shined and hair cut at least once a week.

On page 4, Towne reveals the dramatic situation *visually* in the stage directions: "on the pebbled glass can be read J.J. GITTES and Associates – DISCREET INVESTIGATION." Gittes is a private detective who specializes in divorce work, or "other people's dirty linen" as the cop Loach says about him. Later we'll learn he's an ex-cop who left the force and has mixed feelings about cops; when Escobar tells him he made lieutenant after Gittes left Chinatown, the private detective suffers a twinge of envy.

The dramatic premise is established on page 5 (five minutes into the film), when the phony Mrs. Mulwray (Diane Ladd) informs Jake Gittes, "My husband, I believe, is seeing another woman." That statement sets up everything to follow: Gittes, the ex-cop, "checks out the detailing of Mrs. Mulwray's dress – her handbag, shoes, etc." That's his job, and he's very good at what he does.

When Gittes tracks down and takes pictures of "the little twist" Mulwray is supposedly having an affair with, as far as he is concerned, the case is closed. The next day he's surprised to find the pictures he took on the front page of the newspaper with headlines declaring that the head of the Department of Water and Power has been "caught" in a love nest. He doesn't know how his pictures got into the paper. When he returns to his office he is further surprised to find the *real* Mrs. Mulwray (Faye Dunaway) there to greet him, the plot point at the end of Act I.

"Do you know me?" she asks.

"No," Gittes replies. "I would have remembered."

"Since you agree we've never met, you must also agree that I haven't hired you to do anything – certainly not spy on my husband," she says. As she leaves, her attorney hands Gittes a complaint that he could take his license away and smear his name and reputation.

Gittes doesn't know what's going on. If Faye Dunaway is the *real* Mrs. Mulwray, *who* was the woman who hired him and *why*? More important, *who* hired the woman to hire him? Somebody, he doesn't know who or why, has gone to a lot of trouble to set him up. And nobody sets up Jake Gittes! He's going to find out who's responsible and why. That is Jake Gittes' dramatic need, and it drives him through the story until he solves the mystery.

The dramatic premise – "My husband, I believe, is seeing another woman" – sets up the *direction* of the screenplay. And, direction, remember, is "a line of development."

Gittes accepts the case, and finds Hollis Mulwray at City Hall. In the council chambers, a discussion is in progress about the proposed Alto Vallejo dam and reservoir.

In an interview I did with Robert Towne at Sherwood Oaks, he said he approached *Chinatown* from the point of view that "some crimes are punished because they can be punished. If you kill somebody, rob or rape somebody, you'll be caught and thrown into jail. But crimes against an entire community you really can't punish, so you end up rewarding them. You know, those people who get their names on streets and plaques at City Hall. And that's the basic point of view of the story."

"You know something, Jake?" Curly tells Gittes on page 2. "I think I'll kill her [his wife]."

Gittes responds with the prophetic lines that illustrate Towne's point of view. "You gotta be rich to kill somebody, anybody, and get away with it. You think you got that kind of dough, you think you got that kind of class?" (Ironically, this is one of the scenes cut out when the film was trimmed for television.)

Curly certainly can't get away with murder, but Noah Cross (John Huston), Evelyn Mulwray's father and former head of the Department of Water and Power along with Hollis Mulwray, can and does get away with it. The ending of the film shows John Huston whisking his daughter/granddaughter into the night after Faye Dunaway is killed trying to escape. That is Towne's point of view: "You gotta be rich to kill somebody, anybody, and get away with it."

That brings us to the "crime" of *Chinatown*, a scheme based on the water scandal known as The Rape of the Owens Valley. It is the backdrop of *Chinatown*.

In 1900, the city of Los Angeles, "a desert community" as former major Bagby reminds us, was growing and expanding so fast it was literally running out of water. If the city was to survive, it had to find another source of water. L.A. is right next door to the Pacific Ocean. "You can swim in it, you can fish in it, you can sail on it, but you can't drink it, you can't water your lawns with it, and you can't irrigate an orange grove with it," Bagby argues.

The closest water to L.A. is the Owens River, located in the Owens Valley, a green and fertile area about 250 miles northeast of Los Angeles. A group of businessmen, community leaders, and politicians – some call them "men of vision" – saw the need for water and conceived a marvelous scheme. They would buy up the river rights of the Owens River, by force if necessary, then buy up all that worthless land in the San Fernando Valley, about 20 miles outside L.A. Then they would place a bond issue on the ballot that would fund building an aqueduct from the Owens Valley across 250 miles of blazing desert and jagged foothills to the San Fernando Valley. Then they would turn around and sell the now "fertile" land of the San Fernando Valley to the city of Los Angeles for an enormous sum of money; about 300 million dollars.

That was the plan. The government knew about it, the newspapers knew about it, the local politicians all knew about it. When the time was right, the authorities would "influence" the people of Los Angeles to pass the proposed bond issue.

In 1906, a drought fell upon Los Angeles. Things got bad, then worse. People were forbidden to wash their cars or water their lawns; they couldn't flush their toilets more than a few times a day. The city dried up; flowers died, lawns turned brown, and scare headlines declared "Los Angeles is dying of thirst!" "Save our City!"

To underscore the drastic need for water during the drought and to make certain the citizens passed the bond issue, the Department of Water and Power dumped thousands of gallons of water into the ocean.

When it came time to vote, the bond issue passed easily. The Owens Valley aqueduct took several years to complete. When it was finished, William Mulholland, then head of the Department of Water and Power, turned the water over to the city: "There it is," he said. "Take it."

Los Angeles flourished and grew like wildfire, the Owens Valley withered and died. No wonder it was called The Rape of the Owens Valley.

Robert Towne took this scandal that occurred in 1906 and used it as the backdrop in *Chinatown*. He changed the time period from the turn of the century to 1937, when the visual elements of Los Angeles had the classic and distinctive look of Southern California.

The water scandal is woven through the screenplay, and Gittes uncovers it a piece at a time. That's why it's such a great film. *Chinatown* is a voyage of discovery. We learn things at the same time Jake Gittes learns them. Audience and character are linked together, piecing together bits and pieces of information, and putting them together. It *is* a detective story, after all.

When I was conducting the workshop in Brussels, I had an amazing insight into *Chinatown*. I had read the script and seen the movie maybe a half dozen times, but there was still something about it that was bothering me. I had a feeling I was missing something, something I couldn't put into words, something important. While I was in Brussels, I was taken to several of the marvelous art museums of Belgium and got turned on to a group of fifteenth and sixteenth century painters known as the Flemish Primitives: Bosch, Jan van Eyck, Breughel, painters who paved the way and laid down the foundations of modern art.

One weekend I was visiting Bruges, a marvelous fifteenth century city filled with wonderful architecture and canals, and I was taken to a museum featuring early Flemish art. My friend casually pointed out a certain painting. It was bright, colorful and showed two people (the patrons) in the foreground, standing against a beautiful landscape of rolling hills and the sea. It was beautiful. She told me the background I admired was really an Italian landscape. I was surprised and asked her how she knew. She explained it was the custom of the early Flemish painters to travel to Italy to sharpen their skills, to study color and texture, and refine their technique. They sketched and painted Italian landscapes, and then returned to Brussels or Antwerp. When they painted their patrons, they used these landscapes as "backdrops" for their paintings. The paintings are remarkable in style and content.

I looked at that particular painting for a long time, at the patrons in the foreground, admiring the Italian landscape in the background. That's when the light bulb flashed, and suddenly I understood *Chinatown*! I finally understood what had been nagging me about the film. Robert Towne took a scandal that occurred at the turn of the century and used it as the backdrop for a screenplay that takes place in 1937! That's what the Flemish painters did!

That's film! It is a cinematic process that enriches the story.

That's when I knew I had to know more about the Owens Valley. So I researched Bob Towne's research. I learned the origin, background, and the facts of the Owens Valley scandal. The next time I read the script and saw the film it was like seeing it for the first time.

The water scandal that Noah Cross conceives and executes, the crime that causes the deaths of Hollis Mulwray, Leroy the drunk, Ida Sessions, and finally Evelyn Mulwray, the scandal that Jake Gittes uncovers, is woven with great subtlety and skill throughout the entire screenplay, like a fifteenth century Belgian tapestry.

And Noah Cross gets away with murder.

All this is established and set up on page 8 when Gittes is in the council chambers, and we hear Bagby arguing that "eight and a half million dollars is a fair price to pay to keep the deserts from our streets – and not on top of them."

Mulwray, the character modeled on William Mulholland, replies the dam site is unsafe as proven by the previous Van der Lip Dam disaster and says, "I won't build it. It's that simple – I am not making that kind of mistake twice." By refusing to build the dam, Hollis Mulwray becomes a target for murder; he is an obstacle that must be eliminated.

Again, on page 10, the dramatic question of the screenplay is raised: "You steal the water from the Valley, ruin the grazing, starve my livestock – " yells the farmer who invades the chambers. "Who's paying you to do that, Mr. Mulwray, that's what I want to know!"

So does Gittes.

It is *the* question that propels the story to its final resolution and is all *set up* from the very beginning, in the first ten pages, and moves in a *linear* direction to the end.

By introducing the main character, stating the dramatic premise, creating the dramatic situation, the screenplay moves with precision and skill to its own conclusion.

"Either you bring the water to L.A., or you bring L.A. to the water," Noah Cross tells Gittes.

That is the foundation of the entire story. That's what makes it so great.

It's that simple.

Reread the first ten pages of *Chinatown*. See how the backdrop of the action, the scandal, is introduced. See if you can design your opening ten pages in such a way that you introduce the main character, state the dramatic premise, and sketch the dramatic situation in the most cinematic way.

THE PROBLEM SHEET

Set-Ups and Pay-Offs
- Incidents and characters are not paid off
- Scenes lack direction (a line of development)
- No transitions between scenes
- Scenes are too long and too expository
- Tempo is too slow
- Too much or not enough information is being revealed
- Too many plot twists, turns, and contrivances
- Story line seems unstructured, with too much, or not enough, action
- The character's conflict is too internal

In the first few pages of *Thelma & Louise*, Thelma is "packing," literally throwing stuff into a suitcase for their weekend excursion into the mountains, and the last thing she does is open the nightstand drawer next to the bed, and "we see a gun, one Darryl bought her for her protection. It is unloaded, but there is a box of bullets. She picks up the gun like it's a rat by the tail and puts it in her purse ..."

This little scene, more like a mention, doesn't seem like much at the time, just part of her ditzy character, like eating a frozen candy bar for breakfast one bite at a time. Later, when Thelma and Louise are driving toward their anticipated weekend, Thelma hands the gun to Louise saying, "You take care of this." Louise is shocked: "What in the hell did you bring that for?" "Oh, you know ..." Thelma replies. "In case there's any crazy psycho killers on the loose," and they both laugh at her outrageous behavior. Louise tells her to "put it in my purse."

In reality, this little bit seems like a "throwaway," something to shed light on the character, nothing that's really too important. It's only later, when Harlan is in the parking lot, forcing himself on Thelma, that the gun comes into play. Louise takes it out of her purse, orders him to stop, which he does reluctantly, and when he exchanges words with her, she loses it and blows him away.

This gun is integral to the plot of the screenplay. If Thelma had not taken the gun with her, had not given it to Louise, Harlan would not have been killed. They would not become fugitives from the law, and the whole story wouldn't have happened; in short, if there were no gun there wouldn't have been any *Thelma & Louise*.

Setting up some of the various story elements of the screenplay is essential to the art of Problem Solving. Whether a particular element, an object or an event, deals with setting up the story, setting up a character, or character trait, understanding when and when not to establish a story point is the difference between a script that works and one that does not.

The setting up of these story elements often becomes the "glue" that holds everything together, which is why it's a problem of *Structure*, not *Plot* or *Character*. If it ain't on the page, it ain't on the stage is the old Hollywood expression, and knowing when to set something up and then pay it off is fundamental to the craft of screenwriting.

Different things must be set up, then incorporated into the story line – that's one of the principal rules of all writing. One of the most important elements is setting up the *dramatic premise* of the screenplay; that is, *what the story is about*. The Set-Up also refers to setting up the first ten pages of the screenplay, establishing the inciting incident, as well as providing enough exposition to move the story forward. Setting up these elements gives texture and direction, the natural line of development to the narrative.

Characters also have to be set up, along with their characteristics and their manners of behavior. Character aspects serve a variety of dramatic functions, like Louise knowing how to handle a gun. What happened to her in Texas when she was growing up, the *Circle of Being*, is a character element that is essential to know. It was Louise, the young girl raped in Texas, who really pulled the trigger, not the Louise of the present.

If certain elements of character are set up, then they have to be paid off. In *The Shawshank Redemption*, Andy Dufresne had been a respectable banker in a Portland, Maine, bank, before being convicted of his wife's murder, so he knows enough about the system to create a fictitious identity, to establish a phony driver's license, birth certificate, and passport, as well as duplicate a set of account books. So we believe he could take the warden's money – which he has laundered and deposited in banks all over the Portland, Maine, area – to Mexico. "On the outside," he says to Red, "I was an honest man. I had to come to prison to learn how to be a crook." And that information, which had been set up early in the screenplay, was not finally paid off until the end of the Second Act. So it really doesn't matter where the story point is paid off, as long as it is set up properly, whether it's related to the character or the plot.

There are other elements that need to be set up in a screenplay, specific objects, for example, like the gun in *Thelma & Louise*, or the rock hammer in *The Shawshank Redemption*. These particular objects are essential to the story line, so they need to be planted in the screenplay at different points within the landscape of the story. In *The Shawshank Redemption* we have seen the warden giving Andy clothes to take to the prison laundry, and shoes to shine, so when he gives Andy his clothes and shoes on the night he makes his escape, it's totally believable, meaning it's paid off. The "willing suspension of disbelief" has been set up and we buy it. It's good writing.

So understanding how to set up characters, situations, and objects in a screenplay and then paying them off is necessary to the Problem-Solving process.

This was something I had to learn in my own screenwriting experience. When I first started writing screenplays, I didn't know anything. I didn't know what a screenplay was, I didn't know what it meant to tell a story with pictures, I had no idea about structure or building a story, and didn't know anything about setting up a story or situation, or paying it off, for that matter. Though I had been an English major at UC Berkeley, as well as a published film and book reviewer, I still didn't have the foggiest notion about the nature and craft of screenwriting.

So I did the only thing I could do: I got hold of some screenplays from the filmmakers I admired the most and started reading and rereading the material. I have mentioned Jean Renoir's contribution to my understanding of film education in both *Screenplay* and *The Screenwriter's Workbook*.

But I consider two writer-directors to have been my teachers, and both were masters of the cinema. One of them was the great Sam Peckinpah (*The Wild Bunch*, *Pat Garrett and Billy the Kid*, and *The Ballad of Cable Hogue*, to name just a few).

The other filmmaker I studied was the magnificent, revolutionary, and influential Michelangelo Antonioni. The Italian director is a master of setting up and weaving emotional attitudes and characterizations throughout his films.

These filmmakers taught me everything. And I was so struck with Peckinpah's *Ride the High Country* that I decided that this was what great screenwriting was all about. So when I managed to get hold of the script of *Major Dundee* (written by Peckinpah with Oscar Saul) I think I must have read it at least a hundred times, analyzing it, taking it apart, memorizing it scene by scene, action by action, character by character, trying to understand what made it tick and what made it work so successfully. It was a wonderful education and illustration of how to set up the dramatic premise of the story line.

There are several good examples of how you set things up in order to pay them off later. If you do want to set something up, think of it as a "*noun*"; you're going to be setting up a "*person, place, or thing*," either a character, or a situation, or an object. *Thelma & Louise* is a great example: the gun Thelma puts into her purse at the beginning of the film is paid off at Plot Point I when Harlan is shot in the parking lot.

In that case it was setting up an object, or "thing." Setting up her character, in order to expand the situation, is revealed later when Louise was raped in Texas. As a matter of fact, when you read the screenplay of this film, everything is carefully set up from the very beginning; Louise's relationship with her boyfriend, Jimmy, actually the back story that results in the two women going to the mountains for the weekend; and tracing the emotional arc of Thelma's growth from being locked in her marriage with Darryl in the opening allows her to grow into a free-thinking, independent woman.

When and where to set up things in a scene, sequence, or act, and when, where, and how to pay them off, means knowing your story and characters well. If you don't know the basic and essential elements of your story line, or if you're vague and unclear about the progression of events, or the character's arc, this lack of information, this lack of preparation will often create problems in the screenplay. This is really what writing's all about, asking yourself the right questions so you can reach levels that keep the story moving forward with depth and dimension. It creates a framework of universality around your work. This is your responsibility as writer; if you don't know what's going on in your story, then who does?

There are times in the screenplay when a particular piece of information, or a physical item, is set up in one scene, and then paid off in the very next. Or the information or object can be paid off several scenes later, or even later than that, as is the case in *Crimson Tide*.

In this, the story is set up from the opening scene of the screenplay. A news reporter is shown at sea on an aircraft carrier, and he explains, with the help of actual newsreel footage, that a band of Russian rebels have taken over the government and are threatening to launch a nuclear attack against the US. In response, the nuclear sub *Alabama* is ordered to sea, and Act I is devoted to setting up the Russian threat, introducing and setting up the Denzel Washington character – Hunter, XO – and the Gene Hackman character – Ramsey, the captain of the vessel – and preparing the sub. At Plot Point I the sub casts off and begins its underwater mission. That basically sets up the story.

THE DEFINITIVE GUIDE TO SCREENWRITING

The First Half of Act II deals with expanding the characters and clarifying their points of view. There's a little dialogue exchange that succinctly summarizes the differences in their philosophies of war. It also shows us the differences in their points of view, because it is this conflict that fuels the entire film. If the differences in their points of view had not been set up and established, the entire story would fail to work; there would be no conflict, no mutiny attempt, no story, and the *Alabama* would just cruise the waters until the situation in Russia resolved itself. Basically, their differing points of view would be like two parallel lines moving toward infinity without ever connecting. That's not how you build the structure of a screenplay.

Crimson Tide reflects the nature of the classic "tragic situation." Hegal, the nineteenth-century German philosopher, always proclaimed that the true nature of tragedy is not a conflict between "good and evil," or "right and wrong," but resides in the conflict between "good versus good," or "right versus right." Both sides of the conflict are right in the actions they pursue. And *Crimson Tide* personifies this in an exciting and entertaining presentation. It's a very good film.

The setting up and paying off of story points is integral to the art and craft of screenwriting. Every scene, every sequence, every Plot Point and story point, must be set up, established, and then, at the right moment, paid off. Nothing can be set up without later being paid off.

For every action, remember, there is an equal and opposite reaction.

THE SCENE

8

The scene is the single most important element in your screenplay. It is where something happens – where something *specific* happens. It is a specific unit of action – and the place you tell your story.

Good scenes make good movies. When you think of a good movie, you remember *scenes*, not the entire film. Think of *Psycho*. What scene do you recall? The shower scene, of course. What about *Butch Cassidy and the Sundance Kid*? *Star Wars*? *Citizen Kane*? *Casablanca*?

The way you present your scenes on the page ultimately affects the entire screenplay. A screenplay is a reading experience.

The purpose of the scene is to *move the story forward*.

A scene is as long or short as you want. It can be a three-page dialogue scene, or as short as a single shot – a car streaking down the highway. The scene is what you want it to be.

The story determines how long or how short your scene is. There is only one rule to follow; trust your story. It will tell you everything you need to know. I've noticed many people have a tendency to make a rule for everything. If there are eighteen scenes and two sequences in the first thirty pages of some screenplay or movie, they feel *their* first thirty pages must have eighteen scenes and two sequences. You can't write a screenplay following numbers as you do a drugstore painting.

It doesn't work – trust your story to tell you what you need to know.

We're going to approach the scene from two sides: we're going to explore the *generalities* of the scene, that is, the *form*, and then we'll examine the *specifics* of the scene; how you create a scene from the elements or components you have within that scene.

Two things are in every scene – PLACE and TIME.

Where does your scene take *place*? In an office? A car? At the beach? In the mountains? On a crowded city street? What is the *location* of the scene?

The other element is *time*. What time of day or night does your scene take place? In the morning? Afternoon? Late at night?

Every scene occurs within a specific *place* at a specific *time*. All you need to indicate, however, is DAY or NIGHT.

Where does your scene take place? *Inside* or *outside*; or INT. for interior, EXT. for exterior. So the form of the scene becomes:

> INT. LIVING ROOM – NIGHT

or

> EXT. STREET – DAY

PLACE and TIME. You need to know these things before you can build and construct a scene.

If you change either *place* or *time* it becomes a new scene.

We saw, in the first ten pages of *Chinatown*, Curly in Jake's office, upset because of his wife. Gittes gives him a drink of cheap whiskey, then they walk out of his office into the reception area.

When they move from Nicholson's office into the reception area, it is a new scene; they have changed *place*.

Gittes is called into his associate's office and hired by the phony Mrs. Mulwray. The scene in the associate's office is a new scene. They have changed the *place* of the scene – one scene in Gittes' office, another in the reception area, and another in his associate's office. Three scenes in the *office sequence*.

If your scene takes place in a house, and you move from the bedroom to kitchen to living room, you have three individual scenes. Your scene might take place in the bedroom between a man and a woman. They kiss passionately, then move to the bed. When the CAMERA PANS to the window where the sky changes from night to day, then PANS back to our couple waking up, it is a new scene. You have changed the *time* of your scene.

If your character is driving a car up a mountain road at night and you want to show him at different locations, you must change your scenes accordingly: EXT. MOUNTAIN ROAD – NIGHT to EXT. MOUN- TAIN ROAD, FURTHER – NIGHT.

There's a reason for this; the physical necessity of changing the position of the CAMERA for each scene or shot in the new location. Each scene requires a change in CAMERA position (Note: the word CAMERA is always capitalized in the screenplay) and therefore requires a change in lighting. That's why movie crews are so large and the cost of filming a movie is so expensive. As the price of labor esca- lates, the cost per minute increases and we end up paying more at the box office.

Scene changes are absolutely essential in the development of your screenplay. The scene is where it all happens – where you tell your story in *moving pictures*.

A scene is constructed in terms of beginning, middle, and end, just like a screenplay. Or, it can be presented in part, a portion of the whole like showing only the end of the scene. Again, there's no rule – it is your story, so you make the rules.

Every scene reveals at least one element of necessary story infor- mation to reader or audience. Very rarely does it provide more. The infor- mation the audience receives is the nucleus, or purpose, of the scene.

Generally, there are two kinds of scenes: one, where something happens *visually*, like an action scene – the chase that opens *Star Wars*, or the fight scenes in *Rocky*. The other is a *dialogue* scene between one or more persons. Most scenes combine the two. In a dialogue scene, there's usually some action going on, and in an action scene, there's usually some dialogue. A dialogue scene is usually about three pages long or less. That's three minutes of screen time. Sometimes it's longer, but not often. The "aborted" love scene in *Silver Streak* is nine pages long; a few scenes in *Network* are seven pages long. If you write a dialogue scene between two people, try to keep it under three pages. There's no room in your screenplay to be "cute," "clever," or "gimmicky." You can tell your life story in three minutes if you have to; most scenes in contemporary screenplays are only a few pages long.

Within the body of your scene, something specific happens – your *characters* move from point A to point B; or your *story* moves from point A to point B. Your story always moves forward. Even in "flash-back." *Julia*, *Annie Hall*, and *Midnight Cowboy* are structured to include the flashback as an integral part of the story. The flashback is a technique used to expand the audience's comprehension of story, characters, and situation.

How do you go about creating a scene?

First create the *context*, then determine *content*.

What happens in the scene? What is the *purpose* of the scene? Why is it there? How does it move the story forward? What happens?

An actor sometimes approaches a scene by finding out what he's doing there, where he's been and where he's going after the scene. What is his purpose in the scene? Why is he there?

As writer, it's your responsibility to know why your characters are in a scene, and how their actions, or dialogue, move the story forward. You've got to know what happens to your characters *in* the scenes, as well as what happens to them *in between* the scenes; what happened between the office Monday afternoon, and Thursday evening at dinner? If you don't know, who does?

By creating *context*, you determine dramatic purpose and can build your scene line by line, action by action. By creating *context*, you establish *content*.

OK. How do you do that?

First, find the *components* or *elements* within the scene. What aspect of your character's *professional* life, *personal* life, or *private* life is going to be revealed?

Let's go back to the story of three guys holding up the Chase Manhattan Bank. Suppose we want to write a scene where our characters definitely decide to rob the bank. Up until now, they've only talked about it. Now, they're going to do it. That's *context*. Now, *content*.

Where does your scene take place?

In the bank? Home? Bar? Inside a car? Walking in the park? The obvious place to set it would be in a quiet, secluded location, perhaps a rented car on the highway. That's the obvious place for the scene. It works, but maybe there's something more visual we can use; this is, after all, a movie.

Actors often play "against the grain" of a scene; that is, they approach the scene not from the obvious approach, but the *unobvious* approach. For example, they'll play an "angry" scene smiling softly, hiding their rage or anger beneath a façade of niceness. Brando is a master at this.

In *Silver Streak*, Colin Higgins writes a love scene between Jill Clayburgh and Gene Wilder in which they talk about flowers! It's beautiful. Orson Welles, in *The Lady from Shanghai*, had a love scene with Rita Hayworth in an aquarium, in front of the sharks and barracudas.

When you're writing a scene, look for a way that dramatizes the scene "against the grain."

Suppose we use a crowded pool hall, at night, as the setting for the "decision" scene in our Chase Manhattan Bank story. We can introduce an element of suspense in the scene; as our characters shoot pool and discuss their decision to rob the bank, a policeman enters, wanders around. It adds a touch of dramatic tension. Hitchcock does it all the time. Visually, we might open with a shot of the eight ball, then pull back to reveal our characters leaning over the table talking about the job.

Once the *context* is determined – the purpose, place, and time – then the *content* follows.

Suppose we want to write a scene about the ending of a relationship. How would we do it?

First, establish the purpose of the scene. In this case it is the ending of a relationship. Second – find out *where* the scene takes place and *when*, day or night. It could take place in a car, on a walk, in a movie theater, or a restaurant. Let's use a restaurant; it's an ideal place to end a relationship.

Here's *context*. Have they been together long? How long? In relationships about to end, usually one person wants it to end and the other hopes it won't. Let's say *he* wants to end it with *her*. He doesn't want to hurt her; he wants to be as "nice" and "civilized" as he can.

Of course, it always backfires. Remember the breakup scene in *An Unmarried Woman*, where Michael Murphy has lunch with Jill Clayburgh, but can't force himself to say the words. He waits until they're on the street, after lunch, then breaks down and blurts out the words.

First, find the components of the scene. What is there in a restaurant that we can use dramatically? The waiters, the food, someone sitting nearby; an old friend?

The *content* of the scene now becomes part of the *context*.

He doesn't want to "hurt" her, so he's quiet and uncomfortable. Use the *uncomfortableness*: run-on sentences, staring off into the distance, watching nearby diners; perhaps the waiter overhears a few remarks, and he's a surly Frenchman, possibly gay. You get to choose!

This is a method that allows you to stay on top of your story, so the story's not on top of you. As a writer, you must exercise *choice* and *responsibility* in the construction and presentation of your scenes.

Look for conflicts; make something difficult, more difficult. It adds tension.

Remember the scene at the outdoor restaurant in *Annie Hall*? Annie tells Woody Allen that she just wants to be his "friend," and not continue their relationship. Both are uncomfortable and this adds tension to the scene by heightening the comedic overtones; when he leaves the restaurant he collides with several cars, tears up his driver's license in front of a policeman. It's hysterical! Woody Allen utilizes the situation for maximum dramatic effectiveness.

Comedy works by creating a situation, then letting people act and react to the situation and each other. In comedy, you can't have your characters playing for laughs; they have to believe what they're doing, otherwise it becomes forced and contrived, and therefore, unfunny.

Remember the Italian film *Divorce, Italian Style*, with Marcello Mastroianni? A classic film comedy, only a thin lines separates it from being a classic tragedy. Comedy and tragedy are two sides of the same coin. Mastroianni is married to a woman who makes enormous sexual demands on him and he can't cope with it. Especially when he meets a voluptuous young cousin who's crazy about him. He wants a divorce but, alas, the Church won't recognize it. What's an Italian man to do? The only way the Church will recognize the end of the marriage is for the wife to die. But she's as healthy as a horse.

He decides to kill her. Under Italian law, the only way he can kill her with honor and get away with it is if she's unfaithful; he has to be cuckolded. So he sets out to find a lover for his wife.

That's the situation!

After many, many funny moments, she *is* unfaithful to him, and his Italian honor demands he take action. He tracks her and her lover to an island in the Aegean Sea, and searches for them, gun in hand.

The characters are caught within the web of circumstances and play their roles with exaggerated seriousness; the result is film comedy at its best.

Woody Allen generates beautiful situations. In *Annie Hall*, *Sleeper*, and *Play It Again, Sam*, he creates a situation and then lets his characters react to it. In comedy, says Woody Allen, "acting funny is the worst thing you can do."

Comedy, like drama, depends on "real people in real situations."

Neil Simon creates marvelous people who operate at cross-purposes, then lets the "sparks fly" as they encounter obstacle after obstacle. He establishes a strong situation, then puts strong, believable people in it. In *The Goodbye Girl*, Richard Dreyfuss sublets an apartment from a friend, and when he arrives to take possession, in the midst of a driving rainstorm at three o'clock in the morning, he finds the apartment occupied by Marsha Mason and her daughter. She refuses to leave because "possession is nine-tenths of the law!"

What follows is scene after scene of verbal humor; they hate each other, tolerate each other, finally love each other.

When you set out to write a scene, find the purpose of the scene, then root it in place and time. Then find the elements or components within the scene to build it and make it work.

One of my favorite scenes from *Chinatown* is when Jack Nicholson and Faye Dunaway are at her house after the Mar Vista Home for the Aged sequence. During the previous eighteen hours, Gittes has almost drowned, been beaten up twice, had his nose sliced, lost one Florsheim shoe, and has had no sleep at all. He's tired and hurts all over.

His nose hurts. He asks her if she has any peroxide to clean his nose wound, and she takes him into the bathroom. She daubs his nose, and he notices something in her eye, a slight color defect. Their eyes hold, then he leans forward and kisses her.

The next scene takes place after they've made love. It's a beautiful illustration of what you should look for when you plan a scene. Find the *components* within the scene to make it work; in this case, it was the hydrogen peroxide in the bathroom.

Every scene, like a sequence, an act, or an entire screenplay, has a definite beginning, middle, and end. But you only need to show *part* of the scene. You can choose to show only the beginning, just the middle, or only the end.

For example, in three-guys-holding-up-the-Chase-Manhattan-Bank, you can start the scene in the *middle* when they're playing pool. The beginning of the scene, where they arrive, get a table, practice, then start the game, does not have to be shown unless you choose to show it. The ending of the scene, when they leave the pool hall, doesn't have to be shown either.

Very rarely is a scene depicted in its entirety. The scene, more often than not, is a fragment of the *whole*. William Goldman, who wrote *Butch Cassidy and the Sundance Kid* and *All the President's Men*, among others, once remarked that he doesn't enter his scenes until the last possible moment; that is, just before the ending of some specific action in the scene.

In the bathroom scene in *Chinatown*, Towne shows the *beginning* of the love scene, then cuts to the *ending* of the bed scene.

You, as writer, are completely in control of how you create your scenes to move your story forward. You *choose* what part of the scene you are going to show.

Colin Higgins is a writer of unique film comedies. (With *Foul Play* he's become a director as well.) *Harold and Maude* is a fantastic comic situation – a young man of twenty and a woman of eighty create a special relationship together. *Harold and Maude* is a case where the audience gradually found the film and over a period of years made it an underground "classic" of the American cinema.

In *Silver Streak* Higgins creates a marvelous love scene that is "against the grain." Gene Wilder, as George, and Jill Clayburgh, as Hilly, have met in the dining car, like each other, and get drunk together. They decide to spend the evening together. She gets the room, and he gets the champagne. The scene opens as George returns to his compartment, flushed with alcohol and expectation.

(page 19 of screenplay)

INT. THE CORRIDOR – NIGHT

Giggling to himself and humming "The Atchison, Topeka and the Santa Fe," George makes his way down the corridor. Suddenly one of the Fat Men steps out of his compartment at the far end and begins walking toward George. George stops and leans against a door to let him pass. It is a very tight and difficult maneuver for the Fat Man to pass and in the struggle George's hand lands on the door handle.

Immediately the door flies open and George staggers back into the room. He turns to see a large, ugly MEXICAN LADY in her nightshirt kneeling at her bed saying her prayers. She takes one look at George and in violent Spanish begins panic-praying to ward off the oncoming rape.

George freaks, and bowing and mumbling apologies, hurriedly exits to the safety of the corridor, closing the door behind him. He pauses for a moment to regain his composure, burps, and then starts off again. Immediately the second Fat Man exits from his compartment and makes his way toward George.

George sighs but not wishing to go through the whole scene again he backs up past the Mexican Lady's door, and knocks on the next door down. He opens it, steps inside for a second to let the Fat Man pass, then turns to the occupant. He is a very distinguished gentleman, suavely attired, who looks up from the papers he has been reading. This is ROGER DEVEREAU.

GEORGE

Excuse me.

Not waiting for a response George smiles and quickly closes the door. He continues on down the corridor.

INT. GEORGE'S CORRIDOR

George arrives outside his door and knocks.

HILLY'S VOICE

Come in.

George enters.

INT. GEORGE'S COMPARTMENT

True to her word Hilly has gotten the porter to push back the partition and make their two rooms into one. The effect is remarkably spacious – and very romantic as the two couches have been turned into beds. George looks around and smiles.

GEORGE

This is *very nice.*

Hilly is lying on her bed with her shoes on. She is putting a tape into her portable cassette player.

(20)

HILLY

Wait. I'm still working on the lights and music. All they offer on the intercom is a choice between classical and popular. This is the classical.

She presses a button by her bed and we HEAR the cannon finale from Tchaikovsky's "1812."

HILLY

And this is the popular.

She presses another button and we hear Guy Lombardo playing "The Donkey Serenade."

GEORGE

That's the popular? I think we're in a
time warp.

George has taken off his coat and tie and goes to
the bathroom to get a towel for the champagne.
Hilly puts her cassette player down by the bed and
turns it on.

HILLY

So I'm settling for this.

From the cassette player we hear the lilting love song
known as "Hilly's Theme."

GEORGE

Beautiful.

He comes out of the bathroom and sits beside her on
the bed.

GEORGE

I love that song. And now whenever I
hear it I'll be thinking of you.

He leans over and kisses her softly on the cheek.
Hilly likes it.

HILLY

You put that very nicely.

GEORGE

Thank you. Some champagne?

HILLY

Please.

George begins undoing one of the bottles.

(21)

GEORGE

I can't get over the size of this place with
the partition down.

HILLY

They are small rooms individually ... but
perfect for juggling.

GEORGE

For what?

HILLY

Juggling. When you practice the balls
would always bounce off the walls.

She demonstrates with three imaginary balls. George
smiles and pops the cork. He fills the glasses.

GEORGE

You juggle a lot?

HILLY

(slyly)
I know what goes where – and why.

George stops, looks her in the eye, and she smiles
back innocently. He grins and they begin chuckling
with an easy fun-filled sensuality. George offers her a
glass of champagne.

                    GEORGE
Yours.

                    HILLY
Thank you.

                    GEORGE
And mine.

He leans back on the bed and they face each other.

                    GEORGE
To us. And the romance of the railroad.

                    HILLY
Trains that pass in the night.

They sip.

                    HILLY
Why don't you take your shoes off?
You're sup-

(22)

posed to put them in that little locker
and the porter will have them shined for
you in the morning.

                    GEORGE
Really? That's terrific.

While taking off his shoes he glances at the
Rembrandt book on the chair.

GEORGE

This the master's work?

HILLY

Uh huh. He gave me that copy for safe-
keeping. Want to read it?

George puts his shoes in the little locker near the
door.

GEORGE

Later.

He turns off the overhead lights, leaving on the blue
night lights and the orange reading lamps. It is a
romantic combination and Hilly smiles her approval.

HILLY

Grab your pillow and we can look at the
desert in the moonlight.

GEORGE

Great idea.

George takes the pillow from his bed, which lies
parallel with the window, over to Hilly's bed, which
lies vertical with the window.

GEORGE

Slide over.

They snuggle on the bed so that they are both lying
on their backs with George's arm around Hilly's
shoulder. For a moment they just stare out the

window, watching the cactus and the desert hills of
the Mojave zip by under the stars.

> **HILLY**
>
> Beautiful, isn't it?

> **GEORGE**
>
> Very.

He puts down his glass and kisses her hair. She rolls
over and faces him.

(23)

> **HILLY**
>
> George?

> **GEORGE**
>
> Yes.

> **HILLY**
>
> Do you really edit sex manuals?

> **GEORGE**
>
> I really do. But I have a confession to make.

> **HILLY**
>
> Oh?

> **GEORGE**
>
> I'm actually much better at books on
> gardening.

> **HILLY**
>
> *(smiling)*
> Really?

GEORGE

Oh, yes. That's my special field.

HILLY

An authority?

GEORGE

Absolutely.

Hilly begins unbuttoning his shirt.

HILLY

Well then, is there anything you might
want to pass on?

GEORGE

You mean a few tips on gardening techniques?

HILLY

Yes. Some helpful hints for the beginner.

GEORGE

Well, when gardening one rule to
remember is – be nasty to nasturtiums.

Hilly kisses his naked chest and giggles.

HILLY

Is that so?

(24)

GEORGE

Oh, yes.

HILLY

They like it rough, huh?

GEORGE

The rougher the better.

She kisses his chin.

HILLY

Great. What else should I know?

GEORGE

There's the secret for treating azaleas.

HILLY

Tell me. I'm all ears.

She snuggles into his neck and begins biting his ear.

GEORGE

Treat them the same as begonias.

HILLY

No kidding?

GEORGE

It's gospel.

HILLY
(wanting to get it straight)
So you're saying: "What's good for
azaleas is good for begonias."

> **GEORGE**
> I couldn't have expressed it better
> myself.

Hilly leans up on one elbow.

> **HILLY**
> George, this is fascinating.

> **GEORGE**
> Didn't I tell you.

> **HILLY**
> I'd like to delve deeper.

> **GEORGE**
> Be my guest.

(25)

> She goes back to kissing his chest and begins
> working her way down toward his navel.

> **HILLY**
> Well, then, what would happen if you
> treated an azalea like a nasturtium?

George glances at the window – and freezes.

NEW ANGLE – SHOCK CUT

Out the window the dead body of a man suddenly
slams into FRAME. He dangles grotesquely, held up
by his coat caught on a protruding bolt. George
gasps. The train WHISTLE screams.

We see clearly the face of the dead man – an older gentleman with a white moustache and goatee. He has been beaten and shot in the head and the blood trickles down the side of his face.

George jumps off the bed. The body sways for another second then falls away. The WHISTLE stops and all is still once more.

INT. GEORGE'S COMPARTMENT – ANOTHER ANGLE

Hilly has seen nothing but she looks up at George, staring transfixed at the empty window.

> **HILLY**
> George. What is it? I'm sorry I asked the question.

> **GEORGE**
> Did you see that? That man?

George flips on the light and rushes to the window, trying to look back down the tracks.

> **HILLY**
> What man?

> **GEORGE**
> There was a man out the window. He'd been shot in the head.

> **HILLY**
> What?

GEORGE

(very excitedly)

Hilly, I'm not joking. A dead man fell off the

(26)

roof. His coat was caught. I saw it. What should I do? I've got to report it. Maybe they can stop the train.

HILLY

Hey, hey, hey! Lighten up!

She gets off the bed and takes hold of him.

HILLY

C'mon now. Sit down. You need a little more champagne.

GEORGE

I'm not kidding, Hilly. I saw it.

HILLY

Okay. Here.

George sits and Hilly pours him some champagne. George drinks it down in one gulp.

GEORGE

Wow! I can't believe it.

HILLY

Me neither.

GEORGE

But I saw it, really I did.

HILLY

Of course you did. You saw something.
But who knows what it was. An old
newspaper. A kid's kite. A Halloween
mask. It could have been anything.

GEORGE

No, I'm sure it was a body – a dead
man. His eyes were so clear.

HILLY

More clear than your head. George, you
imagined it.

GEORGE

No, I'm positive I didn't.

HILLY

All right then, call the conductor and tell
him your story. We've still got another
bottle of champagne.

(27)

GEORGE

He'll think I've been drinking.

HILLY

Where would he get that idea?

GEORGE

But, Hilly, it was so vivid.

HILLY

Come here.

Hilly fluffs up his pillow and urges him to put his legs up. George rubs his forehead.

GEORGE

Wow, I feel kind of dizzy.

HILLY

Lie down.

George falls back on the bed with a sigh. Hilly picks up the cassette recorder, which stopped playing when George knocked it over, and looks around for a place where it will be safe. She starts the music ("Hilly's Theme") and puts it on a high overhanging rack near the window.

GEORGE

Boy, if that's what the DTs are like, I'm
giving up the bottle for life.

HILLY

The mind plays funny tricks all the time.
You know that. Just relax and forget it.

Hilly turns off the lights and lies alongside George. He looks at her for a long moment.

GEORGE

That sure is a pretty song.

> **HILLY**
> Yes, it is.

He kisses her gently on the lips and then looks at her with a great deal of tenderness.

> **GEORGE**
> You are very beautiful, Hilly.

Hilly despite her sophistication is not used to this tenderness. Tears well in her eyes.

(28)

> **HILLY**
> I like you, too.

He moves forward again and they kiss long and passionately. This is the first time they have showed their real need and mutual desire and when the kiss is broken they both look at each other knowing that this feeling between them is truly something special.

> **GEORGE**
> Are you sure I'm not dreaming?

> **HILLY**
> Maybe we both are.

She falls into his arms and he hugs her longingly.

Notice how the scene incorporates a beginning, middle, and end. This is also the plot point at the end of Act I, so find "the incident or event" that takes us into Act II. Notice the subtly expressed warmth between the two characters. On screen, Wilder and Clayburgh breathed life into it, and it became a lovely moment.

It's a perfect example of a scene that works!

Create a scene by creating a *context* and then establishing *content*. Find the purpose of the scene, then choose the *place* and *time* for the scene. Find the *components* or *elements* within the scene to create conflict and dimension and to generate drama. Drama, remember, is conflict; seek it out.

Your story always moves forward, step by step, scene by scene, toward the resolution.

THE PROBLEM SHEET

The Flash Point
- Characters are too talky and explain too much
- Main character is not very sympathetic
- The main character is a loner and has no one to talk to
- The main character has no point of view
- The action is too thin
- The emotional stakes are not high enough
- Something seems to be missing
- The story line is too episodic, too jerky, and needs transitions
- The story seems confusing
- The story wanders and gets bogged down in too many details

What's the best way to use a flashback? When does it work the best and when is it most effective?

These are some of the most common questions I encounter regarding the flashback; it really doesn't matter what country I'm in, or whether the writers are students or professionals. For some reason, the use of flashbacks in a screenplay seems to elicit indecision and insecurity. So, when I'm asked what's the best way to use a flashback, I listen patiently then ask why the screenwriter wants to use one in the first place. The person usually becomes very serious and states that the flashback gives information that's essential to the story.

That's cool, I respond, but if you use the flashback in this particular situation, does it move the story forward? Or, does it reveal something about the character? Remember, the flashback is simply a tool, a device, which the screenwriter uses to provide the reader with information that he or she cannot incorporate into the screenplay any other way. That's something most writers don't understand or take into consideration. That's why there seems to be so much confusion about whether to use a flashback or not.

The purpose of the flashback is simple: it is a device that *bridges time and place either to reveal information about the main character, or to move the story forward*.

When flashbacks are done well and integrated into the narrative line of the story, as in *How to Make an American Quilt*, *Courage Under Fire* (Patrick Duncan), and *The English Patient* (Anthony Minghella), the flashback works wonderfully. But when a flashback is thrown into the screenplay because the writer doesn't know how to move the story forward any other way, or decides to show something about the main character that could be better stated in dialogue, then the flashback only draws attention to itself and becomes intrusive. That's when it doesn't work.

The flashback is a tool; it should be used to give the viewer information about the character or story that he can't get any other way. It can reveal *emotional* as well as *physical* information (as with Andy Dufresne's breakout from Shawshank), though it often does both, and can show different points of view of the same event, as in *Courage Under Fire*. Or it can reveal thoughts, memories, or dreams, as in *The English Patient*.

That's when the flashback is most effective. If it is incorrectly used, as the *Problem Sheet* reveals, it only highlights flaws: characters who are too thin and weak, action too subtle or episodic, and the story itself seeming to wander around searching for itself, like a dog chasing its tail.

I firmly believe that flashbacks are an aspect of *Character*, not story. As a matter of fact, I tell my students that a flashback is really a *"flash-present*," because what we're really seeing is what the character is thinking and feeling in *present time*, whether a memory, an event, or fantasy, or the illumination of the character's point of view. What we see in a flashback is shown through the eyes of the character, so we're seeing what he or she is seeing, thinking, or feeling in present time; in this time and in this place. No matter what it is. Take a look at *The English Patient* again; the action all takes place in present time with the character remembering moments in the past. The *"flashpresent"* is anything the character is thinking and feeling in the present moment, whether a thought, a dream, a memory, or a hope, a fear, or a fantasy, for time has no restraints or limits. In the character's head the *"flashpresent"* could be past, present, or future.

In *Courage Under Fire*, for example, the same incident is seen through the eyes of different characters, and each one views it differently. The *subject* of the script is honor; it dramatizes how a person must learn to live with a mistake he made that resulted in the death of a friend. Not only that, but the Denzel Washington character is forced to lie to the dead man's family at the urging of the military. The *context* of the film, what holds it together, the circumstances or situation, is the Gulf War of 1991. Each particular flashback reveals what happened when a medic helicopter on a rescue mission was shot down by Iraqi soldiers.

What happened when the helicopter went down? That's the assignment of the officer in charge, Colonel Serling, played by Denzel Washington. The pilot who flew the mission is being considered for the Medal of Honor, America's highest and most prestigious military award. But it turns out there are some discrepancies in the survivors' stories, and to add further fuel to the fire, the captain of the medic helicopter is a woman, played by Meg Ryan. Colonel Serling is told by the White House that it is important politically for her to receive the medal, for it will be the first time a woman would have been so honored for courage under fire.

The script begins with an incident in the Gulf War (1991) that takes place at night in the heat of battle. Colonel Serling makes the decision to fire at a tank that does not respond to his message. Only after the tank is destroyed, and all men lost, does he learn the tank was one of his own, captained by his friend. That's the *inciting incident* of the screenplay, the incident or event that catapults the story into motion. When he returns to the States, he's given the assignment of investigating the woman's actions, and is forced to look into the mirror of his own soul to examine his own actions under fire, which he cannot forgive or forget.

So we explore the subject of "courage under fire." As he's investigating the actions of the Meg Ryan character, he forces himself to seek out the truth, while under constant pressure from the White House and the military. He finds that for each step he takes, his actions are reflected back at him through his own experience.

But it's the perfect setup for using the flashback. This is the kind of story I call an "emotional detective story," for each member of the surviving crew sees the action differently. It's a *Rashomon-type* story, and it's up to the Denzel Washington character to sort things out and find "the truth." His search becomes a journey of transformation and self-forgiveness.

It's true there are two different stories in this screenplay, but both stories reflect the emotional scar that remains unhealed in Colonel Serling's heart, and his dramatic need is to resolve the conflict within himself.

If your screenplay was not conceived to incorporate flashbacks and doesn't seem to be working, see whether "the problem" exhibits some of the symptoms listed on the *Problem Sheet*. If the answer is yes, and you think a flashback may solve the problem, whatever it is, then the simple rule "If you can say it, don't show it" may apply.

Now, I'm sure this sounds like a contradiction, because the object of a screenplay is to tell the story in pictures, not words. The dialogue only becomes an adjunct to the visual information that moves the story forward; either that, or it reveals information about the character. Suppose, for example, you want to show an event that has affected your character, and you decide to incorporate it into the script. So you go through the scene and find a place to lead into the flashback, which naturally results in your cutting away from the middle of the scene to insert the flashback. What happens? In the case of *The English Patient* it works wonderfully, because the patient is a mystery, and slowly we begin to learn who he is, and about his affair with Katherine, but each time we cut away there is a natural and solid transition point. Plus, the entire love affair, though told in flashback, is really the structural foundation of the entire film. We learn what happened to the English patient at the same time Hana (Juliet Binoche) does. It works wonderfully.

Using a "*flashpresent*" is also effective showing memories, or visually giving expression to a thought or expectation or to wishful thinking; remember that scene in *True Lies* (James Cameron) where Arnold is driving in the Corvette with the salesman who thinks he's having an affair with his wife and he busts him in the nose? Only wishful thinking. You can show that, no problem. You can also also use the flashback to show how, or why, an event happened, or maybe flashforward to an event that may or may not happen in the near future. These all are ways to incorporate the "*flash point*" into your screenplay and *make it work*.

But there's also an *emotional* use of the flashback. In *How to Make an American Quilt* there are six different stories that deal with the various aspects of love. The subject of the quilt, "Where Love Resides," is what the story is about. The screenplay itself is structured very much like a quilt; piece by piece, story by story, and each of the quilters' particular stories reflects a certain emotional aspect in relationship to love and commitment. What works so well is the lead-in point where the flashback dovetails into the present time, and it's this weaving of narrative story line between past and present that illuminates Finn's dilemma so well. Each piece of the quilt the women are making gives us some insight and understanding into the nature of love. There is something Finn must learn from all the stories so she can resolve the conflict of "where love resides" within herself. This is a very good example of the way flashback reveals the emotional conflict that resides at the core of Finn's character.

Which brings us back to the basic question of this chapter: when can you use a flashback to solve a particular problem?

The examples given illustrate the basic context of the flashback; either physical or emotional. It is the point at which you slide into the *"flashpresent."* If you feel you have a problem the flashback creates or can solve, what do you perceive the problem to be? First, ask yourself what you want to use the flashback for. Is it to reveal character? Or is it to show *how* an event reveals the character, in terms of their actions and reactions? What incident are you going to show, and what does it reveal about the character, and how is it going to move the story forward?

If, for example, you have a situation where you think your story is wandering around in circles, or your character is too talky and explains too many things, you might consider using a flashback to reveal a certain aspect of your character. If your character is too passive and reactive, or feels too thin or one-dimensional, you could use a flashback to provide more depth and dimension to your story line.

But – and it's a very big *but* – you just can't insert a flashback because you think it will work to expand character. You need to go back into the character and define those forces that are working on him or her during the screenplay; if need be, write essays about the relationships between the characters just to clarify them in your own mind.

"What is character but the determination of incident? And what is incident but the illumination of character?"

These are questions you must ask yourself as you start contemplating the use of flashback to solve a particular problem. If you decide to use it, think of it in terms of a *"flashpresent"*; what is your character thinking or feeling in the present moment? If you can get into your character's head, and find some thought, memory, or event that reflects, or acts, upon the present moment, and, through it, show how it affects your character, you gain an optimal advantage. Go into your character's *Circle of Being* and see what you can find.

The best use of the flashback is to provide some kind of emotional insight and understanding for your character. I always think of a flashback as a "flashpresent." It's what's inside your character's head at the present moment; it either moves the story forward or reveals information about the main character.

Could you have used a flashback in *Thelma & Louise* to show her *Circle of Being*? Possibly. There might have been an opportunity to show what happened to Louise when she was raped in Texas. It might have helped clarify why she killed Harlan in the parking lot. But would it have been as effective? Not really. There's no sense spoon-feeding the reader or audience. We've become too sophisticated in terms of movie culture to do that. As far as I'm concerned, a flashback revealing this event in Louise's life would have been redundant and surely not be as effective as the way Callie Khouri originally conceived it.

So be careful when you use a flashback.

Some films incorporate the flashback as a major part of the story; they use it to "*bookend*" their main story line, meaning they open the script with an incident or event, and then flashback to the actual story, then end it in the present time again. A few films that do this well are: *The Bridges of Madison County*, *Sunset Boulevard*, *Annie Hall*, and *Citizen Kane*. And, of course, *Pulp Fiction*.

Should you decide to use a flashback, make sure it doesn't intrude upon the flow of the action, or get in the way of the story, or draw too much attention to itself.

If you can say it, maybe you don't have to show it after all.

THE PROBLEM SHEET

Enter Late and Get Out Early
✎ Dialogue is too wordy, too explanatory

- ✎ The scenes are too long, with not enough action
- ✎ Story line is thin and episodic
- ✎ Plot elements and story points have to be explained over and over again
- ✎ The script is too long
- ✎ The story is not visual enough
- ✎ Conflict is expressed through dialogue, not action
- ✎ Characters are reactive, rather than active
- ✎ The Second Act is weak and much too long
- ✎ The writing is too easy, it can't be good

In William Goldman's book *Adventures in the Screen Trade*, he talks about the best place to enter the scene, and to hypothetically illustrate his point he gives an example. Suppose, he says, you're writing a scene in which a reporter is interviewing a subject and it's laid out like this: the reporter arrives at the place of the interview, the two introduce themselves to each other, get comfortable, chat for a while, and after a few moments the reporter suggests they start the interview. So he turns on the cassette recorder, pulls out his notepad, and starts asking his questions. They discuss the topic, going back and forth for a while until the reporter is satisfied and terminates the discussion. He turns off the recorder, thanks the subject, picks up his belongings and prepares to leave, says his goodbyes, and walks to the door. But when he reaches the door, he suddenly stops as if struck with an afterthought, turns back to the subject, and says, "Oh, by the way. One last question ...!"

Where is the best place for the screenwriter to enter the scene? When the reporter arrives? When he turns on his recorder? At some point during the interview? At the end? None of the above, Goldman says. Instead, he feels the best place for the screenwriter to enter the scene is when the reporter is standing at the door, on his way out, and remembers "one last question."

A good rule of thumb is *"enter late and get out early."* Which means that in many scenes (depending on their purpose) it's best to enter the action at the last possible moment. I usually tell my students that you enter the scene about two lines before the purpose of the scene is revealed. In this way you only need a minimum of dialogue to state the dramatic purpose.

Now this, of course, is only a *general rule*; it doesn't apply to every scene in the screenplay, because the dramatic function of each scene is unique. Some scenes have to constructed, in terms of their beginning, middle, and end, and it always depends on what information you need to communicate, either to move the story forward, or to satisfy the dramatic purpose of the particular scene. Where you enter the scene is absolutely an *individual decision*, and hopefully the scene itself will dictate the best point to enter. If you're able to see it.

The same principle applies to ending the scene. At what point do you leave one scene so you can move into the next? The main things to remember about getting out of one scene and into the next are: first, get out with a sense of tension so the reader will want to see what happens next. Second, make the transition from one scene into the next interesting, visually arresting, smooth.

If you write a scene that is complete unto itself, it will have a definite beginning, middle, and end, and if you do that consistently, you'll end up with an episodic, or sequential screenplay. Every scene has a definite end, a definite place to get out; you just have to find it, and it doesn't matter whether it's transitional, or deliberate (like a fade-out). Every scene should lead into the next one. The connection between these units of dramatic action, whether affected by picture-to-picture, sound-to-sound, dialogue-to-dialogue, or special-effects to special-effects transitions, should always be pulling and guiding you from one scene into the next. The story must always move forward from beginning to end, beginning to end.

In order to keep the tension going, and keep the reader turning pages, enter late and get out early. That's what screenwriting is all about.

If you don't pay attention to the point at which you enter the scene there is a possibility that your screenplay will drag and sag, or be too long, so that the sense of tension and suspense is lost, and if that happens, the chances are you'll be overwhelmed with problems of a script that is not working.

How do you determine the best place to enter the scene? The only way to gauge this is to ask yourself what happens before the scene begins, what happens during the scene, and what happens after the scene is over. Whether it takes place in an office, or at a concert, or in a car, where does the scene begin, what is its middle, and how does it end?

Let's say you have an important scene that's too long, too wordy, and drags the action down. And let's say, just as an example, that your scene takes place in an office. The first question to ask yourself is where is your character coming from before the scene begins? From his or her office? From a meeting outside the office? From home or the airport? What is the purpose of the scene, and what function does it serve? In other words, why is it there? And from the other characters' point of view, what are they doing when your character enters the office? Are they in the middle of a phone call or conversation? What's the back story to the scene? Are there any pleasantries exchanged? Or are the characters irritated and in a foul mood? When the characters enter the office, maybe your main character might be asked to wait before entering in turn. Conflict, remember? Getting your character into the office would be the beginning of the scene. So you could enter the scene anywhere along the flow of the physical action of getting into the office.

The middle would be the actual conversation taking place. What's the converation about? How does it fit within the context of the story? What function does it serve? Does it move the story forward or does it reveal information about the character? Is it a dramatically charged scene, or is it mainly subtext, meaning that what's not said is more important that what is said?

Then what happens at the end? Does the character say his or her goodbyes and simply leave? Does the character go back to his or her own office, leave the building, or get into a cab and then we move into the next scene? In other words, what's the ending of the scene?

With this kind of problem, I have my students break down the scene and lay out the parameters of beginning, middle, and end. Again, what is the purpose of the scene? Where does it take place? How does the character get into the scene? When those answers are known, then I have them list these events on a separate piece of paper so they can determine which elements lead up to the character's entering the scene, what events take place during the scene, and what happens when the scene is over. When they have completed this little exercise on a separate piece of paper, they have three complete columns of *beginning*, *middle*, and *end*. For these events lead up to, are part of, and conclude the scene.

Then I ask them to examine the characters' emotional state. What are the characters thinking and feeling before they enter the scene? Is there an emotional subtext? What is their dramatic need in this particular scene? What do they really want to say (basically stating the purpose of the scene), and what is said to them? If there's any doubt or question in the students' minds, I have them write the scene out in an obvious and direct way. What is the scene really about? Just write it and don't worry about whether it says what you want it to say. There's still time for all that. Sometimes I'll have them do this in a free-association essay, of a couple of paragraphs or a page. This is only background to the scene.

Then, move on. What is the character's point of view during the scene? Does it alter or affect the scene? How so? What about the other person(s) in the scene? What are their thoughts, feelings, and emotions before the scene begins? And what is their point of view during the scene? What is their dramatic need in the scene? Do they achieve it? Every character in the scene has a different agenda, a different dramatic need, and it's absolutely essential for writers to know what that need is so they can express it either visually or through dialogue.

If you're unclear about what the relationship is between the characters interacting in the scene, go through the free-association process again.

Structuring your scene so you enter late and get out early makes good reading and is what keeps the action moving forward smoothly, seamlessly. When I read a good screenplay, the reading experience is smooth and easy, and the pages have an almost liquid texture, with each scene continually moving the story forward. The only way I can describe it is like "honey on the page."

And a good read is what we're all looking for.

THE SEQUENCE 9

"Synergy" is the study of systems; the behavior of systems as a whole, independent of their working parts. R. Buckminster Fuller, the noted scientist and humanitarian, creator of the geodesic dome, stresses the concept of synergy as the *relationship* between the whole and its parts; that is, a system.

The screenplay is comprised of a series of elements that can be compared to a "system"; a number of individually related parts arranged to form a unity, or whole; the *solar system* is composed of nine planets orbiting the sun; the *circulatory system* works in conjunction with all the organs of the body; a *stereo system* is made up of amplifier, pre-amp, tuner, turntable, speakers, cartridge, needle, and possibly cassette deck. Put together, arranged in a particular way, the system works as a whole; we don't measure the individual components of the stereo system, we measure the system in terms of "sound," "quality," and "performance."

A screenplay is like a system; it is comprised of specific parts related and unified by action, character, and dramatic premise. We measure it, or evaluate it, in terms of how well it "works" or "doesn't work."

The screenplay, as "system," is made up of endings, beginnings, plot points, shots and effects, scenes, and sequences. Together, unified by the dramatic thrust of action and character, the story elements are "arranged" in a particular way and then revealed visually to create the totality known as "the screenplay." A story told with pictures.

As far as I am concerned, the *sequence* is the most important element of the screenplay. It is the skeleton, or backbone, of your script; it holds everything together.

A SEQUENCE is *a series of scenes tied together, or connected, by one single idea.*

It is a unit, or block of dramatic action unified by *one single idea*. Remember the *chase* sequence in *Bullitt*? The *wedding* sequence that opened *The Godfather*? The *fight* sequence in *Rocky*? The *prom* sequence in *Carrie*? The *tennis* sequence in *Annie Hall* where Woody Allen meets Diane Keaton? The *UFO* sequence at the Devil's Tower in *Close Encounters of the Third Kind*? The *destruction of the Death Star* sequence from *Star Wars*?

A series of scenes connected by one single idea: a wedding, a funeral; a chase; a race; an election; a reunion; an arrival or departure; a coronation; a bank holdup. The sequence is a specific idea which can be expressed in a few words or less. The specific idea, like a "race" – the Indianapolis 500, for example – is a *unit*, or *block*, of *dramatic action* contained within the idea; it is the *context*, the space that holds the *content*, like an empty coffee cup. Once we establish the *context* of the sequence, we build it with *content*, or the specific details needed to create the sequence.

The sequence is the skeleton of the screenplay because it *holds* everything in place; you can literally "string" or "hang" a series of scenes together to create chunks of dramatic action.

You know those Chinese "block" games? You hold a large block in your hand, release it, and a number of blocks flip-flop to the floor, all held by the block you hold in your hand.

That's what a sequence is like: a series of scenes connected by one single idea.

Every sequence has a definite beginning, middle, and end.

Remember the football sequence from *M*A*S*H*? The teams arrive, put on their uniforms, warm up, growl at each other, and the coin is tossed. That's the beginning. They play the game. Back and forth they go; a play here, another there, a touchdown here, an injury there, and so on. After an exciting fourth quarter the game is finally over, the M*A*S*H team victorious, the opponents snarling in defeat. That's the middle of the sequence. The end comes when the game is over; they go to the locker rooms and change into their street clothes. That's the end of the "football" sequence in *M*A*S*H*.

A series of scenes tied together, or connected, by one single idea with a definite beginning, middle, and end. It is a microcosm of the screenplay, the same way a single cell contains the basic properties of the universe.

It's an important concept to understand in writing the screenplay. It is the organizational framework, the *form*, the *foundation*, the *blueprint* of your screenplay.

The contemporary screenplay, as practiced by such "modern" screenwriters as Alan Ball, Richard LaGravenese, Paul Schrader, Robert Towne, Steven Kloves, Frank Darabont, Ron Bass, James Cameron, to name a few, might be defined as *a series of sequences tied together, or connected, by the dramatic story line*. John Milius's *Dillinger*, for *example*, is episodic in structure, as is Kubrick's *Barry Lyndon*, or Spielberg's *Close Encounters of the Third Kind*.

A sequence is a whole, a unit, a block of dramatic action, complete within itself.

Why is the sequence so important?

Look at the *paradigm*:

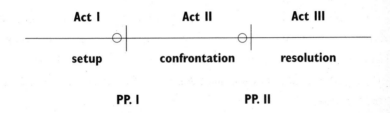

Before you can begin writing your screenplay, you need to know four things: the *opening*, the *plot point* at the end of Act I, the *plot point* at the end of Act II, and the *ending*. When you know what you're going to do in these specific areas, and you've done the necessary preparation on action and character, then you're ready to start writing. Not before.

Sometimes, but not always, these four story points are sequences, a series of scenes connected by one single idea; you might open your film with a *wedding* sequence as in *The Godfather*. You might use a sequence like Robert Redford discovering his *dead coworkers* in *Three Days of the Condor* as the plot point at the end of Act I. You might want to write a *party* sequence for the plot point at the end of Act II, as Paul Mazursky does in *An Unmarried Woman*, where Jill Clayburgh leaves with Alan Bates. You might use a *fight* sequence to end the film, as Sylvester Stallone does in *Rocky*.

Knowledge of the sequence is essential in writing a screenplay. Frank Pierson wrote *Dog Day Afternoon* with just twelve sequences. It should be noted that there are no specific number of sequences in a screenplay; you don't need twelve, eighteen, or twenty sequences to make a screenplay. Your story will tell you how many sequences you need. Frank Pierson started off with four: opening, plot points at the end of Acts I and II, and ending. He added eight sequences and built that into a complete screenplay.

Think about it!

Suppose you want to open your film with a wedding sequence. Let's utilize the concept of *context* and *content*. The *context* is wedding. Let's create *content*.

Let's open on the day of the wedding. The bride wakes up in her house or apartment. The groom wakes up in his house or apartment. Perhaps they wake up together? Both prepare for the wedding. They dress, nervous and excited; the family hovers around; the photographer arrives, takes pictures; and they leave for the church or synagogue. That's the beginning of the sequence: it is comprised of five to eight individual scenes.

The middle is arriving at the church or synagogue (this could be a beginning as well), and the wedding ceremony itself. Friends and relatives arrive. The clergyman arrives. Bride and groom create their ceremony and when it's over, file out. An event always has a beginning, middle, and end. Think about it! The end is where they leave as a now-married couple; she throws the traditional bouquet and then they participate in the wedding reception. End it any way you want.

We started with the idea of *wedding*, the *context*, then created the *content*, and we'll end up with five to eight pages of a screenplay.

You can have as many or as few sequences as you want. There's no rule about the number you need. All you need to know is the *idea behind* the sequence, the *context*; and in order to create a series of scenes, the *content*.

Let's create a sequence; suppose we want to write a sequence about a "homecoming."

First, establish the *context*. Suppose our character is returning home after several years in a POW camp in North Vietnam. He's on a plane with several other POWs.

He's going to be met by his family; father, mother, wife, or girlfriend. There's going to be military personnel at the airport, a military band, TV cameras and crew. Remember the first wave of POWs returning home?

Now, *content*. We need an opening for the sequence. Suppose we open on board the plane as it approaches San Francisco from Hawaii. Several military advisors are on board, preparing the POWs for their landing. They've been away for a long time. Things have changed. There's concern, anxiety, fear, apprehension, and relief as the POWs get ready.

We might "crosscut" between the plane and family getting up in the morning. ("Crosscutting" is a cinematic term for two events happening simultaneously; you "crosscut" or "intercut" between them. The opening of *Marathon Man* illustrates this technique. Edwin S. Porter began it in 1903 with *The Great Train Robbery*.)

As his family prepares to leave, they are quiet, tension high, expectation apparent; it's the moment they've been praying for. They leave the house and drive to the airport.

We intercut this with the POWs on the plane, spend time with our character. He's nervous, does not know what to expect.

The family arrives at the airport, parks the car. The military band plays, the personnel prepare to greet the POWs. The media set up their cameras and equipment. This is the end of the beginning portion of the "homecoming" sequence.

Then, the wait.

The plane lands, taxis to the deplaning area, stops. The doors slide open, the POWs depart amidst the blaring of military music. Home again.

You see how it's shaping up?

The reunion of family and friends is a dramatic moment in the sequence. The family embraces; father quiet, possibly with tears in his eyes, his mother laughing and crying as she tells her son how great he looks, even though he's 30 or 40 pounds underweight. The reunion is awkward and heartfelt. There may be some questions from the media.

They leave the airport. Our character searches out a few of his friends and they say their goodbyes; he gets into the car with his family and leaves the airport.

Beginning, middle, and end, all connected by one single idea – "homecoming." It could be ten to twelve pages long.

Remember the "party" sequence in *Midnight Cowboy*? Dustin Hoffman and Jon Voight decide to go to a party. They find the apartment, walk up the stairs, and enter. The party is in full swing, bizarre, unreal. They mingle, exchange words with several people, Jon Voight meets Brenda Vaccaro. Dustin Hoffman leaves, and Jon Voight comes home with Brenda Vaccaro.

Beginning, middle, and end.

In *All the President's Men*, written by William Goldman, from the book by Bernstein and Woodward, there is a sequence dealing with the "list of 100," the Committee to Re-elect the President, known as

CREEP. Deep Throat has told Robert Redford to "follow the money"; obtaining the CREEP list is the first step. Now what?

The sequence begins with Robert Redford and Dustin Hoffman pinpointing the identity of the people. Then, they find out where they live. They approach the people working for CREEP, but no one will talk to them, much less reveal anything. Scene after scene is built up dramatizing this until Woodward and Bernstein are about to call it quits.

That's when it happens. Hoffman meets a bookkeeper who talks and now they have the information they're looking for; the amount of money in the slush fund, and the five people responsible for doling it out. The "CREEP" sequence is fifteen pages long.

The "reservoir" sequence in *Chinatown* is another example. At the beginning of the second act, Jack Nicholson is looking for Mr. Mulwray. Faye Dunaway tells him he might be at the Oak Pass Reservoir, so Nicholson drives there.

At the beginning of the sequence, he arrives at the reservoir and is stopped by the policeman at the gate. He lies to the officer, and hands him a business card he lifted from the Department of Water and Power; he gains entrance and drives to the site of the reservoir.

In the middle of the sequence he arrives at the reservoir and sees an ambulance and rescue vehicle. He meets Lt. Escobar, the man he worked with in Chinatown when he was a cop. The two men don't like each other. Escobar asks Gittes what he's doing there and Nicholson replies he's looking for Mulwray. Escobar points and we see Mulwray's dead body being hauled up the water duct. As Morty, the coroner, says, "Ain't that something? Middle of a drought, and the water commissioner drowns – only in L.A."

A *sequence* is a series of scenes connected by one single idea, with a definite beginning, middle, and end.

What follows is the "I'm – as – mad – as – hell" sequence from *Network*, by Paddy Chayefsky. It is a perfect illustration of a sequence. Howard Beale, played by Peter Finch, has mysteriously disappeared from William Holden's apartment just before he's scheduled to go on the

air. Frantically, Holden and other network executives try to locate him. It's
raining out, and Finch has been wandering around in pajamas and rain-
coat. Note the construction of the sequence. It has a definite beginning,
middle, and end. Notice how it builds, how Faye Dunaway, as Diana,
expands the action dramatically and how it peaks with an emotional high.

(page 78 of screenplay)
> EXT: UBS BUILDING –
> SIXTH AVENUE – NIGHT – 6:40 P.M.
>
> THUNDER CRASHES – RAIN lashes the street.
> PEDESTRIANS struggle against the slashing rain.
> The streets gleam wetly, the heavy TRAFFIC heading
> uptown crushes and honks along, erratic enfilades of
> headlights in the shiny, black streets –
>
> CLOSER ANGLE of entrance to UBS Building.
> HOWARD BEALE, wearing a coat over his pajamas,
> drenched to the skin, his mop of gray hair plastered
> in streaks to his brow, hunched against the rain,
> climbs the steps and pushes the glass door at the
> entrance and goes into –
>
> INT: UBS BUILDING – LOBBY
>
> TWO SECURITY GUARDS at the desk watch
> HOWARD pass –
>
> **SECURITY GUARD**
> How do you do, Mr. Beale:
>
> HOWARD stops, turns, stares haggardly at the
> SECURITY GUARD.

HOWARD
(mad as a loon)
I have to make my witness.

SECURITY GUARD
(an agreeable fellow)
Sure thing, Mr. Beale.

HOWARD plods off to the elevators.

INT: NETWORK NEWS CONTROL ROOM

Murmured, efficient activity as in previous scenes.
DIANA stands in the back in the shadows. On the
SHOW MONITOR, JACK SNOWDEN, BEALE'S
replacement, has been doing the news straight –

SNOWDEN (on console)
… the Vice-President designate was on
the road today and stopped off in Provo,
Utah, and, in a speech in the basketball
arena at Brigham Young University –

PRODUCTION ASSISTANT
Five seconds –

(79)

TECHNICAL DIRECTOR
Twenty-five in Provo –

DIRECTOR
And … two –

SNOWDEN (on monitor)
Mr. Rockefeller had some strong words

to say about the Arab oil-producing
nations. More on that story from Edward
Douglas –

All this is UNDER and OVERLAPPED by HARRY
HUNTER answering a BUZZ on his phone –

HUNTER
(on phone)
Yeah? … Okay –
(hangs up, to DIANA)
He came in the building about five
minutes ago.

DIRECTOR
Get ready to roll her –

PRODUCTION ASSISTANT
Ten seconds coming to one –

DIANA
Tell Snowden if he comes in the studio
to let him go on.

HUNTER
(to the DIRECTOR)
Did you get that, Gene?

The DIRECTOR nods, passes on the instructions to
his A.D. on the studio floor. On the SHOW MONITOR,
we are seeing footage of Rockefeller crowding his
way to the speaker's rostrum, and we are hearing the
VOICE of Edward Douglas in Provo, Utah –

DOUGLAS
(on the phone)
This was Rockefeller's first public
appearance since he was named Vice-
President designate, and he spoke
sharply about inflation and high Arab oil
prices –

On the SHOW MONITOR, Rockefeller flips onto the
screen to say –

(80)

ROCKEFELLER (on monitor)
Perhaps the most dramatic evidence of
the political impact on inflation is the
action by the OPEC countries and the
Arab oil prices in arbitrarily raising the
price of oil four hundred percent –

Nobody in the control room is paying too much
attention to Rockefeller; they are all watching the
double bank of black-and-white monitors which
show HOWARD BEALE entering the studio,
drenched, hunched, staring gauntly off into his own
space, moving with single-minded purpose across
the studio floor past cameras and cables and
nervous CAMERAMEN, SOUND MEN,
ELECTRICIANS, ASSISTANT DIRECTORS, and
ASSOCIATE PRODUCERS, to his desk, which is
being vacated for him by JACK SNOWDEN. On the
SHOW MONITOR, the film clip on Rockefeller has
come to an end.

DIRECTOR

And one –

– and suddenly, the obsessed face of HOWARD
BEALE, gaunt, haggard, red-eyed with unworldly
fervor, hair streaked and plastered on his brow,
manifestly mad, fills the MONITOR SCREEN.

HOWARD (on monitor)

I don't have to tell you things are bad.
Everybody knows things are bad. It's a
depression. Everybody's out of work or
scared of losing their job, the dollar buys
a nickel's worth, banks are going bust,
shopkeepers keep a gun under the
counter, punks are running wild in the
streets, and there's nobody anywhere
who seems to know what to do, and
there's no end to it.

We know the air's unfit to breathe and
our food is unfit to eat, and we sit and
watch our tee-vees while some local
newscaster tells us today we had fifteen
homicides and sixty-three violent crimes,
as if that's the way it's supposed to be.

We all know things are bad. Worse
than bad. They're crazy. It's like everything's going crazy. So we don't go out
any more. We sit in the house, and
slowly the world we live in gets smaller,
and all we ask is, please, at least leave
us alone in our own living rooms. Let me

(81)

have my toaster and my tee-vee and my
hair dryer and my steel-belted radials,

and I won't say anything, just leave us
alone. Well, I'm not going to leave you
alone. I want you to get mad –

ANOTHER ANGLE showing the rapt attention of the
PEOPLE in the control room, especially of DIANA –

HOWARD (contd.)

I don't want you to riot. I don't want you
to protest. I don't want you to write your
congressmen. Because I wouldn't know
what to tell you to write. I don't know
what to do about the depression and
the inflation and the defense budget and
the Russians and crime in the street.

All I know is first you got to get mad.
You've got to say: "I'm mad as hell and
I'm not going to take this any more. I'm
a human being, goddammit. My life has
value." So I want you to get up now. I
want you to get out of your chairs and
go to the window. Right now. I want you
to go to the window, open it, and stick
your head out and yell. I want you to
yell: "I'm mad as hell and I'm not going
to take this any more!"

DIANA

(grabs HUNTER's shoulder)
How many stations does this go out live to?

HUNTER

Sixty-seven. I know it goes out to Atlanta
and Louisville, I think –

> **HOWARD (on monitor)**
> Get up from your chairs. Go to the
> window. Open it. Stick your head out
> and yell and keep yelling –

But DIANA has already left the control room and is
scurrying down –

INT: CORRIDOR
– yanking doors open, looking for a phone, which she
finds in –

(82)

INT: AN OFFICE

> **DIANA**
> *(seizing the phone)*
> Give me Stations Relations –
> *(the call goes through)*
> Herb, this is Diana Dickerson, are you
> watching? Because I want you to call
> every affiliate carrying this live – … I'll be
> right up –

INT: ELEVATOR AREA – FIFTEENTH FLOOR

DIANA bursts out of the just-arrived elevator and
strides down to where a clot of EXECUTIVES and
OFFICE PERSONNEL are blocking an open doorway.
DIANA pushes through to –

INT: THACKERAY'S OFFICE – STATIONS
RELATIONS

HERB THACKERAY on the phone, staring up at
HOWARD BEALE on his wall monitor –

HOWARD (on monitor)
– First, you have to get mad. When
you're mad enough –

Both THACKERAY's SECRETARY's office and his
own office are filled with this STAFF. The Assistant VP
Stations Relations, a 32-year-old fellow names RAY
PITOFSKY, is at the SECRETARY's desk, also on the
phone. Another ASSISTANT VP is standing behind
him on the SECRETARY's other phone –

DIANA
(shouting to THACKERAY)
Whom are you talking to?

THACKERAY
WCGG, Atlanta –

DIANA
Are they yelling in Atlanta, Herb?

HOWARD (on console)
– we'll figure out what to do about the
depression –

THACKERAY
(on phone)
Are they yelling in Atlanta, Ted?

INT: GENERAL MANAGER'S OFFICE – AFFILIATE –
ATLANTA

The GENERAL MANAGER of WCGG, Atlanta, a portly
(83)
58-year-old man, is standing by the open windows
of his office, staring out into the gathering dusk,
holding his phone. The station is located in an
Atlanta suburb, but from far off across the foliage
surrounding the station, there can be heard a faint
RUMBLE. On his office console, HOWARD BEALE
is saying –

HOWARD (on console)
– and the inflation and the oil crisis –

GENERAL MANAGER
(into phone)
Herb, so help me, I think they're yelling –

INT: THACKERAY'S OFFICE

PITOFSKY
(at SECRETARY's desk, on the phone)
They're yelling in Baton Rouge.

DIANA grabs the phone from him and listens to the
people of Baton Rouge yelling their anger in the
streets –

HOWARD (on console)
– Things have got to change. But you
can't change unless you're mad. You
have to get mad. Go to the window –

DIANA
(gives phone back to PITOFSKY; her

> *eyes glow with excitement)*
> The next time somebody asks you to
> explain what ratings are, you tell them:
> that's ratings!
> *(exults)*
> Son of a bitch, we struck the mother
> lode!

INT: MAX'S APARTMENT – LIVING ROOM

MAX, MRS. SCHUMACHER, and their 17-year-old
daughter, CAROLINE, watching the Network News
Show –

HOWARD (on the set)
– Stick your head out and yell. I want
you to yell: "I'm mad as hell and I'm not
going to take this any more!"

(84)

CAROLINE gets up from her chair and heads for the
living-room window.

LOUISE SCHUMACHER
Where are you going?

CAROLINE
I want to see if anybody's yelling.

HOWARD (on TV set)
Right now. Get up. Go to your window –

CAROLINE opens the window and looks out on the
rainswept streets of the upper East Side, the bulking,
anonymous apartment houses and the occasional

brownstones. It is thunder-dark; a distant clap
of THUNDER CRASHES somewhere off and
LIGHTNING shatters the dank darkness. In the
sudden HUSH following the thunder a thin voice
down the block can be heard shouting:

> **THIN VOICES (o.s.)**
> I'm mad as hell and I'm not going to
> take this any more!

> **HOWARD (on TV set)**
> – open your window –

MAX joins his daughter at the window. RAIN sprays
his face –

MAX'S POV. He sees occasional windows open, and,
just across from his apartment house, a MAN opens
the front door of a brownstone –

> **MAN**
> *(shouts)*
> I'm mad as hell and I'm not going to
> take this any more!

OTHER SHOUTS are heard. From his twenty-
third-floor vantage point, MAX sees the erratic
landscape of Manhattan buildings for some blocks,
and silhouetted HEADS in window after window,
here, there, and then seemingly everywhere,
SHOUTING out into the slashing black RAIN of
the streets –

VOICES

I'm mad as hell and I'm not going to
take this any more!

A terrifying enormous CLAP of natural THUNDER,
followed by a frantic brilliant FULGURATION of
LIGHTNING; and now the gathering CHORUS of
scattered

(85)

SHOUTS seems to be coming from the whole,
huddled, black horde of the city's people,
SCREAMING together in fury, an indistinguishable
tidal roar of human rage as formidable as the
natural THUNDER again ROARING, THUNDERING,
RUMBLING above. It sounds like a Nuremburg
rally, the air thick and trembling with it –

FULL SHOT OF MAX, standing with his DAUGHTER
by the open terrace window-doors, RAIN spraying
against them, listening to the stupefying ROARS and
THUNDERING rising from all around him. He closes
his eyes, sighs, there's nothing he can do about it
any more; it's out of his hands.

At the beginning, Howard Beale enters the UBS building, says hello to
the guards, then prepares to "make my witness." He moves to the
Network News Control Room.

The middle is the broadcast and speech, and over this, we see the
reactions he's causing; everywhere, inside and outside, people are
"mad as hell" and yelling out the windows.

The sequence ends as William Holden suddenly acknowledges
the emotional power of Howard Beale. "There's nothing he can do
about it any more; it's out of his hands."

It is a classic sequence – a complete unit of dramatic action; a series of scenes connected by one single idea with a beginning, middle, and end.

Sketch out a sequence in your screenplay; find the idea, create the *context*, add *content*, then design it focusing on beginning, middle, and end. List four sequences you need to write in your screenplay; like the opening, plot points at the end of Acts I and II, and the ending. Design them.

THE PROBLEM SHEET

Sceneus Interruptus

- The scene has no dramatic pay-off
- The action is incomplete; something seems to be missing
- The story line gets lost
- The dramatic need of the main character is unclear
- The scene is loaded with too much explanation
- Dialogue is too direct, too melodramatic
- There are too many characters
- The characters are not true to the emotional reality of the scene
- The tempo of scene is too slow or too fast

Structure is the foundation of screenwriting. The word itself means "to build, or put together" so when you start structuring your script, you're building and putting scenes, sequences, and acts together into a unified whole with a definite beginning, middle and end, though not necessarily in that order. Structure can be either linear or nonlinear, depending on the needs of your story.

The second definition of *structure*, as it relates to screenwriting, is "the relationship between the parts and the whole." Since you have to build, or put together, various parts of the screenplay, whether a scene, or the invidual shots that comprise the scene, or the separate scenes that make up the sequence, or the necessary character elements you need to integrate into the narrative line, the insertion of a flashback or flashforward structure becomes the glue that holds everything together. It's like gravity, the force that sustains the entire physical universe.

When you read and analyze a good screenplay it's like seeing bits and pieces of film joined together to create a series of moving images, the story told in pictures. A clock ticking, a car moving slowly down a crowded city street, a woman peering out of a window, the sound of a baby crying or a dog barking, the car pulling into a parking space, all these bits and pieces of little pictures can be joined together to create a tense and suspense-filled sequence that has the reader, or audience, on the edge of their collective seats.

When we approach the dynamics of *Problem Solving* in screen-writing, all the solutions, to whatever the problem, will utilize *Structure*.

So what kind of problems are you dealing with within the context of *Structure*?

First, you have the context of story. Is your story focused, clear, and precise, or does it seem to wander around trying to find its line of action? Even the most complicated script is clear and concise, at least from the writer's point of view. Does your story seem to skirt on the edge of things and not go deeply enough in terms of action and character? Does it appear that your scenes have no dramatic payoff? Do your characters seem to be wandering around searching for their dramatic need?

All these are symptoms of something that's not quite right with your structure. It could be the scenes are too short, or not paid off, or the story line seems to wander around with no sense of development, which, remember, is defined as "a line of direction." In short, with a problem of *Structure*, something seems to be missing.

I believe that good structure in a screenplay should not be seen. Good structure should simply disappear into the content of the story line. When I first started developing my concepts of structure, I would go to a movie, watch and notebook in hand, and dutifully time the individual Plot Points, because I wanted to clarify and define screenplay form. Form, not formula. Looking back on it now, I see I was trying to locate and define the building blocks of the screenplay, and what I discovered was that structure was like the DNA of screenwriting.

The definition of structure, remember, is to build, or to put something together and, as so often happens, when you correct one problem in a screenplay it always affects something else, so you have to add elements, or remove elements to make it work. That means building, or putting together, a new scene or sequence.

One of the problems I've become aware of in my teaching experience is that writers will sometimes write key scenes, either action or dialogue, which are not paid off; the scenes usually end too early. In a dramatic scene, for example, the screenwriter will cut to the next scene before the purpose of that particular scene is realized. And then, when I'm reading the material, I get the feeling something's missing; the action feels incomplete. It's so important – essential – to determine the purpose of the scene in order to dramatically realize the intention of that scene.

A few years ago I was commissioned to read and analyze a screenplay for a producer/writer. It was an action-thriller set in the Cayman Islands, a marvelous location for this kind of film. The story, about a photographer who accidentally stumbles into a situation where he becomes a target for murder, was interesting and well written. There were good action sequences and the script was well structured.

But as I was reading the screenplay, I kept getting lost in the story line. I was confused and so many characters were pulled into the narrative line, I didn't know who the main character was and what the whole thing was about.

Even though the premise was good, with solid visuals and locations, good action sequences, and interesting characters, somehow I got the feeling that something was missing, something just wasn't right. I couldn't pinpoint the problem, so I started examining it more closely. As I read through the screenplay again, I saw that many of the key scenes were not complete, that the action had stopped before the dramatic requirements of the scenes had been satisfied. In the middle of a confrontation scene, for example, the writer would cut away to another scene, or to another character, and this altered the focus of the story line. I had the impression that something was definitely missing.

With that in mind, I went back and looked at the material again, and saw that this particular trait had become a tendency on the part of the writer. Time after time, a scene or situation would be set up, and then before the purpose of the scene was realized he left it and so it was not really paid off. So while the idea of the scene had been planted, it had never come to fruition, and therefore the action and story line seemed hazy and uncertain.

Now, I had been aware of this phenomenon before, but I never had a name for it. But this was such a clear example of the problem that I labeled it *Sceneus Interruptus*. Leaving the scene too early simply means the *purpose of the scene is unsatisfied, unfulfilled*. It does not accomplish its dramatic function and therefore leaves a gaping hole in the action. And when that happens, something is definitely missing.

The result of *Sceneus Interruptus* can be serious problems in the screenplay. Once the tendency of cutting away prematurely is established, chances are it's going to be reflected in a variety of scenes, and that means it's going to influence the entire story line.

I think the most difficult thing about this problem is simply recognizing it. So many times we read and reread the material looking for ways to improve it, and we have a hard time seeing that a scene ends too early.

Once you become aware that the problem exists, you can fix it. And the way to do that is to break every scene down and restructure it into a beginning, middle, and end. First, what's the purpose of the scene? What's it doing there? What does the character want to win, gain, get, or achieve during the course of the scene? In what way does this scene relate to the character's dramatic need in the screenplay? Where has the character come from, and where is he/she going after the scene is finished? These questions must be addressed and resolved before the scene begins.

If you don't know what's going on during the scene, who does? That means knowing what the thoughts, feelings, and emotions of your character are, and keeping them clearly in mind as the scene plays out.

How do you know when you've satisfied the requirement of the scene? There's no real way of knowing that, of course, except that each scene becomes a link in the chain of dramatic action. Each scene, as mentioned, is like a living cell; it should contain everything within it, either to move the story forward or to reveal information about the character. Just like the DNA molecule in living cells. Every scene serves a particular function, and it's up to you, the screenwriter, to know or determine what that future is. What is its purpose? If you don't know what it is, or what it does, or why it's there, you'll probably have to drop it. Just cut it. The chances are it doesn't belong in the screenplay. You have to be ruthless when you're writing a screenplay, especially when you're trying to solve a problem. Screenwriters all over the world have the same complaint; they always have to cut what they think are their best scenes, their best writing, out of the scripts.

To solve the problems of Sceneus Interruptus, start by rethinking the parameters of the scene. What are the character's thoughts, feelings, or emotions when the scene begins? Where is he or she coming from, and what is the emotional reality working on the character? Does your character have a sore throat and does he seem to be cold? Has he/she just managed to escape from a would-be attacker? Is he/she preparing for a big showdown, or confrontation scene? So, define the emotional forces working on your character when the scene begins.

The next step is to find out what elements you have to work with within the scene. Where does it take place? What time of day or night? Is there anything within the setting of the scene that you can use to your advantage, dramatically? The weather, a crowded art gallery, a crowded restaurant, a market, or on the street? Or is it late at night, where the silence and emptiness of the location seem to create their own ambience? Once you establish the environmental elements, you can break the scene down into beginning, middle, and end.

On a separate piece of paper, break down the scene. To start, where does your character come from before the scene begins? Write it down. If the scene takes place in a library, for example, your character may have come from the office, or maybe an exercise class; if the latter, then it means that he will have to dress, leave the area, walk to the subway or car, ride or drive to the destination, park, get out, walk up the steps, and enter the lobby. That's the beginning. And remember conflict. Maybe something happens on the way to the scene that affects the character, so you might want to create a little back story to the scene.

Then, find a way to dramatize the purpose of the scene. Why is the character at the library? To find a certain book, do some research on the Internet, or have a clandestine meeting?

Isolate the flow of events that make up the middle of the scene. The character arrives, walks into the lobby, searches for someone or something, then finds the person or book he or she is looking for, finds a corner table to sit down at, and then the purpose of the scene begins to unfold. What's the nature of the dialogue? Is it direct, for exposition, so the story can move forward? Or is there a subtext to the dialogue, a hidden meaning, or an indirect threat? Is this a scene that reveals something about the character, that gives us some insight into the emotional or physical landscape of the character? It doesn't have to be much. In *Courage Under Fire* we can tell what Colonel Serling is thinking or feeling when he pulls out a bottle of Scotch and takes a drink. We don't need any more explanation than that.

Then, the end. The character(s) get up, leave the library, and then where do they go or what do they do? Do you follow the main character or the other person? In *Pulp Fiction* the interesting thing about the bar scene in the beginning where Vinnie (John Travolta) meets

Butch (Bruce Willis) is that we could have followed the Butch character just as easily as we do Vinnie on his "date" with Mia Wallace (Uma Thurman). This is all creative choice. Does anything happen on the way to the next scene? How much time elapses between the scene in the library and the next scene?

Look it over. Have you satisfied the purpose of the scene? That is, does it contain the correct information, either visually, or emotionally, or physically, or through the dialogue, to be complete within itself, or to act as a link to another scene? It's always better to enter the scene late and get out early, but the only way you can really do that is if you are totally clear on what each beat or movement is, within the body of the scene.

Is there enough conflict within the scene? Are the characters' points of view clear, concentrated, and focused? That's something you have to be clear about yourself. That's your homework, and nobody can do it for you.

If you're not clear about the relationship between the main character and the person he or she is meeting in the library, then write a short, free-association essay of two or three pages about their relationship. When did they first meet, and where? What happened? What you're really trying to do is to get enough information so you can make sure your scene works and is totally effective for the purpose it serves in the screenplay.

When you complete the necessary preparation, then do your breakdown of beginning, middle, and end, and then select bits and pieces from each category to set up and then pay off the scene. For example, we could start with a shot of the office clock, followed by a shot of the character looking and thinking, then cut to him or her riding in the subway, or driving, then entering the lobby of the library, searching for the other character, their meeting, and then pay it off with a shot of the character leaving, and walking down the steps, or simply go into a transition. Clean, lean, and tight.

In this way you know that the purpose of the scene is satisfied, complete unto itself, providing as well a necessary link in the chain of dramatic action, so the story can move forward with concise skill and visual continuity.

THE PROBLEM SHEET

Something's Missing

- ✎ Story lacks tension and suspense
- ✎ The stakes are not high enough
- ✎ The story line is too plotty, too complex, things happen too fast
- ✎ Story is too thin, too vague, too contrived
- ✎ Too many plot twists and turns
- ✎ Dialogue is too talky, too direct
- ✎ Characters are flat, one-dimensional
- ✎ Main character is not very sympathetic
- ✎ Character always reacts to the situation, and has no real point of view
- ✎ Minor characters stand out more than the main character

When I'm reading a screenplay, I'm always looking for a story line that's lean, clean, and tight. I want the characters to move through the narrative landscape with a strong dramatic need and strong point of view. I want to be surprised and don't want the story to seem contrived or predictable, and I want all scenes or sequences to be related to one another, where nothing, neither a throwaway action nor a line of dialogue, is tossed in just to keep the story moving forward.

It's what I call "the good read." Unfortunately, I am disappointed most of the time. The same goes for almost all the readers in Hollywood, no matter if it's a studio executive, producer, director, development person, or reader. Personally, I am directly involved in the reading and writing of about a thousand screenplays a year; either I'm commissioned to read them by various producers and production companies, or I'm working with my many students and helping them design and develop their screenplays. Over and over again, I find certain tendencies within the screenplay that lead directly to a particular problem; either there is too much material fueling the story, or not enough; something is missing.

Many times during the screenwriting process the screenwriter is faced with the creative choice of whether to write a particular scene or not write it. Sometimes a tendency develops where the writer will skip scenes that they think are unimportant and unnecessary, scenes they think they could do without. If you find that you start asking yourself "whether I really need to write this scene or not," you begin a *critical process of making a judgment*. And while that is a positive and necessary step in the screenwriting process, if overdone it can lead to a creative decision that results in your not writing the scene. And once this process has been formed as part of the writing process, once you get into the pattern of saying, "No, I don't need to write this scene," for whatever reason – you establish the habit of saying no.

Then you're in trouble.

Inevitably, something will be missing in the screenplay; most of the time it will be something important or significant to the action, a key scene or sequence that must be there for the story to move forward. When I was a consultant on *White Palace* (Alvin Sargent), with Susan Sarandon and James Spader, there was a significant transition at the end of the Second Act. The James Spader character makes a decision to follow Susan Sarandon to New York. But the way the script was written did not give us any clue that the character was going to leave; there was a scene, and then the next scene showed him arriving in New York. How he got there, when he made the decision, why he made the decision, was never addressed during this particular draft of the screenplay. Just that he goes.

When I first read this section of the script, I was very confused. It just didn't make sense, especially in light of what happens between the two characters when they encounter each other again. It was a major omission; without this key scene of the Spader character making the decision to leave and follow Sarandon to New York, there was a big, gaping hole in the action. It had to be filled. Such a scene was not only important, it was a structural necessity, for this scene is really the Plot Point at the end of the Second Act.

When something is missing in the screenplay, either a scene or sequence, a character's decision or reaction, it will always get in the way of the action, because we can intuitively feel something is *not there* that should be.

One of my students was writing an action-adventure script about the rescue of an American airman who had been shot down and captured by a guerrilla force in North Korea. And while there were many action scenes, literally one after the other, the writer had omitted saying anything about this character, about what his life was like before his capture, or his family, or what information he had, or his hopes and fears; even in *Crimson Tide* we see the Denzel Washington character at his daughter's birthday party just before he receives the phone call about the Russian threat and in the setup of the Gene Hackman character something is said about the navy being his "real family." We also *see* his relationship with his dog, and that reveals a great deal about him. It's not just action scene after action scene.

Most of the character dynamic that makes a screenplay really effective, no matter if it's an action-adventure, or thriller, or relationship story, was clearly missing in my student's pages. And it was pretty obvious.

Good screenwriting is a *blend of strong action* and *strong character*. They go hand in hand.

How can you correct something like that? In this case I had my student stop his writing and go back and do more character work. First I had him write several essays about the main character, then suggested some character elements that might be woven into the screenplay. In my student's story the main character is a loner; shot down behind enemy lines, captured, no one to talk to – this creates a situation where a flashback, or what I like to call a "*flashpresent*," would work very well. For example, as the character's plane is plummeting to the earth we could possibly see, in very quick cuts, various elements of his life. As he yanks his ejector seat, we could possibly see bits and pieces of his life; a scene with his mother, maybe a shot of his wife, or a child playing with a little dog, or a beautiful sunset. These are just some visual suggestions that could open up the script so as to incorporate character elements into the action. He parachutes into the trees, then there's an action scene of him being hunted down and captured. The screenwriter had become so totally involved in the action elements of the screenplay that he had completely neglected the character.

Any creative decision you make about whether to write a particular scene or not is a necessary and essential step in the screenwriting process. But following the *question* about whether or not you need the scene, instead of following what's needed for the *story* to work, leads to a screenplay that reads "thin," with no tension or suspense, and obvious *plot holes* that need to be explained in order for the story to move forward.

And failure to take care of and fill these particular *plot holes* will often lead to stories, and characters, that are thin and one-dimensional. We call this type of screenplay a "one-line" film.

Sometimes, a one-line film works very effectively: *Speed* (Graham Yost) and *Broken Arrow* are good examples of an idea pushed to its extreme, with just enough character delineation to make it interesting. *Il Postino* is brilliant.

But *The Englishman Who Went Up a Hill but Came Down a Mountain* is a good example of a "one-line" script that doesn't work. The story, about an English surveyor and his partner, assigned to reclassify a hill into a mountain in Wales right after the First World War, is a cute premise, cleverly laid out, but extremely simple in terms of style and execution.

The title says it all; that's what the entire script is about, and there's nothing more to it than this particular situation. That's what this movie really is, a situation, not a story, and for that reason the conflict and tension inherent in the story seems lost; is this mountain really a hill, or is this hill really a mountain? That's the only real tension that powers the story forward.

The stakes are not high enough – that is, the emotional stakes. What's at stake in this story? Not much of anything. The people here have nothing to lose. To make it work more dramatically, more effectively, the emotional intensity has to be higher; that means the conflict has to be increased. Something of value, whether emotional or physical, internal or external, has to be at stake, or at risk. A character's strong dramatic need will generate more conflict only if there are obstacles that must be overcome. If this is the case, you've got to go into the character's life and find the element or elements that can raise the emotional stakes of the situation.

Why? Take a look at Anson, the Hugh Grant character; he is weak and passive and always seems to be reacting to the situation and other characters. We really don't know too much about him, and he literally disappears into the background of the story. There is nothing about his character, or in his character, to draw and focus our attention on him. He has nothing at stake. The barkeeper, Morgan, on the other hand, is a much more dynamic character. Even the character of the Reverend is portrayed with more gusto and life, and stands out more than Anson. The love relationship with the Betsy character seems predictable and contrived, as if it's just thrown in because there has to be a "love interest" in every script. And why she's attracted to this shell-shocked wimp is, at least to my mind, a total mystery. We know he was shell-shocked, but we don't know anything about *him*, and how this has affected him. She is a strong and attractive woman. Why would she consent to be with this kind of a man? Is she his saviour? A rescuer? A distraught mother? We don't know, we can only guess.

So, what's the problem?

Something's missing. First of all, the main character is never really defined. The conflict itself is weak and results in very little tension or suspense because the characters are always reacting to the situation; except for Morgan they are not driven by their passions and emotions, only by their need to make this particular hill fall into the category of being listed as a mountain.

Why is that so important? This is the first hole that needs to be filled. It's never really explained. They talk about it, yes, they discuss it, yes, but there is no underlying reason, or motivation, to take this simple conflict seriously. As a result, the story is thin and contrived, the plot line is weak. Why these Welsh people of Fynnor Gawr cared so much whether the "British" declared their summit a hill or a mountain is never really established. This might have been a fierce struggle, storywise, for the Welsh are a proud and independent people. Couldn't there have been some kind of conflict that spawned the English forcing their laws and their way of life upon the Welsh? The natural rivalry inherent in the story could have been the natural abrasion that might have added more depth and dimension to the story line.

If you feel your story is too thin, or missing something, or if the stakes are not high enough, or if you feel the characters are talking too much, or they all sound alike, or nothing happens, go back over the material and determine whether you've spent enough time setting up the conflict in the story. You can also add color, or create conflict and texture to your characterizations. In *The Englishman* ... the Hugh Grant character is weak because we don't know enough about him. We don't know much about his background, about how his shell-shock experience has affected him, we don't know whether he longs for a secure and loving relationship, or must overcome a long and deep-seated conflict of prejudice against the Welsh. These are all potential areas of character conflict that might have been explored and expanded to offer a more interesting and dramatic dimension to the story. If these areas had been explored, the film would have been much more than a "one-liner." Sometimes, when the material is thin, and something seems to be missing, look for a *subplot* to weave into the action. A subplot is an additional plotline that becomes a secondary branch of the story line. Adding a subplot is a good idea *sometimes*, and sometimes not, depending on the story. Many writers I know are convinced that every story needs a subplot, so they always try to find a way to inject one.

There are two ways to approach creating a subplot; either adding another element to the narrative line of your script through the *action*, or building it from *character*. That's your first creative decision, because all subplots are a function either of *action* or of *character*. The purpose of a *subplot* is to add more solid dramatic possibilities to your story line; to open up the action so the script becomes more visual, and to fill in any pieces of missing action to sharpen and define the conflict.

Because the subplot springs from *action* and *character*, it means you have to create the particular incidents and events and then structure and weave them through the dramatic action. That's why you solve this particular problem by approaching it from *Plot* as well as *Character*.

If you build your subplot based on the *Character*, you will have to create more obstacles to the story line. For example, if your character is a doctor who's searching for a cure for AIDS, and he's almost found it, you might think about creating a subplot about another doctor who is competing with the main character and possibly has found another cure for the same disease. In medical terms it's important to be the first to discover a cure, because that's what attracts the funding and the research dollars. So, maybe the character's dramatic need might be to be the first person to discover the cure. This sets up an additional conflict where the main character is racing against, and challenging, this other character, to be the first to find a cure for AIDS. A subplot like this becomes a very effective way to add and build more dimension into the story line.

How would you go about building this particular subplot? First, you have to create the other character, in this case a doctor doing research with AIDS, and then find out who he or she is by writing a character biography. Maybe these two doctors have had some contact in the past, either before the story starts, or through various research publications; maybe they even went to school together. You can establish this information through the character biography by writing various essays clarifying and defining the dramatic forces working on these two characters. This secondary character will be a major figure in the story, even if he or she is in only a few scenes in the script. Setting up a situation this way allows you to select scenes that will add depth to the plot.

By clarifying and defining what brings a new character into the conflict, and how the main character reacts to this new situation, you generate a whole series of actions and reactions that will hook into the main story line. You are creating additional action to the story, a *subplot* that will give the script a new look and feel. Many writers actually develop the subplot as a separate story, then structure it on the *paradigm* and then weave it through the dramatic action. That's why it's listed more as a problem of *Plot* than of *Character*.

Whenever you feel you need to cut away from the main action, you can now insert scenes from the subplot and create a much stronger narrative line.

If you want to build a *subplot* based on *action*, here's the perfect example: *Ransom*, the Ron Howard film with Mel Gibson and Rene Russo, from an original script by Alexander Ignon, and rewritten by Richard Price (*Clockers*). The script is about the kidnapping of a child of a wealthy family and the physical and emotional toll it takes upon them.

In the first draft of the screenplay the action concentrated on the family and how they dealt with the ordeal, how it affected their relationship. The kidnapping was only the "hook" to focus on the characters during the time of their emotional ordeal. And the point of the story was that people are all the same; rich or poor, man or woman, black, white, brown, or yellow; when the lives of children are at stake, the emotional reality experienced is really the same for everybody. Feelings are feelings.

Which is basically the point of the story. But when Richard Price came on to the project, he became aware that, while it was a great situation as written, something seemed to be missing; the script wasn't as strong as it could be. Ron Howard agreed. When they reread the original material from this perspective, they became aware that during the entire screenplay there was nothing about the kidnappers, nothing about the kidnappers' point of view. Who are these people? Why did they kidnap this particular child? How does the kidnapping affect the parents *and* the kidnappers? This is a bizarre and unique relationship that, if explored, could provide another dimension to the script.

So Price started developing the kidnappers' side of the story, and in the subplot we're able to see who these people are and why they've chosen to commit this crime.

The *subplot* opened up the entire screenplay, giving it a richness it had not had before.

If you want to build and develop a subplot based on *Character*, go back into your character's life and redefine it; you're looking for elements of his or her life that would lend themselves to the story and add another facet to the conflict. You can find them by going into your character's *professional* life, his *personal* life, and his *private* life.

What does your main character do for living? What is his or her profession? What are the relationships between your main character and the people he or she works with? Good? Bad? Are there any conflicts between your character and the people he or she works with? What are they? Has a particular project gone astray? A payment that wasn't made? Does your character socialize with her office mates after work? What does she do? Is she having an affair? Are her parents alive? Is she sick, or healthy? Write an essay of two or three pages laying this all out. Free-associate and just throw all your thoughts and ideas down; again, don't worry about grammar or spelling or writing fragments. Just toss the words down on the paper. This is automatic writing, and you'll be amazed at what you discover. Writing is always an act of discovery, and you never really know what's going to come out. That's what makes it such an exhilarating experience. It's an incredible high.

If you define these elements of your character's *professional* life, you will find some kind of incident or event you can *hook* into to build the subplot.

What about your character's *personal* life? What are the relationships your main character has during the course of the screenplay? Is he married, single, widowed, divorced, or separated? Can you define these relationships? If your character is single, is he or she in some kind of a relationship when the story begins? What state is the relationship in? Is it good, or falling apart? *Think of conflict here*; it's much better, at least dramatically, to have a relationship that's not in the best of shape. Two people who are happy together have very little dramatic value. So create some conflict: perhaps the passion has fallen away, or he's having an affair, or she feels that she's being taken for granted.

If your character is married, what's the relationship like? Is it strong and stable, or is one of the partners questioning his or her commitment? How long have they been married? Are there any children? How many? Define your main character's marriage in a two- or three-page essay and see if you can pull any elements out that may help you build and structure some kind of a subplot. Look for those specific elements that will expand the boundaries of the story line.

You can also do it through your character's *private life*. *Private life* means what your character does when he or she is alone. What hobbies, or interests, does your character have? Taking a class in cooking? A writing class? Looking for "buys" while surfing the net? Working out three or four times a week? What kind of workout? Yoga? Weights? Dance classes? All these areas can be explored and easily offer a variety of creative choices in terms of developing subplots.

Pets are another way you can add incidents and elements to your screenplay. Does your character have any pets? If so, what kind? As mentioned, in *Crimson Tide* the Gene Hackman character comes on board his submarine with his little dog. The serial killer Jame Gumb, in *The Silence of the Lambs*, has a little fat poodle, "Precious." Pets are a wonderful way to add depth and sympathy to your character.

You can even use this dramatically in the story. I had an experience one night a few years ago. I had a very important dinner meeting. But about an hour before I was to leave, I suddenly noticed my cat, about seventeen years old, was not well. She had great difficulty breathing and was unable to move. I dropped everything and immediately took her to receive emergency treatment. I knew I was going to be late for the meeting but as far as I was concerned, I had no choice in the matter. The cat was my first priority. So, I took her to the animal emergency center, the vet examined her, gave her some shots, and kept her overnight. I went on to the meeting and while everything appeared normal, at least on the surface, my thoughts and feelings were with my cat. And it was that situation or incident that could create a dramatic *subplot*. If I was looking for some kind of incident or episode to bulk up my screenplay from the function of Character, this kind of incident or event would be a perfect vehicle.

As I recall, I had a very tough time that night. My cat was given an injection and some pills, and came home the next day. But an incident like this can add depth to your characters and fill in some of the missing holes in your story line.

Just remember that you can approach writing a *subplot* either through *action* or *character*. Each is an effective way to build substance and dimension to the story line, and provides information that moves the story forward visually, rather than verbally. If you have set up the elements of the *subplot*, and they are clearly established and defined, then you can follow them easily as they surface through the story line, like dolphins breaking the waves.

THE PLOT POINT

10

When you're writing a screenplay, you have no objectivity at all – no overview. You can't see anything except the scene you're writing, the scene you've written, and the scene you're going to write. Sometimes you can't even see that.

It's like climbing a mountain. When you're moving toward the top, all you see is the rock directly in front of you, and the one above you. Only when you reach the top can you gaze at the panorama below.

The hardest thing about writing is knowing what to write. When you're writing a screenplay you have to know where you're going; you have to have a *direction* – a line of development leading to the resolution, the ending.

If you don't you're in trouble. It's very easy to get lost within the maze of your own creation.

That's why the *paradigm* is so important – it gives you direction. Like a road map. On the road, through Arizona, New Mexico, on through the vast reaches of Texas and across the high plains of Oklahoma, you don't know where you are, much less where you've been. All you can see is the flat, barren landscape broken only by silver flashes from the sun.

When you're *in* the *paradigm*, you can't *see* the *paradigm*. That's why the plot point is so important. The PLOT POINT is an incident, or event, that "hooks" into the action and spins it around into another direction.

It moves the story forward. The plot points at the end of Acts I and II *hold the paradigm* in place. They are the anchors of your story line. Before you begin writing, you need to know four things: ending, beginning, plot point at the end of Act I, and plot point at the end of Act II.

Here's the *paradigm* again:

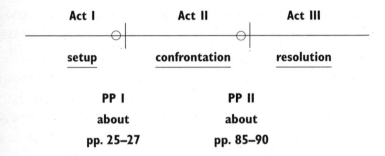

Throughout this book, I stress the importance of the plot points at the end of Acts I and II. You must know the plot points at the end of each act before you begin writing. When your screenplay is completed, it may contain as many as fifteen plot points. How many you have, again, depends upon your story. Each plot point *moves* the story *forward*, toward the resolution.

Chinatown is structured from plot point to plot point; each plot point carefully moves the action forward.

The script, as we've seen, opens with Gittes being hired by the phony Mrs. Mulwray to find out who her husband is having an affair with. Gittes follows Mulwray from council chambers to reservoir, later discovers him in the company of a young woman. He takes pictures, returns to the office, and, as far as he's concerned, the case is closed.

When he's getting a haircut he learns someone has released the story, along with pictures, to the newspaper.

Who did it? And why?

Gittes returns to his office and a young woman is waiting to see him. Has he ever seen her before? she asks. No. He would have remembered.

She tells him if he doesn't know her, then how could *she* hire him? *She* is Mrs. Evelyn Mulwray, the *real* Mrs. Mulwray (Faye Dunaway); since she did not hire him, she's going to sue him for libel and take away his detective license. She leaves.

Gittes is stunned. If that's the *real* Mrs. Mulwray, who hired him? And why? With the "love scandal" front-page news, he knows he's been set up – framed. Someone, he doesn't know who, wants him to take the "fall," and there's no way Jake Gittes is going to take a fall for anybody. His ass is on the line and he's going to find out who set him up. And why.

End of Act I.

What moment in that block of dramatic action "hooks" into the action and spins it around into another direction? Is it when the phony Mrs. Mulwray hires him? When the story is released to the newspaper? Or when the real Mrs. Mulwray shows up?

When Faye Dunaway enters the picture, the action shifts from a job completed to a possible libel suit and loss of his license. He'd better find out who set him up – then he'll find out *why*.

The *plot point* at the end of Act I is when the *real* Mrs. Mulwray shows up. That event spins the action around, shifts it into another direction. *Direction*, remember, is a line of development.

Act II opens with Nicholson driving up the long driveway to the Mulwray house. Mr. Mulwray is not there. But Mrs. Mulwray is. They exchange a few words, and she tells him her husband might be at the Oak Pass Reservoir.

Nicholson goes to the Oak Pass Reservoir. There he meets Lt. Escobar (both were cops in Chinatown together; Nicholson left and Escobar made lieutenant) and learns Mulwray is dead, apparently as a result of an accident.

Mulwray's death presents another problem, or obstacle, for Gittes. In the *paradigm*, the dramatic *context* for Act II is *confrontation*.

Gittes's dramatic need is to find out *who* set him up, and *why*. So

Robert Towne creates obstacles to that need. Mulwray is dead. Murdered, Gittes finds out later. Who did it? This is a plot point, but not *the* plot point at the end of Act I; it is simply a plot point within the structure of Act II. There are ten such plot points in the second act of *Chinatown*.

Mulwray's death is an incident or event that "hooks" into the action and spins it around into another direction. The story *moves forward*. Gittes is involved, whether he likes it or not.

Later, he receives a phone call from a mysterious "Ida Sessions," the woman, it turns out, who hired him in the beginning; the phony Mrs. Mulwray. She tells him to look in the obituary column of the paper for "one of those people," whatever that means. She hangs up. Soon after, she is found murdered, and Escobar is certain Nicholson is involved.

The theme of "water" has been introduced several times, and Gittes follows it. He goes to the Hall of Records and checks out the owners of land in the Northwest San Fernando Valley. He finds most of the land has been sold within the last few months. Remember the farmer's question on page 10: "Who's paying you [to steal the water from the Valley], Mr. Mulwray?"

When Gittes drives out to investigate an avocado grove, he is attacked by a farmer and his sons and beaten unconscious. They think he's the man who's been poisoning their water.

When he regains consciousness, Faye Dunaway is there – called by the farmers.

Driving back to L.A., Nicholson discovers one of the names in the obituary column mentioned by Ida Sessions is cited as the owner of a large parcel of land in the Valley. Strange. He died at a place called the Mar Vista Home for the Aged.

Together, Gittes and Evelyn Mulwray drive to the Mar Vista old-age home. Gittes learns most of the new owners of land parcels in the Valley are living there, unaware of their purchase. It's phony – the whole thing's a scam. His suspicions confirmed, he's attacked by thugs, but Gittes and Evelyn manage to get away.

They drive back to her place.

These incidents or events are all plot points. They move the story forward.

At her house, Nicholson asks if she has any peroxide to clean his nose wound. She takes him into the bathroom, comments on the severity of the cut, daubs at the wound. He notices something in her eye, a slight color defect. He leans over and kisses her. It's a beautiful scene. They make love.

Finished, they lie in bed making small talk.

The phone rings. She looks at him; he looks at her. It continues ringing. Finally, she answers it, suddenly becomes agitated, hangs up. She tells Gittes he must leave. Immediately. She enjoyed the time spent together, but something important's come up and she has to leave.

Something's come up. What? Gittes wants to find out. He knocks the taillight out of her car and follows her to a house in the Echo Park section of Los Angeles.

End of Act II.

At this point in the story, we still don't know two things; (1) who was the girl Mulwray was with before he was murdered; and (2) who set up Nicholson, and why. Gittes knows the answers to both questions are related, though unresolved.

What's the plot point at the end of Act II?

When Gittes finds the glasses in the pool at Mulwray's house. That's the point at the end of Act II. "An incident, or event, that 'hooks' into the action and spins it around in another direction."

Act III is the *resolution* and what Nicholson learns resolves the story.

Gittes learns the girl is Dunaway's "daughter/sister," sired by her father (John Huston). It also answers the question why Faye Dunaway does not talk to her father, and why John Huston is after the girl. We also learn Huston is responsible for the three murders, as well as everything else; "either you bring the water to L.A., or you bring L.A. to the water," he says.

That's the dramatic "hook" of the movie. And it works, beautifully. The premise of money, power, and influence being a corruptive force is established; as Gittes tells Curly on page 3: "You gotta be rich to kill somebody, anybody, and get away with it." If you've got enough money and power, Towne seems to say, you can get away with anything – even murder.

When Faye Dunaway dies at the end of the film, John Huston spirits his daughter/granddaughter away and "gets away" with everything. Ironically, the incident that drove Gittes off the police-force beat in Chinatown has repeated itself: "I tried to help someone and all I ended up doing was hurting them," he had told Faye Dunaway earlier.

Full circle, turn. Gittes can't deal with it. He has to be restrained by his two partners; the last words of the script are "Forget it, Jake – it's Chinatown."

Do you see how the plot points at the end of Acts I and II "hook" into the action and spin it around into another direction? They move the story forward, to its resolution.

Chinatown moves to its conclusion, step by step, scene by scene, plot point by plot point. There are ten such plot points in Act II, two in Act III.

The next time you go to a movie see if you can locate the plot points at the end of Act I and Act II. Every film you see will have definite plot points. All you have to do is to find them. About twenty-five minutes into the film an incident or event will occur. Discover *what* it is, *when* it occurs. It might be difficult at first, but the more you do it the easier it gets. Check your watch.

Do the same for Act II. Just check your watch about eighty-five to ninety minutes into the film. It's an excellent exercise.

Let's take a look at the plot points in: *Three Days of the Condor*, *Rocky*, *Network*, *Nashville*, *An Unmarried Woman*, and *Close Encounters of the Third Kind*.

Here's the *paradigm*:

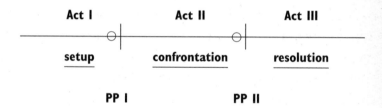

We're looking for the plot points at the end of Act I and II.

In *Three Days of the Condor*, Robert Redford works at "The American Literary Historical Society," a "reading cell" of the CIA. The employees read books. When the film opens, Redford arrives at work, late, and goes about his office routine. He's sent out to get lunch for the staff, and when he returns, everyone's dead, brutally murdered.

Who did it? Why?

Redford doesn't have time to think. He should be dead, too – only because he was "out to lunch" is he still living. It takes him a while to grasp the situation; when he does, he knows someone is going to kill him. He doesn't know who and he doesn't know why – all he knows is that he's going to be killed.

End of Act I.

Lorenzo Semple, Jr., and David Rayfiel, the screenwriters, set up the story the following way: Act I establishes that Redford has uncovered some kind of conspiracy developing within the CIA. He doesn't know *what* it is; all he knows is that his friends and coworkers are dead.

And he's next on the list.

The plot point at the end of Act I is when he *returns* from lunch and discovers everybody dead. It is Redford's *reaction* to this "incident/event" that spins the action around in another direction.

In Act II the dramatic context is *confrontation*. Redford encounters obstacles everywhere. His best friend – also in the CIA – is sent to meet him but is killed, and his death is blamed on Redford. Out of dramatic necessity (you can't have the main character talking to himself – monologues don't work!) he kidnaps Faye Dunaway. Redford is the *victim* all the way through the second act; he spends the next sixty minutes (sixty pages) being hunted down by the hired assassin (Max von Sydow). He constantly reacts to this situation.

When he's attacked in Faye Dunaway's apartment by the mailman killer, he's got to *do* something. He's got to turn the situation around; from being a victim, to being the attacker, the aggressor, in the situation.

Have you ever been a victim? We all have at one time or another. It's no fun. You've got to get "on top" of the situation, and not be run by it. Redford does turn it around, and Faye Dunaway helps him to do it. She enters the CIA headquarters, pretending to apply for a job. She "accidentally" blunders into Cliff Robertson's office, the man in charge of the "Condor affair," sees what he looks like – Redford has never seen him before – apologizes, and leaves.

Over lunch at a restaurant, Redford and Dunaway abduct Cliff Robertson. Redford questions him intently and tells the CIA man the information that will ultimately lead to his discovery of what's really going on – there is a CIA within the CIA.

The plot point at the end of Act II is when Redford turns the action around – from being a victim to being the attacker, from being hunted to being the hunter. By abducting Cliff Robertson, Redford "spins the action around into another direction."

In Act III Redford follows his lead to the man responsible for the scheme – Lionel Atwell. Redford confronts Atwell at his house, finds he has set up a CIA within the CIA and is the man behind the deaths of the others. The reason – oilfields. Max von Sydow enters, abruptly kills the high-ranking CIA official, and spares Redford. At least for now. The assassin is back in the employ of "the company," the CIA.

When you are writing your screenplay, the plot points become signposts, holding the story together and moving it forward.

Are there any exceptions to this rule? Do all movies have plot points? Maybe you can think of some that don't?

What about *Nashville*? Is that an exception?

Let's take a look. First, who's the main character of the film? Lily Tomlin? Ronee Blakeley? Ned Beatty? Keith Carradine?

I had the opportunity to hear Joan Tewkesbury, the screenwriter, talk at Sherwood Oaks about writing *Nashville*. She spoke about the difficulty of writing several characters at once, and how she had to find some unifying theme in the film to hold it together. She went to Nashville twice to do research before writing the film – both times for several weeks. She realised the main character of the film – that is, who the movie is about – is the city of Nashville. *It* is the main character. When she said that, I suddenly realized the *plot point is a function of the main character*. Follow the main character in a story and you'll find the plot points at the end of Acts I and II.

Nashville is the main character because it holds everything together, like a *context*; everything occurs within the city. There are several major characters in the film and they all move the action forward.

The film opens at Nashville Airport as the major characters arrive. We are introduced to them, catch glimpses of their characters and personalities, their hopes and dreams. After Ronee Blakeley arrives, they the airport simultaneously but in separate cars, and like Keystone Kops, bumble into each other in the snafu of a freeway traffic jam.

The plot point at the end of Act I is when they leave the airport. The action shifts direction, from airport to freeway, and allows the action of the story to *move forward* as needed by the characters.

Act II details their characters and interactions; the dramatic need of each character is established, the conflicts generated, courses plotted. At the end of the second act, Michael Murphy, the political front man, convinces Allan Garfield to let Ronee Blakeley sing at the political rally.

That's the plot point at the end of Act II. It is the "incident, or event, that spins the story around" and takes us into Act III and the resolution.

Act I takes place at the airport; Act II in various locations; Act III at the Parthenon, just outside Nashville. We follow the main characters as they arrive at the Parthenon. The rally begins, and ends with the assassination attempt that seriously wounds or kills Ronee Blakeley.

In that final flurry of action, as the throng of people react fearfully, Barbara Harris takes the microphone and leads everyone in song. Together, they sing in harmony as sirens screech and panic reigns. Nashville, after all, *is* a city of music.

Robert Altman, the director, is a master craftsman of dramatic structure; his films may look randomly composed but in reality they are executed with sculpted finesse. *Nashville* fits the *paradigm* to a tee.

What about *Network*? Is that an exception? No. It follows the *paradigm* perfectly. Most people get hung up in trying to decide *who* the main character is. Who is the main character? William Holden? Faye Dunaway? Peter Finch? Robert Duvall?

No. The "network" is the main character. It feeds everything, like a system; the people are parts of the whole, replaceable parts, at that. Network continues on, indestructible; people come and go. Just like life.

In the same way that Nashville is the main character, so is Network the main character. If you grasp this, everything follows naturally.

When the film opens a narrator states that this story is about Howard Beale (Peter Finch), and we find William Holden and Finch getting drunk in a bar. The best of friends, Holden is head of the news department and must fire newscaster Finch after fifteen years because of poor ratings. When Finch goes on the air and states he's being replaced, "a victim of the ratings," he makes the dramatic pronouncement he's going to kill himself on the air!

It becomes a front-page story and creates havoc. The ratings go up. The network, in the form of executive Robert Duvall, is paranoid about Finch's statement; Duvall wants him off the air immediately.

But Faye Dunaway, as director of programming, sees a unique opportunity. She convinces Robert Duvall to put Finch back on the air as a kind of mad prophet who's had it with the "bullshit" we bitterly call a "lifestyle" or "standard of living."

Finch goes back on the air. The ratings improve and soon Howard Beale's is the number-one show on TV. Then, he oversteps himself and exposes the pending acquisition of the network by Saudi Arabian investors.

Finch is hauled "on the carpet" by the president of the corporate network, CCA; Ned Beatty, in a magnificent scene, raves that Peter Finch has "tampered with the natural order of things"; the Arabs took a lot of money out of this country, he tells Finch, and now they have to put it back in. It's a natural flow, like gravity, or the ocean tides.

Ned Beatty convinces Peter Finch to spread the gospel as seen by the president of CCA – the individual is dead, but the corporation lives! The people don't buy it; Finch's ratings drop. As in the beginning, Network wants to get Finch off the air, but Ned Beatty, the president, refuses. Robert Duvall, Faye Dunaway, and the others have a problem. How do they get Finch off the air? The film ends with Peter Finch being assassinated on the air – in a variation on what he had threatened at the beginning of the film. Endings and beginnings, right?

What are the plot points at the end of Acts I and II?

Howard Beale is going to be fired, but gets another chance when Faye Dunaway convinces Robert Duvall to put him back on the air. That's the plot point at the end of Act I. It occurs 25 minutes into the film. It "hooks" into the action and spins it around. Because of Faye Dunaway, Peter Finch has a top-rated show until he oversteps himself with the "takeover speech." That speech is the plot point at the end of Act II.

That "incident" results in Ned Beatty telling Peter Finch to change his message and spread the gospel according to Beatty. This leads to the resolution; Finch must be taken off the air because of poor ratings, and the only way to do that is to kill him. And they do it. It is biting satire and very funny.

Knowledge of the plot point is an essential requirement in writing a screenplay. Be aware of plot points, look for them in the films you see, discuss them in the scripts you read.

Every film has them.

What about the plot points in *Rocky*? In Act I, Rocky is a down-and-out fighter who "wants to be someone"; in reality, he's a "bum" who picks up some odd dollars as the muscle for a childhood friend.

By coincidence, Rocky gets the opportunity to fight the Heavyweight Champion of the World. Is that a plot point or is that a plot point! It occurs about 25 minutes into the film.

Rocky overcomes the barriers of laziness and inertia, forces himself into shape, knowing all the time he can't win. Apollo Creed is just too good. If he can stay on his feet for fifteen rounds with the world's champion, however, it becomes a personal victory. And that becomes his "goal," his dramatic "need" – we could all take a lesson from Rocky.

The plot point at the end of Act II is when Rocky races up the steps of the museum and dances around in victory to the tune of "Gonna Fly, Now." As the script reads, he's as ready as he'll ever be to fight Apollo Creed. He's done all he can – whatever's going to happen is going to happen.

Act III is the fight sequence. It has a definite beginning, middle, and end, and Rocky, with inspiring strength and courage, rights Apollo Creed for fifteen rounds. It is a personal victory.

When you see the movie you'll find Rocky selected to fight Apollo Creed approximately twenty-five minutes into the film; Rocky is "ready" to fight about eighty-eight minutes in. The rest of the movie is the fight.

Check it out!

An Unmarried Woman is another example. Act I, the setup, dramatizes the *married* life of Jill Clayburgh and Michael Murphy. Everything *seems* fine in their relationship, but if you look closely you can clearly see the strain on her husband. About 25 minutes into the film, Michael Murphy suddenly announces to Jill Clayburgh that he's in love with another woman; that he wants to live with her, possibly marry her. He wants out of the marriage.

Is that a plot point?

The second act deals with Jill Clayburgh's attempts to adjust to her new situation; formerly a married woman, she is now an unmarried woman, and a single parent.

Then she meets and has a one-night stand with artist Alan Bates. He wants to see her again; she refuses. She's getting used to the idea of being single. Shortly after they've had sex together, they meet again, at a party.

At the party, Bates scuffles with another artist over Clayburgh, and the two of them leave together. They like each other and decide to see each other again; it's not long before they create a relationship.

The party occurs eighty-five minutes into the film. Is that a plot point? Of course. Act I deals with the situation of "the marriage," Act II with being "single" and forging a relationship with Alan Bates and a new sense of identity.

When you see a movie, determine the plot points. See whether the *paradigm* works or not.

As a form, the screenplay is constantly changing. In recent years, screenwriters have been raised on TV – pictures, not words – which has redefined and expanded the art of the screenplay. What works in terms of style and execution is constantly evolving.

Historically, of course, there have always been significant changes in the American film. From the romantic comedies and social dramas of the thirties, to the war movies and romantic detective stories of the forties, to the fantasy fluff of the fifties, the violence of the sixties, and the political coverups and expansion of the woman's consciousness in the seventies, American movies have consistently evolved in terms of form and content.

From the early sixties – the time of *Hud* and *The Hustler*, two films, I think, that most heavily influenced the contemporary screenplay by refining the dramatic structure into three independent act divisions – the screenplay has become leaner, tighter, and more visual in style and execution.

Hollywood has undergone a period of transition. Studios continue to experiment with new sound systems, new equipment, and new visual techniques, devices that force the filmmaker to expand and improve his craft. Film, like any living art form, evolves, a fusion of scientific advancement and artistic achievement.

There are two editions of Steven Spielberg's *Close Encounters*; the first edition, his original cut to meet the studio deadline, and then his recutting of the film, made a few years after the original release. As far as I'm concerned, the original *Close Encounters* is a film of the future. In terms of style, form, and execution, it transforms the structure of film and shows us tomorrow, today.

Take a look at the *paradigm*:

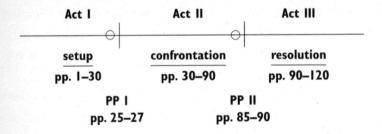

Approximately twenty-five minutes into the film Richard Dreyfuss is sitting in his truck when the power goes out and he is jolted from his seat. It is a wonderful and unusual event: Plot Point I. About eighty-eight minutes into the film, Dreyfuss reaches the Devil's Tower and manages to make his way inside the protected area. Plot Point II. Act III is his experience with the UFO.

This is the structure of Spielberg's recut version of the film. But the first edition is different: The original edition of the film is leaner, more visual, more episodic in form and structure. The advertising for the movie states that a "Close Encounter" of the First Kind is the visual *sighting* of a UFO; of the Second Kind is *physical evidence* of a UFO; and a "Close Encounter" of the Third Kind is *contact*.

Sighting, physical evidence, and contact. The film visually dramatizes these concepts; Act I is the visual *sighting* of the UFOs, Act II is the *physical evidence*, and Act III is *contact*.

Here's the *paradigm* for *Close Encounters*:

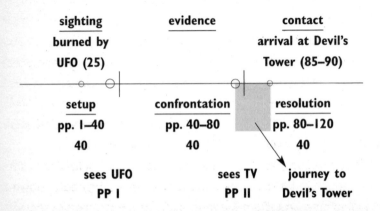

Act I is 40 pages, Act II is 40 pages, and Act III is 40 pages. (In reality, the film is 135 minutes, most of it in the form of additional action happening on the journey between the plot point at the end of Act II and the beginning of Act III.)

Twenty-five minutes into the film, Richard Dreyfuss is sitting in his truck at the railroad crossing, and is suddenly exposed to the blinding lights of a UFO; the experience is so intense he's literally "blown out" of his seat. This corresponds to the plot point at the end of Act I.

He's inexplicably "drawn" to a wooded hillside highway, and watches a group of UFOs streaking through the night sky. One man holds a sign; "stop and be friendly." It's a nice touch. He tries to convince his wife (Teri Garr) of the reality of his experience, but she doesn't believe him. Nobody believes him. He goes back to the hill, and waits. When the lights come, army helicopters swoop out of the sky. That's the end of Act I, *sighting*; it comes about 42 minutes into the film.

Act II deals with that *physical evidence*; at the end of Act I, Richard Dreyfuss is standing with Melinda Dillon, and we see her child (Cary Guffey) building an image of the mysterious mountain that comes to haunt them throughout the second act.

The act opens with Dreyfuss stuffing his pillow into the shape of a mountain; soon he becomes obsessed with it; numbers are received from the UFO and are analyzed as being the geographic coordinates of the Devil's Tower in Wyoming. When Dreyfuss *sees* the mountain on TV (while constructing the very same mountain in his living room) it is the plot point at the end of Act II. It occurs approximately 75 to 80 minutes into the film. That's where he must go.

He leaves his wife and family behind, overcomes obstacle after obstacle, and finally reaches the Devil's Tower. This corresponds to the plot point on pages 85–90 at the end of Act II. Dreyfuss and Melinda Dillon are "captured" by the army units, but manage to break away and race toward the mysterious mountain. The resolution begins.

Act III, *contact*, shows Richard Dreyfuss and Melinda Dillon climbing the mountain to their appointed rendezvous. They edge down to the landing site, and like a stage in evolution where nature "selects" the surviving organism, Richard Dreyfuss goes on alone. In the splendor and wonder of some of the most magnificent special effects ever conceived (by Douglas Trumbull) earthling and alien greet each other and communicate spiritually through the universal language of music. Music, indeed, is the Seventh Wonder.

Within the structure of *Close Encounters* the paradigm holds, but is shifted to create a complete 40-minute unit, or block, of dramatic action contained within the cinematic context: Act I, *sighting*; Act II, *physical evidence*; and Act III, *contact*.

The *form* is the future.

Knowledge and mastery of the plot point are an essential requirement of writing a screenplay. The plot points at the end of each act are the anchoring pins of dramatic action; they hold everything together. They are the signposts, goals, objectives, or destination points of each act – forged links in the chain of dramatic action.

Go to a film and find the plot points at the end of Acts I and II. Look at your watch. Time them. See whether the *paradigm* works. If you can't find them, look again. They're there.

Do you know the plot points at the end of Acts I and II in your screenplay?

BUILDING THE SCREENPLAY

11

Up until now, we've discussed the four basic elements needed to write a screenplay – ending, beginning, plot point at the end of Act I, and plot point at the end of Act II. Those are the four things you need to know before you put one word on paper.

Now what?

How do you go about putting all those things together to build a screenplay?

How do you construct a screenplay?

Take a look at the *paradigm*:

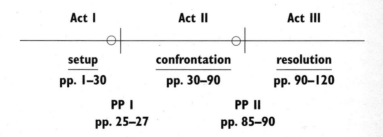

Act I, Act II, Act III. Beginning, middle, and end. Each act is a *unit*, or *block*, of dramatic action.

Look at Act I:

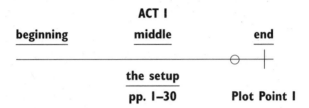

ACT I

| beginning | middle | end |

the setup

pp. 1–30   Plot Point I

Act I extends from the *opening* of the screenplay to the *plot point* at the end of Act I. Therefore, there is a beginning of the *beginning*, a middle of the *beginning*, and an end of the *beginning*. It is a self-contained *unit*, a block of dramatic action. It is approximately thirty pages long, and about page 25 or 27 a *plot point* occurs, an incident or event that "hooks" into the action and spins it around into another direction. What happens in Act I is the dramatic context known as the *setup*. You have approximately thirty pages to *set up* your story; introduce the *main character*, state the *dramatic premise*, and *establish the situation*, visually and dramatically.

Here's Act II:

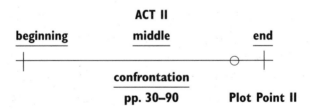

ACT II

| beginning | middle | end |

confrontation

pp. 30–90   Plot Point II

Act II is the *middle* of your screenplay. It contains the bulk of action. It goes from the beginning of Act II to the plot point at the end of Act II. So we have a beginning of the *middle*, a middle of the *middle*, and an end of the *middle*.

It is also a *unit*, or block, of dramatic action. It is approximately sixty pages long, and about page 85–90 another plot point occurs which "spins" the story around into Act III. The dramatic *context* is confrontation, and your character will encounter obstacles that keep him from reaching his goal. (Once you determine the "need" of your character, create obstacles to that need. Conflict! Your story then becomes your character overcoming all obstacles to achieve his or her "need.")

Act III is the end, or resolution, of your screenplay.

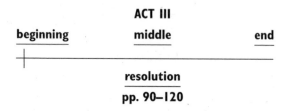

ACT III

beginning	middle	end

resolution

pp. 90–120

Like Acts I and II, there is a beginning of the *end*, a middle of the *end*, and an end of the *end*. It is approximately thirty pages long, and the dramatic *context* is the *resolution* of your story.

In each act, you start from the beginning of the act and move toward the plot points at the end of the act. That means each act has a *direction*, a line of development from beginning to the plot point. The plot points at the end of Acts I and II are your destination points; that's where you're going when you're building or constructing a screenplay.

You build your screenplay in terms of units – Act I, II, III.

How do you build your screenplay?

Use 3 x 5 cards.

Take a pack of 3 x 5 cards. Write the idea of each scene or sequence on a single card, and maybe a few brief words of description to aid you when you're writing. For example, if you have a sequence about your character in a hospital, you can indicate several scenes, one per card; *arrival* of your character at the hospital; *he or she checks in* at the admitting office; the *doctors examine him*; lab work is done; various medical tests, like X rays, EKG or EEG, are conducted; family members or friends visit him; his hospital roommate may be someone he dislikes; the doctors might discuss the case with relatives; your character might be in the intensive care unit. All this can be specified in a few words on each card.

Each description can be written into a scene, all within the sequence marked "Hospital."

You can use as many cards as you like: Edward Anhalt, who adapted *The Young Lions* and *Becket*, used fifty-two cards to build his screenplays. That's how many cards there are in a package. Ernest Lehman, who wrote *North by North West*, *The Sound of Music*, and *Family Plot*, used anywhere from fifty to a hundred, however many he needs. Frank Pierson wrote *Dog Day Afternoon* in twelve cards; he wove the story around twelve basic sequences. Again, there is no rule about how many cards you need to have to build your screenplay; use as many as you want. You can also use different-colored cards; blue for Act I, green for Act II, and yellow for Act III.

Your story determines how many cards you need. Trust your story! Let *it* tell you how many cards you need, whether it be 12, 48, 52, 80, 96, 118; it doesn't matter. Trust your story.

The cards are an incredible method. You can arrange scenes any way you want, rearrange them, add some, omit others. It is a method that is simple, easy, and affective, and gives you maximum mobility in building your screenplay.

Let's begin to build a screenplay by creating the dramatic *context* of each act, so we can find the *content*.

Remember Newton's Third Law of Motion from physics – "for every action there is an equal and opposite reaction." The principle works in building the screenplay. First, you must know the *need* of your main character. What is the *need* of your character? What does he or she want to achieve, get, satisfy, or win, within the body of your screenplay? Once you establish your character's need, then you can create obstacles to that need.

Drama is conflict.

And the essence of character is action – action is character.

We live in a world of action-reaction. If you're driving a car (action) and someone cuts you off or cuts in front of you, what do you do (reaction)? Swear, usually. Honk your horn indignantly. Try to cut the other driver off, tailgate him. Shake your fist, mutter to yourself, step on the gas! It's all a *reaction* to the *action* of the driver cutting you off.

Action-reaction, it's a law of the universe. If your character *acts* in your screenplay, somebody, or something, is going to *react* in such a way that your character *reacts*. Then, he will usually create a *new* action that will create another reaction.

Your character *acts*, and somebody *reacts*. Action-reaction, reaction-action – your story always moves toward that plot point at the end of each act.

Many new or inexperienced writers have things happening to their characters, and they are always *reacting* to their situation, rather than *acting* in terms of dramatic need. The essence of character is *action*; your character must *act*, not react.

In *Three Days of the Condor*, Act I sets up the office routine of Robert Redford. When Redford returns from lunch, everyone is dead. That is the plot point at the end of Act I. Redford *reacts*: he calls the CIA; they tell him to avoid all places where he's known, especially home. He finds the absent coworker dead in bed, and doesn't know where to go or whom to trust. He is *reacting* to the situation. He *acts* when he phones Cliff Robertson and tells him he wants his friend Sam to meet him and bring him into headquarters. When that fails, Redford *acts* by forcing Faye Dunaway to take him to her apartment at gunpoint: he's got to rest, collect his thoughts, find out what action to take.

Action is *doing* something, *reacting* is having it happen.

In *Alice Doesn't Live Here Anymore*, Alice, after the death of her husband, is going to Monterey, California, to become a singer and satisfy a childhood dream. In order to survive with her young son, she seeks a job as a singer in various bars. At first no one will give her a chance. She becomes desperate, despondent, hoping for a break. She is *reacting* to her situation – the circumstances surrounding her – and this makes her a passive and not very sympathetic character. When she does get a chance to sing, it's not what she expected at all.

Many inexperienced writers have things happen to their characters; they *react* rather than *act*. The essence of character is *action*.

You've got thirty pages to set up your story, and the first ten pages are crucial.

Within the first ten pages, you must establish the *main character*, set up the dramatic *premise*, and establish the *situation*.

You know what your opening is, and you know the plot point at the end of the first act. It's either a scene or a sequence, an "incident" or an "event."

If you think about it, you've already got about five or ten pages of your script written with those two elements. So, you've got about twenty pages to write in order to complete Act I. Not bad, especially since you haven't written anything yet.

Now you're ready to build your screenplay. Start with Act I.

It is a complete unit of dramatic action; it begins with the opening scene or sequence and ends at the plot point at the end of the act.

Take the 3 x 5 cards. Write down a few words or descriptive phrases on each card. If it's an office sequence, write "office," and what happens there: "embezzlement of $250,000 discovered." On another card: "emergency meeting of top executives." The next card: "introduce Joe as main character." Next card: "the media learn about it."

Next card: "Joe nervous, insecure." Use as many cards as you need to make the "office sequence" complete.

What happens next?

Take another card and write the next scene: "Joe questioned by police."

Then what happens?

A scene with "Joe and family at home." Another card: "Joe receives phone call; he is a suspect."

Next card: "Joe driving to work." Next card: "Joe arrives at work, the strain evident."

What happens next?

"Joe questioned further by police." A scene can be added where the "media question Joe." Another card: "Joe's family knows he's innocent; will stick by him." Another card: "Joe with attorney. Things look bad."

Step by step, scene by scene, build your story to the plot point at the end of the act, "Joe indicted for embezzlement." That's the plot point at the end of Act I. It's like putting together a jigsaw puzzle.

You may have eight, ten, fourteen or more cards for Act I. You've indicated the flow of dramatic action to the plot point. When you've completed the cards for Act I, take a look at what you've got. Go over the cards, scene by scene, like flash cards. Do it several times. Soon you pick up a definite flow of action; you'll change a few words here and a few words there to make it read easier. Get used to the story line. Tell yourself the story of the first act, the *setup*.

If you want to write a few extra cards because you discover a few holes in your story, do so. The cards are for you. Use them to construct your story, so you always know where you're going.

When you've completed the cards for Act I, put them on a bulletin board, on the wall or on the floor, in sequential order. Tell yourself the story from the beginning to the plot point at the end of Act I. Do it over and over again and pretty soon you'll begin to weave the story into the fabric of the creative process.

Do the same with Act II. Use the plot point at the end of the act to guide you. List the sequences you have lined up for the act.

Remember the dramatic *context* of Act II is *confrontation*. Is your character moving through the story with his "need" firmly established? You must keep obstacles in mind all the time in order to generate dramatic conflict.

When you've finished the cards, repeat the process from Act I; go through the cards from the beginning of Act II to the plot point at the end of Act II. Free-associate, let ideas come to you, put them on cards and go over and over them.

Lay them out. Study them. Plot your story progression. See how it's working. Don't be afraid to change anything. A film editor I once interviewed told me an important creative principle; he said that within the context of the story "the sequences tried that *don't work* are the ones that tell you *what does work*."

It's a classic rule in film. Many of the best cinematic moments happen by accident. A scene *tried* that doesn't work when first tried will ultimately tell you what *does* work.

Don't be afraid to make mistakes.

How long should you spend on the cards?

About a week. It takes me four days to lay out the cards. I spend one full day on Act I, about four hours. I spend two days on Act II; the first day for the first half of the act, the second day for the last half. And, one day laying out Act III.

Then, I'll put them on the floor or bulletin board. I'm ready to start working.

I spend a few weeks going over and over the cards, getting to know the story, the progression, the characters, until I feel comfortable. That means about two to four hours a day spent with the cards. I'll go through the story, act by act, scene by scene, shuffling cards around, trying something here, moving one scene from Act I into Act II, a scene from Act II into Act I. The card method is so flexible you can do anything you want, and it works!

The card system allows you maximum mobility in structuring your screenplay. Go over and over the cards until you feel ready to begin writing. How do you know when to start writing? You'll know; it's a feeling you get. When you're ready to start writing, you'll start writing. You'll feel secure with your story; you'll know what you need to do, and you'll start getting visual images of certain scenes.

Is the card system the only way to construct your story?

No. There are several ways to do it. Some writers simply list a series of scenes on the page, numbering them (1) Bill at the office; (2) Bill with John at bar; (3) Bill sees Jane; (4) Bill leaves for party; (5) Bill meets Jane; (6) they like each other, decide to leave together.

Another way is to write a *treatment*; a *narrative synopsis* of what happens in your story incorporating a little dialogue; a treatment is anywhere from four to twenty pages long. An *outline* is also used, especially in television, where you tell your story in a detailed narrative plot progression; dialogue is an essential part of the *outline*, and it is anywhere from twenty-eight to sixty pages in length. Most *outlines*, or *treatments*, should not be longer than thirty pages. Do you know why?

The producer's lips get tired.

That's an old Hollywood joke, and there's a great deal of truth to it.

No matter what method you use, you are now ready to move from telling the story on cards to writing the story on paper.

You know your story from start to finish. It should move smoothly from beginning to end, with plot progression clearly in mind so all you have to do is look at the cards, close your eyes, and *see* the story unfolding.

All you've got to do is write it!

Determine your ending, opening, and plot point at the end of Acts I and II. Get some 3 x 5 cards, different colors if you choose, and start with the opening of your screenplay. Free-associate. Whatever comes to mind for a scene, put it down on the cards. Build toward the plot point at the end of the act.

Experiment with it. The cards are for you – find your own method to make them work for your story. You might want to write a *treatment* or *outline*. Do it.

THE PROBLEM SHEET

Too Much, Too Soon
- The story is told in words, not pictures
- The action does not move the story forward
- The dramatic premise is not clear
- Who is the main character?
- Characters are too expository

✎ Main character is too passive and reactive

✎ There are too many characters

✎ Everything has to be explained

✎ The first act is too long

✎ The story line is too choppy and disjointed

✎ Too much happens too fast

As a general rule, if you want to find the origin of any problem you have to start looking for it from page one, word one.

If you do that and analyze the material, you may begin to notice some things. For example, there may be too many characters, or you don't really know who the main character is, who the story is about. Or maybe it just feels like the script is too talky and the action progresses more through dialogue and exposition than the visual image. Or so much seems to be happening that the focus of the story, what it's really about, seems choppy, sloppy, and disjointed.

Look at the material again and you will probably realize that there is so much information being given and the story moves so fast, you might not really know what's going on.

All these elements are symptoms of too much information being given too early in the story; too much is happening too soon. The result: not enough depth or insight into the characters and not enough conflict or drama in the narrative line. And it's definitely a problem.

If you want to look for the cause or the source of this particular problem, it will almost always be found in Act I and, more specifically, in the first ten pages of the screenplay.

A good screenplay is set up from page one, word one. Act I is a unit of dramatic action that begins with the opening scene and continues until the Plot Point at the end of the act. It is held together with the dramatic context known as the *Set-Up*; because all the elements of the story, the characters, the dramatic premise and situation, the relationships between them, must be established within this particular unit of dramatic action. Act I is a unit of action in which all the elements of the story must be carefully integrated and set up; all the incidents and events in this unit of action must lead directly to the Plot Point at the end of Act I, the true beginning of your story.

If the script is not set up correctly, then there is a certain tendency to keep adding characters and events to the story line to make it move faster. The story seems to skate on the surface of the action without penetrating its layers of texture and depth, creating the feeling that the story is trite, contrived, and predictable.

Why does this happen? It seems like many writers approach their screenplays without enough preparation; they're so anxious to begin writing the script that they don't take the time to explore and develop the relationships between the actions and characters. So they begin from the smallest kernel of information and then feel their way through the First Act. Most of their time is spent trying to figure out what the story is about and what happens next, so they throw down as many story points as they can in the First Act, hoping the story will manifest itself.

It doesn't work. Seeds are planted, but not cultivated, watered, or nourished. The writer tells his or her story in the first ten pages, then is lost and doesn't know what to do next.

Preparation and research are essential to the screenwriting process. It is the responsibility of the screenwriter to know and clearly define who the *main character* is, what the *dramatic premise* is – what the story is about – and what the *dramatic situation* is – the circumstances surrounding the action. If you don't know the story well enough, if you haven't spent enough time doing the required research, then you run the risk of inserting more incidents and events into the story line just to try to make it work, and then the narrative thread of the story usually goes awry; the stuff just isn't working.

Sometimes the problem exists because the story line is too thin, and more "plot" has to be found, but the solution is not creating more interesting incidents or characters to be put into the screenplay. Creating more "things" to happen, more obstacles to confront, doesn't do anything except expand the problem.

The trouble is often traceable to a writer's impulse to get the script off to a fast and provocative start. If you've only got ten pages to grab the attention of the reader or audience, then the tendency is to make sure the story captures the reader's interest. And often that means dumping the characters, their obstacles, and their relationship with the other characters into this ten-page unit of dramatic action.

It's too much, too soon. More is not necessarily better. If you take great screenplays like *The Shawshank Redemption*, *Thelma & Louise*, *The Silence of the Lambs*, or *Apollo 13*, all the major ingredients of the story line are either there in place, or referred to, within the first ten-page unit of dramatic action. That's why the context of Act I is the Set-Up.

The Shawshank Redemption is a great example. Since the story deals with Andy in prison, we have to set up the murder of Andy's wife and lover as well as the trial and verdict, before he enters the prison. We have to know why he's there and what *crime* he has committed. The three threads of the story line – murder, trial, and verdict – are brilliantly intercut, so we *see* the events leading to his conviction even though we don't actually see him committing the murders.

Many screenwriters would approach the story from the perspective of dialogue; they might begin with Andy entering the prison, and then, during his relationship with Red, he would tell the story in bits and pieces. As Red informs us in voice-over, Andy didn't seem to belong in the prison population; when he walked "he strolled, like a man in a park without a care or worry." During their first few scenes together, he could explain to Red about the murder of his wife. In terms of setting up the story the approach would work, but then the tendency might be *to explain* rather than *reveal*.

In *Apollo 13* the first ten pages set up all the narrative threads that are needed to establish the situation. After newsreel shots of the fire that killed the three astronauts of Apollo 1 (the transition from newsreel to present time, TV to TV, is very much like the flashback transitions in *How to Make an American Quilt*, except the quilt is used as the visual motif), the script opens with a friendly partylike gathering watching Neil Armstrong's first walk on the moon. In just a few words we learn these people are astronauts in the current NASA program and the dream of Jim Lovell (Tom Hanks) is to land on the moon. In just a few pages we know everything we need to know, including the suspicion that his wife has some deep fear about his going into space again.

The dramatic hook occurs on page 10, when Lovell returns home and surprises his family with the news that his space mission has just been moved up to the Apollo 13 position. (Originally, a scene had been written showing Lovell with the NASA officials getting the assignment, but it slowed everything down so it was cut.)

Once he gets the assignment, we can focus, in the second ten pages, on his training and preparation for the mission, so we can see what the astronauts had to go through to prepare for their flight. Plot Point I is the lift-off into space.

Apollo 13 is an excellent example of classic screenwriting that sets up character and story from page one, word one, both through action and dialogue. The script could easily have started with Lovell and his crew being informed their mission was being pushed up, and if it had been written that way, most of the expository information would have to be established in the first ten-page unit of the dramatic action.

In *Sense and Sensibility*, based on Jane Austen's nineteenth-century novel, it would have been very easy to put in too much too soon. In the first few pages we could set up the back story, the relationships within the family, the death of the father, how it affects the three sisters, but this normally would be too much information for Act I. Nevertheless, it's got to be there for us to set up the story correctly.

How did Emma Thompson handle this? In voice-over we hear about the family, see the father on his deathbed, and we learn the fortunes of the family are to be automatically inherited by the son. And he promises his dying father that he will take care of his three sisters. But after the funeral, the son's wife has other plans for her husband's inheritance.

That's a lot of information to present in the first ten pages. But it's been set up in both narration and pictures, so we see the father's widow and his three daughters are literally without the roof over their heads. The rest of Act I deals with how the family is going to cope with this situation, and we see them play it out in scene after scene. The girls have to be married, of course, for in those days women needed husbands to take care of them. And when the possible match between the Emma Thompson character with Hugh Grant doesn't happen, the girls give up the house to their brother and move to the country. Plot Point I.

If all this back-story information had been executed through dialogue, there would have been way too much explanation in the story. It would have been too *wordy*, the characters *passive* and *reactive*, the *scenes too long* and *expository*, with the result that the narrative action would not *move the story forward*.

Take a look at the *Problem Sheet*. It's all there.

That's why each element of the story line must be carefully laid out before you even begin writing. Believe it or not, most problems in screenwriting are there because not enough research was done; the story, the characters, and all the dramatic forces working on the story have not been thought out enough.

The inclination to put too much, too soon, into your story line is, I find, usually the result of a number of different things, but the primary cause is that most writers don't spend enough time doing character research. A biography of the main character may not have been written, or maybe not enough was written, with the result that the character seems thin or unsympathetic. The result: a weak character so busy reacting to all the incidents and events of the plot that he or she becomes passive and seemingly disappears off the page. The main character will have no point of view, and some of the lesser, or minor, characters take over. The main character becomes lost in the background.

If you examine the *Problem Sheet* you'll see that almost all the symptoms seem to stem from the writer not knowing the characters well enough. Too many plot twists and turns have to be explained, and the action wanders – as in *Diehard 3* – the dramatic premise forgotten or unclear. This happens in *Broken Arrow* (Graham Yost), the John Woo film in which character is sacrificed for action. What carries the film, of course, is not the story or the characters, but the action.

This particular problem of too much, too soon, is defined as a problem of *Plot*, but the symptoms we've been analyzing stem from *Character*. Why is that?

Because to fix this kind of problem you've got to open up, develop, and enlarge the incidents of the story line, adding new *Plot* elements even though the problem evolves from *Character*.

For example, a woman was writing a story that takes place in the sixteenth century about a band of traveling musicians. The main character is a young woman, deeply in love and recently married, whose husband, when the story opens, is accidentally killed in a river accident. Right after the funeral, her father is determined to marry her to an old man, a very rich and respected merchant, but she refuses and will not obey his commands or honor his wishes. She doesn't know what to do, but when she's invited to a lord's estate to cure his young son (she's set up to be a natural healer), she allows herself to be seduced by him. Her action permits her to get out of the unbearable situation with her father, but sets her apart from the others in the band. She is filled with pride and independence and no one is going to tell her what to do. Especially when it concerns her feelings.

The nobleman is enchanted with her, but when he learns she has used him (he was only a solution to a problem, after all) he vows that if he can't have her, no one else will either. So he sets into motion a plan that will keep her as a prisoner in his castle. And we know that if she ever goes to prison, this free spirit will literally wither and die.

That's basically the story, and it works well. When my student began writing the screenplay, she began hurrying the action, putting in too much information because she thought she had to explain how the musicians lived, what their society was like, and their interrelationships within this musical clan. She structured Act I this way, opening with the group crossing a raging river, when suddenly the husband falls into a swirling eddy and can't swim against the mighty current and drowns. The young wife rushes to him but it's too late. The funeral follows, and immediately following the ceremony her father tells her that he has sold her to the old man, the merchant, and she must marry him. She can't deal with it and flees, but after a few weeks the young widow is summoned to the nobleman's estate to cure his son. The son recovers, the nobleman becomes infatuated with her, and she determines that he is the answer to her prayers and lets herself be seduced.

Being seduced by the nobleman is the Plot Point at the end of Act I. It gives us enough time to set up the death, the relationships within the band, and establish the dramatic premise. The dramatic and visual possibilities are strong, the emotional opportunities rich. The narrative flow of events gives us a good insight into the arena of life of the traveling musicians.

But the woman was still insecure about the story and wrote everything that should happen in Act I into the first ten pages. She literally shoved everything together so the main character meets the nobleman by page 10. As a result, everything happens so fast that nothing is really developed; all the insights that could give us a full and rich portrait of the characters were omitted. In terms of story, there was too much information being given too soon. Everything was mashed together and the events simply rode on the surface of the story like a leaf floating on the water.

When I explained that she had too much information in these first pages, she did not really know how to fix it. I told her she had to go back into her characters in order to get more material, so as to develop Act I more completely. So I gave her an exercise: I had her write a free-association essay about the main character's emotional state; what her feelings were for her husband/lover during their courtship and marriage.

Then I had her develop an emotional back story to her character; what happened between wife and husband immediately before the story begins. Maybe they had an argument the morning before crossing the river; maybe they had just finished making love and vowed their love for each other. I had her describe the character's feelings of grief and loss, her anger at being left behind without him, and so on.

The exercise helped the woman approach some of those emotional bridges that have to be crossed in order to develop character. When she became more familiar with her character's emotional life, I had her take each one of the events she had written in those first ten pages, and separate them into individual sequences with a beginning, middle, and end. I had her write them all out, in a page-or-two essay; when she finished, she could add and create new material that would allow her to open up the fertile landscape of her story.

A sequence, remember, is a series of scenes connected by one single idea with a definite beginning, middle, and end. A funeral, a wedding (*Four Weddings and a Funeral* is really five sequences strung together), a chase, a shootout, and suchlike.

Here's how we broke it down for Act I: The band moving toward the river then crossing the river is one sequence; being swept away and the chase leading to the young husband's death, another; her reaction to the loss, her mourning, the funeral, another. All these sequences are complete within themselves and can be structured individually into beginning, middle, and end. Because the new material has to be expanded, structured, and woven into the story line, it brings more depth and dimension to the emotional needs of the character.

That's why it's a problem of *Plot*, though it encompasses elements of both *Structure* and *Character*. The solution to this particular problem is more easily approached from the perspective of *Plot*; that is, we add events to the story line in order to develop the dramatic action more fully. I am sure it would be easier if we could clearly and conveniently separate each problem into its own little category complete unto itself, but that's not the way it works. In life, as in screenwriting, everything is related to everything else.

Because *Plot*, *Character*, and *Structure* are the foundations of screenwriting, they will always be interrelated, though certain problems can be approached more easily via one category than another.

You could also solve this kind of problem by approaching it from the category of *Structure* or *Character*. It really doesn't matter how you approach the problem as long as you identify and define it.

What's most important is to find the right way to set up your story; find the picture, or the scene, that best illustrates the story *and* the character. As mentioned, in *Apollo 13*, the script opens with Jim Lovell (Tom Hanks) and other astronauts at a party, watching Neil Armstrong's landing on the moon. The picture on TV and the simple comments by the characters let us know immediately that these people are involved in the space mission to the moon. Within the first ten pages we know that Jim Lovell's dream, his dramatic premise, is to return to the moon.

All this information has been set up simply and economically by the screenwriter's knowledge of who these characters are, what their dramatic need is, what the story is about, and the circumstances surrounding the action. What's set up in Jim Lovell's case is that he knows he may never fly to the moon again because of the accident in the Apollo spacecraft.

This is just good screenwriting. Everything we need to know, we know within this first ten-page unit of dramatic action. It sets up the story so that Plot Point I, the true beginning of the story, is the blastoff into space for the Apollo 13 mission. And thus the temptation to set up the story through dialogue has been avoided.

When you think you have a problem, go back into the material and reread it from the point of view that *maybe too much is happening too soon*. Is the front end of your screenplay, the first ten pages, overloaded with information, characters, or events? Is so much happening so fast that the reader becomes lost or does the major focus of the story line seem lost?

WRITING THE SCREENPLAY 12

The hardest thing about writing is knowing what to write. Look back and take a look where we've come from. Here is the *paradigm*:

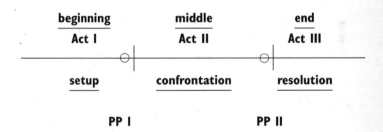

beginning	middle	end
Act I	Act II	Act III
setup	confrontation	resolution
PP I		PP II

We've talked about a *subject*, like three guys holding up the Chase Manhattan Bank, and broken it down into *action* and *character*. We talked about choosing a *main* character, and two *major* characters, and channeling their action into robbing the bank. We talked about choosing our *ending*, our *beginning*, and the *plot points* at the end of Acts I and II. We've talked about *constructing the screenplay* with 3 x 5 cards, and are familiar with the *direction* of the story.

Look at the *paradigm*: WE KNOW WHAT TO WRITE!

We've completed a form of preparation applicable to all writing in general, and the screenplay in particular; it is form and structure. You are now able to select the elements of your story that fall inside the *paradigm* of screenplay form. In other words, you know what to write; all you've got to do is *write it*.

Writing a screenplay is an amazing, almost mysterious phenomenon. One day you're up on top of things, the next day you're down, lost in confusion and uncertainty. One day it works, the next day it doesn't; who knows how or why. It is the creative process; it defies analysis; it is magic and it is wonder.

Whatever has been said or written about the experience of writing from the beginning of time, it still boils down to one thing – writing is your own, personal experience. Nobody else's.

A lot of people contribute to the making of a movie, but the writer is the only person who sits down and faces the blank sheet of paper.

Writing is hard work, a day-by-day job, sitting in front of your computer or notepad day in, day out, getting words on the screen or on paper. You've got to put in the time.

Before you begin writing, you've got to *find the time* to write.

How many hours a day do you need to spend writing?

That depends on you. I work about four hours a day, six days a week. John Milius writes one hour a day, seven days a week, between 5 and 6 p.m. Stirling Silliphant, who wrote *The Towering Inferno*, sometimes writes twelve hours a day. Paul Schrader works on a story in his head for months, telling it to people until he *knows* it completely; then he "jumps in" and writes it in about two weeks. Then, he'll spend weeks polishing and fixing it.

You need two to three hours a day to write a screenplay.

Look at your daily schedule. Examine your time. If you're working full time, or caring for home and family, your time is limited. You're going to have to find the best time for you to write. Are you the kind of person who works best in the morning? Or does it take you until early afternoon to be wide awake and alert? Late at night may be a good time. Find out.

You may get up and write a few hours before you go to work; or, come home from work, unwind, and then write a few hours. You may want to work at night, say about 10 or 11 p.m., or you may go to bed early and wake up about 4 a.m. to write. If you're a housewife and have a family, you may want to write when everyone's gone for the day, either midmorning, or midafternoon. You be the judge of what time, day or night, you can get two to three hours alone.

And a few hours alone is a few hours alone. No telephone, no friends for coffee, no idle chatter, no chores, no demands made on you by husbands, wives, lovers, or children. You need two to three hours alone, without interruption.

It may take you a time to find the "right" time. Fine. Experiment, make sure it's the best time for you to work.

Writing is a day-by-day job. You may write your screenplay shot by shot, scene by scene, page by page, day by day. Set goals for yourself. Three pages a day is reasonable and realistic. That's almost 1,000 words a day. If a screenplay is 120 pages long, and you write three pages a day, five days a week, how long will it take you to write a first draft?

Forty working days. If you work five days a week, that means you can get a first draft in about six weeks. Once you start the writing process, you'll have days when you write ten pages, days when you do six, and so on. Just make sure you get three pages a day. Or more.

If you're married, or in a relationship, it's going to be difficult – you need some space and private time, as well as support and encouragement.

Women with families can have a more difficult time than others. Husbands and children are not always very understanding or support-ive. No matter how many times you explain that you're "going to be writing," it doesn't help. Demands are made that are difficult to ignore. I have even had married women students tell me their husbands threaten to leave them unless they stop writing, and their children turn into monsters; the domestic routine is being interfered with, and they don't like it. It's tough to handle; emotions of guilt, anger, or frustra-tion get in the way of your need for the time, space, and freedom to write, and if you don't watch out you could easily become a victim of your emotions.

When you're in the writing experience, you're near your loved ones in body, but your mind and concentration are a thousand miles away. Your family doesn't care or understand that your characters are in a highly charged situation; *you* can't break your concentration to deal with the snacks, meals, laundry, and shopping that you normally do.

Don't expect to. If you're in a relationship your loved ones will *tell* you they understand and support you, but they won't – not really. Not because they don't want to, but because they don't understand the writing experience.

Don't feel "guilty" about taking the time *you need* to write your screenplay. If you expect your wife, husband, or lover to "get upset," or "not understand" when you're writing, it won't bother you when it happens. *If* it does. You have to be "at choice" when you're writing; expect a "tough time" and it won't bother you if it happens.

A note to all husbands, wives, lovers, friends, and children: if your husband, wife, lover, or parent is writing a screenplay, they need your love and support.

Give them the opportunity to explore their desire to write a screenplay. During the time they're writing, anywhere from three to six months, they're going to be moody, explosive, easily upset, preoccu- pied, and distant. Your daily routine is going to be interfered with, and you're not going to like it. It's going to be uncomfortable.

Are you willing to give them the space and the opportunity to write what they want to write? Do you love them enough to support them in their efforts even if it interferes with your life?

If the answer is "no," talk about it. Work out a way so that both sides can win, and then support each other. Writing is a lonely, soli- tary job. For a person in a relationship, it becomes a joint experience.

Establish a writing schedule: 10:30 to 12 noon; or 8 to 10 p.m.; or 9 to midnight. With a schedule, the "problem" of discipline becomes easier to handle.

Decide *how many* days you're going to be writing. If you're working full time, at school, or involved in a marriage or relationship, you can't expect to write a screenplay working one or two days a week. Creative energy is lost that way. You've got to focus and concentrate clearly on the script you're writing. You need at least four days a week.

With your writing schedule set up you can get down to work; and one fine day you sit down to write.

What's the first thing that's going to happen?

Resistance, that's what.

After you write FADE IN: EXT. STREET – DAY you'll suddenly be seized with an incredible "urge" to sharpen your pencils or clean your work area. You'll find a *reason* or *excuse* not to write. That's resistance.

Writing is an experiential process, a learning process involving the acquisition of skill and coordination; like riding a bicycle, swimming, dancing, or playing tennis.

Nobody learns to swim by being thrown into the water. You learn to stay afloat, to survive. You learn to swim by perfecting your form, and you can only do that by actually swimming; the more you do the better you get.

It's the same thing with writing. You're going to experience some form of resistance. It shows itself in many ways and most of the time we aren't even aware it's happening.

For example: when you first sit down to start writing you may want to clean the refrigerator. Or wash the kitchen floor. You may want to jog, change the sheets, take a drive, eat, or have sex. Some people go out and buy $500 worth of clothes they don't want! Or, get angry, impatient, and yell at everybody and anybody for nothing in particular.

They're all forms of resistance.

One of my favorite forms of resistance is sitting down to write and suddenly getting an idea for *another* screenplay. A *much better* idea; an idea so original, so exciting, you wonder what you're doing writing "this" screenplay. You really think about it.

You may get two or three "better" ideas. It happens quite often; it may be a great idea, but it's a form of resistance! If it's really a good idea, it will keep. Simply write it up in a page or two and file it away. If you decide to pursue this "new" idea and abandon the original project, you'll discover the same thing happening; when you sit down to write, you'll get *another new idea*, and so on and so on. It's resistance; a mind-trip, a way of avoiding writing.

We all do it. We're masters at creating *reasons* and *excuses* not to write; it's simply a "barrier" to the creative process.

How do you deal with it?

Simple. If you know it's going to happen, simply acknowledge it when it does. When you're cleaning the refrigerator, sharpening pencils, or eating, just know that's what you're doing; experiencing resistance! It's no big thing. Don't put yourself down, feel guilty, or punish yourself. Just acknowledge the resistance – then you move right through to the other side. Just don't *pretend* it's *not happening*. It is! Once you deal with your resistance, you're ready to start writing.

The first ten pages are the most difficult. Your writing is going to be awkward and probably not very good. It's OK. Some people won't be able to deal with that; they'll make a decision that what they're writing is no good. They'll stop, righteous and justified, because they "knew they couldn't do it."

Writing is a learning coordination; the more you do the easier it gets.

At first, your dialogue's probably not going to be very good.

Remember that dialogue is a function of character. Let's review the purpose of dialogue. It

✎ moves the story forward;
✎ communicates facts and information to the reader;
✎ reveals character;
✎ establishes character relationships;
✎ makes your characters real, natural, and spontaneous;
✎ reveals the conflicts of the story and characters;
✎ reveals the emotional states of your characters; and
✎ comments on the action.

Your first attempts will probably be stilted, clichéd, fragmented, and strained. Writing dialogue is like learning to swim; you're going to flounder around, but the more you do the easier it gets.

It takes anywhere from 25 to 50 pages before your characters start talking to you. And they *do* start talking to you. Don't worry about the dialogue. Just keep writing. Dialogue can always be cleaned up.

Those of you looking for "inspiration" to guide you won't find it. Inspiration is measured in moments, a few minutes, or hours, a screenplay in weeks and months. If it takes you a hundred days to write a screenplay, and you're "on" for ten of those days, consider yourself lucky. Being "on" for a hundred days, or twenty-five days, just doesn't happen. You may "hear" that it does, but in truth it's the pot at the end of the rainbow – your're chasing a dream.

"But" – you say.

But what?

Writing is a day-by-day job, two to three hours a day, three or four days a week, three pages a day, ten pages a week. Shot by shot, scene by scene, page by page, sequence by sequence, act by act.

When you're *in* the *paradigm*, you can't *see* the *paradigm*.

The card system is your map and your guide, the plot points your checkpoints along the way, the "last-chance" gas station before you hit the high desert, the ending, your destination. What's nice about the card system is that you can forget it. The cards have served their purpose. You'll suddenly "discover" a new scene that works better, or hadn't been thought of. Use it.

It doesn't matter if you want to drop scenes or add new ones; do it. Your creative mind has assimilated the cards so you can throw out a few scenes and still be following the *direction* of your story.

When you're doing the cards, you're doing the cards. When you're writing, you're writing. Forget a rigid adherence to the cards. Let them guide you, don't be a slave to them. If you feel a spontaneous moment that gives you a better, more fluid story, write it.

Keep writing. Day by day, page by page. And during the writing process you're going to discover things about yourself you never knew.

For example, if you're writing about something that happened to you, you may re-experience some of those old feelings and emotions. You may get "wacky" and irritable and live each day as if you were on an emotional roller coaster. Don't worry. Just keep writing.

You're going to move through three stages of your first-draft screenplay.

The first stage is the "word on paper" stage. This is when you put it all down. If you're in doubt about writing a scene or not writing it, write it. If in doubt, write. That's the rule. If you start censoring yourself you might wind up with a 90-page screenplay, and that's too short. You'll have to add scenes to a tight structure to bring it to length, and that's difficult. It's easier to cut scenes out than add them to an already structured screenplay.

Keep moving forward in your story. If you write a scene and go back to clean it up, to polish it and "make it right," you'll find you've dried up by about page 60, and might shelve the project. Many writers I know who've tried to write a draft this way have failed to complete it. Any major changes you need to make, do in the second draft.

There will be moments when you don't know how to begin a scene, or what to do next. You know the scene on cards, but not how to get into it visually.

Ask yourself "what happens next?" and you'll get an answer. It's usually the *first* thought skittering across your mind. Grab it, and throw it down on paper. It's what I call the "creative grab," because you've got to be quick enough to "catch it" and put it down.

Many times you'll try to improve that first idea to "make it better." If your first thought is to have the scene in a car driving down the highway, and you decide to make it a walk in the country or a walk on the beach, you'll lose a certain creative energy. Do it too many times and your script will reflect a "contrived," deliberate quality. It won't work.

There's only one rule that governs your writing; not whether it's "good" or "bad," but does it work? Does your scene work? If it does, keep it in, no matter what anybody says.

If it works, use it. If it doesn't, don't.

If you don't know how to get in or out of a scene, free-associate. Let your mind wander; ask yourself the best way to get into the scene; trust yourself; you'll find the answer.

If you created a problem, you'll be able to find a solution to that problem. All you have to do is look for it.

Problems in a screenplay can always be solved. If you create it, you can solve it. If you're stuck, go back to your people; go into your character biography and ask your character what he or she would do in that situation. You'll get an answer. It may take a minute, an hour, a day, several days, a week, but you'll get the answer; probably when you least expect it, and in the most unusual place. Just keep asking yourself the question: "What do I need to do to solve this problem?" Run it through your head constantly, especially before you go to sleep. Occupy yourself with it. You'll find an answer.

Writing is the ability to ask yourself questions and get the answers.

Sometimes you'll get into a scene and not know where you're going, or what you're looking for to make it work. You know the *context*, not the *content*. So you'll write the same scene five different times, from five different points of view, and out of all these attempts you may find one line that gives you the key to what you're looking for.

You'll rewrite the scene using that one line as your anchor thought, and eventually be able to create something dynamic and spontaneous. You just have to find your way.

And trust yourself.

Around page 80 or 90, the resolution is forming and you'll discover the screenplay is literally writing itself. You're just like a medium, putting in time to finish the script. You don't have to do anything; it writes itself.

Does this method work in adapting a book, or novel, into a screenplay?

Yes.

When you adapt a book or novel into a screenplay, you must consider it an *original* screenplay *based* on other material. You can't adapt a novel literally and have it work, as Francis Ford Coppola learned when he adapted *The Great Gatsby* by F. Scott Fitzgerald. Coppola – *Patton*, *The Godfather*, *Apocalypse Now* – is one of the most arresting and dynamic writer-directors in Hollywood. In adapting *The Great Gatsby* he wrote a screenplay that is absolutely faithful to the novel. The result is a visually magnificent failure. Dramatically, it didn't work at all.

It's an apples-and-oranges situation.

When you adapt a book into a screenplay, all you need to use are the main characters, the situation, and some, but not all, of the story. You may have to add new characters, drop others, create new incidents or events, perhaps alter the entire structure of the book. In *The English Patient*, the entire movie was conceived from a few paragraphs in the novel. And then Anthony Minghella did some twenty-seven rewrites on the material, shaping it into what became the final film. In *Julia* Alvin Sargent created an entire movie out of an episode from *Pentimento* by Lillian Hellman.

Writing a screenplay is writing a screenplay. There are no shortcuts.

It may take you six to eight weeks to complete your first "words on paper" draft. Then you're ready to move into the second stage of your first draft; taking a cold, hard, objective look at what you've written.

This is the most mechanical and uninspiring stage of writing a screenplay. You'll take what is perhaps a 180–200 page draft of your script and reduce it to 130–140 pages. You'll cut out scenes, add new ones, rewrite others, and make any changes you need to get it into a workable form. It might take you about three weeks to do this. When you're finished, you're ready to approach the third stage of your first-draft script. This is where you see what you've got, where the story really gets written. You'll polish it, accent it, hone and rewrite it, trim to length, and make it all come to life. You're out of the *paradigm* now so you can see what you've got to do to make it better. In this stage you may rewrite a scene as many as ten times before you get it right.

There will always be one or two scenes that don't work the way you want them to, no matter how many times you rewrite them. You know these scenes don't work, but the reader will never know. He reads for story and execution, not content. I used to read a script in forty minutes, seeing it in my head, rather than reading it for prose style or content. Don't worry about the few scenes you know don't work. Let them be.

You discover the scenes you like the *most*, those clever, witty, and sparkling moments of action and dialogue, might have to be cut when you reduce it to workable length. You'll *try* to keep them in – after all, it *is* your *best* writing – but in the long run you've got to do what's best for your screenplay. I have a "best scene" file where I put the "best" things I've ever written. I had to cut them out to tighten the script.

You have to learn to be ruthless writing a screenplay, to sometimes cut out what you know is the best thing you've ever written; if it doesn't work, it doesn't work. If your scenes stand out and draw attention to themselves, they might impede the flow of action. Scenes that stand out *and* work are the scenes that will be remembered. Every good film has one or possibly two scenes people always remember. These scenes work within the dramatic context of the story. They are also the trademark scenes that later become immediately recognizable. In *High Anxiety* Mel Brooks made a movie out of famous Alfred Hitchcock scenes. As a reader, I could always spot variations on "famous scenes" from the movie past. They usually don't work.

If you don't know whether your "choice" scenes work, they probably don't. If you have to think about it, or question it, it means it's not working. You'll know when a scene's working. Trust yourself.

Keep writing; day by day, page by page. The more you do the easier it gets. When you're almost finished, perhaps ten or fifteen pages from the end, you might find you're "holding on." You'll spend four days writing one scene or one page, and you'll feel tired and listless. It's a natural phenomenon; you simply don't want to finish it, to complete it.

Let it go. Just be aware you're "holding on," then let it go. One day you'll write "fade out, the end" – and you're done. *It's* done.

It's a time of celebration and relief. When it's over, you're going to experience all kinds of emotional reactions. First, satisfaction and relief. A few days later, you'll be down, depressed, and won't know what to do with your time. You may sleep a lot. You've got no energy. This is what I call the "postpartum blues" period. It's like giving birth to a baby; you've been working on something for a substantial period of time. It's been a part of you. It's gotten you up in the morning and kept you awake at night. Now it's over. It's natural to be down and depressed. The end of one thing is always the beginning of something else. Endings and beginnings, right?

It's all part of the experience of writing the screenplay.

DAZED, LOST, AND CONFUSED? IT COULD BE WRITER'S BLOCK

There may be times during the screenwriting process when you experience a kind of sinking sensation welling up inside and suddenly there is a cloud of negativity and confusion on the waters of your creativity. And it seems to come out of nowhere.

Most writers, including myself, try to ignore the feeling, to push it away, hide it under the carpet, and the more we try to dispel it, to pretend it's not there, to hover behind a false bravado, the more we realize we're stuck, lost somewhere within the maze of our own creation.

This is when we hit the "wall." Almost all writers, at some time or other, experience this wall, or block, and try to force their way through it. Sometimes it works, and sometimes it doesn't.

Most of the time it doesn't. And no matter where you are in the screenwriting process, the first words-on-paper draft or the rewrite, it doesn't take much to be overwhelmed by the writing process. We handle this kind of problem in many different ways, of course, like suddenly finding more important things to do; like cleaning the kitchen, or going to the market, or washing the dishes, or going to the movies. Whatever.

After all, some parts of the story are more difficult than others. And some scenes need more work than others. But after a few days struggling with these particular pages, struggling with some of these thoughts and feelings, you may notice some doubts about your abilities as a writer begin to surface. You may find yourself thinking too much, asking yourself questions like: What am I going to do? How am I going to get back on track? I wonder if I'm in *Writer's Block*? You'll question yourself, your talent, your ability to get the job done.

Then one morning you'll wake up and suddenly recognize that a heaviness of haze and uncertainty hangs around your neck, and the feeling that's been tugging at you for the last few days erupts and you know you really don't know what you are doing. You finally admit that you don't know how to help yourself or where to go and the only thing that makes any sense at all is surrendering to the state you are in – dazed, lost, and confused.

Welcome to the world of screenwriting.

It's one of those common problems that strike fear in the hearts of screenwriters everywhere.

In one of my screenwriting workshops a student came into class one night with a strange and somewhat tortured look on her face. When I asked her what was wrong, her eyes welled up with tears and she became very serious, and said, "I don't know where I'm going. I'm totally lost, I'm confused, and my pages are garbage. All that's happening is talk, talk, talk. I keep going around in circles and I don't know what to do. I'm so upset, I could cry."

It's a universal problem. How you get out of it varies from person to person, script to script, but the first thing to do is to admit *you have a problem* and it's not going to go away until you deal with it, and confront it head-on. That's just one of the truths of life.

In my student's case she was so close to the material, she couldn't see it anymore, so the first thing I wanted her to do was just stop writing. When you reach this kind of crisis point, you're so overwhelmed and frustrated that you have to regroup. Just stop writing. Put down your computer, pen and paper, tape recorder, however you're working, and spend some time contemplating your story: What is your story about? What is the dramatic need of your main character? How are you going to resolve the story line? The answers to these questions are the key to getting back on track.

If you are writing a story and do not know what emotional forces are working on your character, it is very easy to run up against "the wall" and keep "going around in circles," ultimately falling into the well of *Writer's Block*.

Here's the way it usually works. You're totally immersed in the day-to-day process of screenwriting, but there may be one scene or sequence that does not work as well as it should and you might begin to wonder why it's not working. It's just a random thought and you probably pay no attention to it. But if the scene still does not work, you might become aware of a subtle shift occurring within yourself, maybe some doubts about why this scene or sequence is failing to come together. Then you might find that you're talking to yourself, having a little conversation about *The Problem*. The first thing that usually happens is you start questioning yourself. "If I weren't so stupid, I could do this," you might think to yourself, and the more you wrestle with the problem, the more your image as a screenwriter begins to erode, and then you might start making disparaging comments about yourself and your ability. That's when you begin sliding into "the pit," and soon an entire litany of negative judgments descends upon you.

"I knew I should have stayed away from this subject," you might think to yourself; or "I'm no good at writing." Soon you'll begin to expand and enlarge on your own insecurities, thinking, "I don't know whether I should be writing this script," or "Maybe I just don't have the talent to do this," or "Maybe I should just find a partner and write it with someone else." It goes on and on.

But underneath all these thoughts, comments, or judgments you're making is the common thread that somehow this is all "your fault." If you could do it, you would, and if you can't, it's because you don't have the talent or ability to do it. In short, we turn it inside and blame ourselves.

No wonder it's called *"Writer's Block."*

If you're in this particular dilemma, and your creative voice is smothered by this blanket of doubt and negativity, then it's time to *give the critic a voice*. That means giving that judgmental, critical, and negative voice that's roaming around inside your head the opportunity to speak his or her mind.

First, go to your screenplay pages then take out a separate piece of paper and label it *The Critic's Page*. As you start writing, every time you become aware of a negative comment or judgment coming up, write it down on *The Critic's Page*. Number the comments, label them, just as if you were making a shopping list. For example, you might become aware that "These pages are terrible," or "I don't really know what I'm doing," or "This isn't working," or "Maybe somebody else should finish it for me." Maybe "These characters all sound the same," and it's apparent that "I've lost my vision," and so on. Whatever your thoughts and comments are about your pages, just lay them down; 1, 2, 3, 4, 5 ...

The first day you're doing *The Critic's Page*, you may write two pages of screenplay, and four pages of critic. On the second day maybe you'll write three pages of screenplay and two or more pages of critic. The third day maybe four or five pages of screenplay and a page or two of the critic.

At that point, stop writing. Take *The Critic's* pages, put them in order, and just read them; day one, day two, day three. As you think about these comments, mull them over in your mind. You'll discover something very interesting; the critic *always says the same thing*. It doesn't matter what kind of scene it is, or who the characters are, or what you write, whether it's the pages from day one, two, or three, or whether it's a dialogue scene or an action scene, the critic says the same thing – the same words, the same phrases, the same expressions. It's all the same. No matter *what* you write, this is what your critic is going to be telling you. It stinks, it's no good, you should be doing something else.

That's the nature of the mind, to judge, to criticize, to evaluate. The mind can either be our best friend or our worst enemy. It's so easy to get plugged into judgments of right or wrong, good or bad.

Now, it could be that what the critic says is accurate. Maybe the pages *are* terrible, the characters *are* thin and one-dimensional, and you're going around in circles. So what? *Confusion is the first step towards clarity.* What you try that doesn't work always shows you what does work. As you struggle through any problem area, just get something down on paper. Just write lousy pages. You'll always be able to go back and make them better. That's the process all writers go through. So what if you've "hit a wall" and are going around in circles, dazed, lost, and confused?

Give the critic a voice. If you don't give the critic a voice, it'll turn inside and begin to fester, getting worse and worse until it bursts. It's easy to let yourself become your own victim.

Until you become aware of the critic's voice running around at the back of your mind, you're going to become a victim of that voice. Recognizing and acknowledging that voice is the first step through the block; it's not necessary to act upon, or make a decision about, the judgments and evaluations the critic makes – whether the critic is right or not. No matter what stage you are at in the writing process, whether it's first words on paper, or rewriting, don't get too serious about what the critic tells you. One of the things we have to accept is that we always get lost within the maze of our own creations.

Writer's Block is a powerful enemy and can hammer you into submission; the mere thought of writing turns you off; and because you're not writing you'll feel guilty, so whenever you sit down to work, you suddenly feel this "blanket of heaviness" settle over your head. You'll lose all objectivity and fall into despair.

Writer's Block. It happens all the time. To everybody. *The difference is how you deal with it. How you see it.*

There are two different ways to look at this "problem." One is to see your dilemma as a real problem, a real block, something to "overcome," or "break through," a physical and emotional obstacle that locks you into a creative straitjacket.

That's one way of looking at it.

But there's another way of looking at it. And that is to see the ordeal as *part of the writer's experience*; everybody goes through it. It's nothing new or unusual. If you recognize and acknowledge that, you've reached a creative crossroads. The realization becomes a creative guide to another level of your screenwriting craft. If you can look at it as an opportunity, you will find a way to strengthen and broaden your ability to create characters and story. It shows you that maybe you need to go deeper into your story, and strive for another level of richness, full of texture and dimension.

"*A man's reach should exceed his grasp*," the poet Robert Browning wrote.

If you understand that being dazed, lost, and confused is only a *symptom*, this "problem" becomes an opportunity to test yourself. Isn't that what life's all about – putting yourself on the line in a situation where you test yourself to rise to another level? It's simply an evolutionary step along the path of the screenwriting process.

If you accept this point of view, it means you're going to have to dig deeper into your material; you're going to have to stop writing, go back into your character's life and action, and define and clarify different elements of your character's life. You're going to have to go back and do new character biographies; define or redefine the characters and their relationships to each other that are the hub of your story line.

If you're working on a particular scene, for example, you may need to rewrite the scene, or change the points of view of your characters; you may need to change locations, or create new actions, new episodes or events, for your character. Sometimes you may have to restructure the action for a particular scene or sequence by restructuring an entire act!

If you're adapting a book, or an article, into a screenplay, at least there's a story line to follow, a thread of narrative that weaves itself through the incidents and events of the dramatic action. Sometimes there's a tendency to let the dialogue of the book, or play, whatever the original material is, dictate the story; if you rely on this too much it becomes an obstacle that will impede the screenplay. You may be trying to be too true to the source material.

That doesn't work at all. You've got to make the material your own, and that means breaking down the book, creating incidents of characters that complement the film's story line; so whatever you do, leave the book behind, and create whatever you need to make it work.

Whenever you feel lost, dazed, or confused, it only becomes a problem if you let it become a problem.

The things you try that don't work always show you what does work.

THE NATURE OF DULL

Have you ever read something you've written and realized it's the dullest and most boring writing you've ever read? The pages seem worthless, trite, and your worst fears are confirmed: you have no talent, no ability, and the whole experience is like a bad dream.

It's not an uncommon feeling, and while it may be true some of the time, it's not true all of the time. When you take a look at what you've written, and made the judgment that it's dull and boring, what can you do to fix it?

In other words, what is the *nature of dull*?

To really understand it, we have to explore the *symptoms of dull* – those traits in your writing style that may lead to writing dull and boring pages. And since this book is about recognizing and identifying the *symptoms* of various screenwriting problems, we're going to take a look at what makes up the essence of dull writing.

That means examining the relationship between bad writing and good writing. And since *relationship* means a connection between two or more things, it means we can't define dull and boring writing until we know what makes up good writing.

When you read a well-written screenplay, "a good read," the words leap off the page at you. Part of it is style, part of it is structure, but the real dynamic of good screenwriting is creating strong and active characters, combined with a unique, stylized visual narrative that constantly moves the story forward. Many films reflect this very well: *The Shawshank Redemption*, *How to Make an American Quilt*, *Sense and Sensibility* (Emma Thompson), blend story with character, and a situation many people can relate to. *Twelve Monkeys* (David and Janet Peoples) blends a strong visual style with an interesting dramatic premise, but it's a "one-line" script (it lacks depth and dimension) that moves the story forward to its contrived and somewhat predictable ending. *Blade Runner* (Hampton Fancher and David Peoples) treats this same kind of theme with more imagination, as does *The Fugitive* (Andrew Davies).

Strong action and strong characters. That's what makes good screenwriting.

So what are some more of those qualities that make up good screenwriting? Several things: perhaps the most important is to understand that the foundation of all good dramatic writing is *conflict*. All drama is conflict; without conflict you have no character; you have no action; without action you have no story. And without story you have no screenplay.

Dramatic conflict can either be internal or external; an emotional story like *The Hours*, or *How to Make an American Quilt*, or *American Beauty*, has internal (and external) conflict. External conflict is a story where the conflict is outside the character, and the characters face physical (and of course, emotional) obstacles, such as *Apollo 13* or *Jurassic Park* (Michael Crichton and David Koepp). Creating conflict within the story, through the characters and events, is one of those simple, basic "truths" of all writing whether it be novel, play, or screenplay.

So what is *conflict*? If you look at the word it means to be "in opposition"; and the hub of any dramatic scene is having the character or characters be in opposition to some*one* or some*thing*. Conflict can be anything, a struggle or a quarrel, a battle or a chase scene, internal or external, any kind of confrontation or obstacle, and it really doesn't matter whether it's emotional, physical, or mental.

Conflict must be at the very hub of your story, because it is the core of strong action and strong character. If you do not have this conflict, this foundation to your writing, you'll find yourself more often than not caught in a quagmire of dull writing.

If you want to examine "the stuff" that makes dull writing, what would you say? What is the *nature of dull*? What does it look like? What does it taste like, and what is its *essence*, the seed that sprouts into the tree?

There are *symptoms* that can be identified if you know what to look for, and they usually give a pretty good indication of what the problem is, whether the script is slow and heavy, or too long, or all the characters sound the same. If that's the case, then how do you fix it, or shape it, transform it from a "bad read" into a "good read"?

For example, if your dramatic premise seems weak and not clearly articulated and defined within the first ten pages, then the chances are that the *Set-Up* is weak and the material is going to wander around in different directions and lack a dramatic focus. That's a *symptom*; let it go on too long and you've got a dull screenplay; just as a scratchy irritation in the throat is sometimes a symptom of a cold or flu. Symptoms reveal things, and in the "art" of medicine, if you read the symptoms correctly, then you can find the cause, and heal the disease, whatever it might be. At least, in theory.

In screenwriting you cure the problem by knowing and understanding its symptoms. For example, suppose a writer wants to create a strong action line and, in so doing, sets up the story so fast, he or she simply skims over, or omits, necessary and essential character information? It won't take the writer long to realize the character's been sacrificed for action.

We can identify this because the character will be so busy reacting to the events or the situation that we don't have an opportunity to learn anything about him or her. That's a *symptom*. And it always seems to lead to a dull and boring read.

An easy way to spot one of the *symptoms of dull* is through the main character. Good screenwriting always shows itself in strong character and strong action. So, if you use your main character as an indicator, and feel that he or she is not strong enough, or there's too much dialogue and not enough visual action, you're probably right in assuming that the character is weak and reactive. In this case the character appears to ride the surface of the story line, and there's not enough information to go deeper into the psyche of the character to see what's really going on.

Think about creating an incident that works upon your character in such a way that his or her reaction reveals a more forceful and illuminating dimension of character.

Another symptom of dull screenwriting is when the screenwriter *enters the scene too early* and too much time is spent talking about something totally unrelated that will not move the story forward. For example, entering a scene too early usually results in the characters talking about something totally unrelated to the purpose of the scene. Enter the scene just before the purpose is revealed; enter late and get out early is the general rule.

The art of screenwriting is in finding places where silence works better than words. Recently, one of my students told me that after he had completed writing a scene, the thought occurred to him to go back and take another look at it. Something was bothering him about it and he didn't know what it was. So he read and reread the scene, and suddenly understood how he could make it work more effectively with just *two lines of dialogue*! That's just good screenwriting. You don't need pages and pages of dialogue to set up, explain, or move your story forward; just a few lines will do, if you enter the scene at the right point.

In *How to Make an American Quilt*, past and present are woven together by questions and answers. And even though there are many different stories, they are all connected with the theme of the film: Where Love Resides. Each story deals with an affair of the heart, and each reflects another aspect of Finn's dilemma regarding her commitment to Sam. The quilt is a metaphor for the entire film.

Another symptom: having the character always react to situations or events. If that happens too much, the character becomes passive and reactive. An important ingredient of good character creation is finding the best way to *introduce* that character. If your character is too egotistical or uncaring, he or she will be unsympathetic. Just look at *Diehard 3*; we meet the Bruce Willis character drunk, in a van, not having seen his wife in a year. We don't really care too much about him.

Sometimes a screenplay starts off too quickly and if the action happens too fast, the reader doesn't know who the character is or why he or she is participating in this action or event. If the story starts off too slowly, then everything has to be explained through dialogue, so there is no dramatic tension to pull the reader through the story line. It leads to a dull screenplay.

One of the things I've discovered about the nature of dull is that while scenes may be structured well, with the dialogue clean and sharp, there is no payoff to the scene. We don't see the natural conclusion of the scene because the screenwriter cuts away before the purpose of the scene is fulfilled. I've read so many screenplays where the writer seems to forget why the scene is in there in the first place. Each scene is related to every other, and you've only got 120 pages to tell your story, so you can't waste time writing scenes that are not paid off. Characters, incidents, events, decisions, all need to be set up at some time in the story. It doesn't have to be in the scene before, or in the same scene, or in the scene after; it can be anywhere because all aspects of a story line are related to one another and therefore information can be planted anywhere. It can be set up in the first ten pages, then paid off in Act II or III. What really matters is when you set something up in the screenplay, you have to pay it off, either visually or verbally; either through pictures or dialogue.

Another aspect of the *nature of dull* is overwritten scene description. People ask me how long a descriptive paragraph should be, and I reply that any descriptive paragraph, whether it's action or character, or any combination of the two, should not be longer than four sentences.

Why four? There are many reasons. First, when you're writing a screenplay there has to be a lot of white space on the page. Long, bulky, single-spaced paragraphs that take up a half page or more are just too difficult to read. I tell my students that I don't care what the particular action is, they just can't put it all into one descriptive paragraph. Break the paragraph up into four or five sentences. A reader reads the screenplay as if he or she is seeing the movie on the screen, so pages have to be lean, clean, and tight, and not bogged down with a lot of descriptive comments that will never make their way to the screen.

The quickest way to make a reader put down a screenplay is to stop him with a lot of thick and bulky paragraphs that fill up the page. It turns the reader off, and becomes another symptom in the *nature of dull*.

SCREENPLAY FORM 13

When I was head of the story department at Cinemobile, and reading an average of three screenplays a day, I could tell you in the first paragraph whether the script was written by a professional or amateur. An abundance of CAMERA angles like long shots, close shots, instructions about zooms, pans, and dollies immediately revealed a novice screenwriter who didn't know what he or she was doing.

As a reader, I was always looking for an excuse not to read a script. So when I found one – like excessive CAMERA instructions – I used it. I didn't have to read ten pages. You can't sell a script in Hollywood without the help of a reader.

Don't give the reader an excuse not to read your screenplay.

That's what the screenplay form is all about – what *is* a professional screenplay, and what *isn't*.

Everybody, it seems, has some misconceptions about screenplay form. Some people say if you're writing a screenplay you're "obligated" to write in CAMERA ANGLES; if you ask why they mumble something about "the director knowing *what* to film"! So they create an elaborate and meaningless exercise called "writing in CAMERA ANGLES."

It doesn't work.

Screenplay form is simple; so simple, in fact, that most people try to make it more complex. Richard Feynman, the Nobel Prize-winning physicist from Cal Tech, once remarked that "the laws of Nature are so simple, we have to rise above the complexity of scientific thought to see them." For every action there is an equal and opposite reaction. What could be more simple than that!

F. Scott Fitzgerald is a perfect example. Perhaps the most gifted American novelist of the twentieth century, Fitzgerald came to Hollywood to write screenplays. He failed miserably – he tried to "learn" CAMERA ANGLES and the intricate technology of film, and he let that get in the way of his screenwriting. Not one script he worked on was made without extensive rewriting. His only screenwriting achievement is unfinished, a script called *Infidelity* written for Joan Crawford in the 1930s. It's a beautiful script, patterned like a visual fugue, but the third act is incomplete and it lies gathering dust in the studio vaults.

Most people who want to write screenplays have a little of Scott Fitzgerald in them.

The screenwriter is *not responsible* for writing in CAMERA ANGLES, and detailed shot terminology. It's not the writer's job. The writer's job is to tell the director *what* to shoot, not *how* to shoot it. If you specify how each scene should be shot, the director will probably throw it away. Justifiably so.

The writer's job is to write the script. The director's job is to film the script; to take words on paper and transform them into images on film. The cameraman's function is to light the scene and position the camera so it cinematically captures the story.

I happened to be on the set of *Coming Home*, with Jane Fonda, Jon Voight, and Bruce Dern. Hal Ashby, the director, was rehearsing Jane Fonda and Penelope Milford in a scene, while Haskell Wexler, the director of photography, was preparing to set up the CAMERA.

Here's how it worked. Hal Ashby sat down in a corner with Jane Fonda and Penelope Milford and went over the context of the scene. Haskell Wexler was telling the crew where to put the lights. Ashby,

Fonda, and Milford began blocking out the scene; she moves on this line, Penny enters on this cue, crosses to the bed, turns on the TV, and so on. Once the blocking was established, Haskell Wexler followed them with his "eyepiece," establishing the first camera angle. When Hal Ashby finished working with Fonda and Milford, Haskell Wexler showed him where he wanted to position the camera. Ashby agreed. They set up the camera, the actresses walked through the scene, rehearsed it several times, made minor adjustments, and were ready for a take.

That's the way it is. Film is a collaborative medium; people work together to create a movie. Don't worry about CAMERA ANGLES! Forget about writing scenes describing the intricate moves of a Panavision 70 camera with a 50mm lens on a Chapman crane!

There was a time, though, in the 1920s and '30s, when the director's job was to direct the actors, and it was the writer's job to write in CAMERA ANGLES for the cameraman. It's no longer true. It's not your job.

Your job is to write the script. Scene by scene, shot by shot.

What is a shot?

A shot is what the CAMERA sees.

Scenes are made up of shots, either a single shot or a series of shots; how many, or what kind, is insignificant. There are all kinds of shots. You can write a descriptive scene like "the sun rising over the mountains" and the director may use one, three, five, or ten different *shots* to visually get the feeling of the "sun rising over the mountains."

A scene is written in *master shot*, or *specific shots*. A master shot covers a *general area*; a room, a street, a lobby. A *specific shot* focuses on a specific part of the room. A door, say, or in front of a specific store on a specific street, or building. The scenes from *Silver Streak* and *Chinatown* are presented in master shot. *Network* utilizes specific shots and master shots. If you want to write a dialogue scene in master shot, all you need to write is INT. RESTAURANT – NIGHT, and simply let your characters talk without any reference to the CAMERA or shot.

You can be as general, or specific, as you want. A scene can be one shot – a car racing down the street – or a series of shots of a couple arguing on the corner.

A shot is *what* the CAMERA sees.

Let's take another look at the screenplay form.

(1) EXT. ARIZONA DESERT – DAY

(2) A blazing sun scorches the earth. Everything is flat, barren. In the distance, a cloud of dust rises as a jeep makes its way across the landscape.

(3) MOVING

The jeep races through sagebrush and cactus.

(4) INT. JEEP – FAVORING JOE CHACO

(5)
Joe drives recklessly. JILL sits next to him, an attractive girl in her twenties.

> **(6) JILL**
> **(7)** (shouting)
> **(8)** How far is it?

> **JOE**
> 'Bout two hours. You okay?

(9) She smiles wearily.

> **JILL**
> I'll make it.

(10)

Suddenly, the motor SPUTTERS. They look at each
other, concerned.

(11) CUT TO:

Simple, right!

This is the proper, contemporary, and professional screenplay
form. There are very few rules, and these are the guidelines:

Line 1 – called THE SLUG LINE is the general or specific locale.
We are outside, EXT., somewhere in the ARIZONA DESERT; the time
is DAY.

Line 2 – double-space and then give your description of people,
places, or action, single-spaced, from margin to margin. Descriptions
of characters or places should not be longer than a few lines.

Line 3 – double-space; the general term "moving" specifies a change
in camera focus. (It is *not* a camera instruction. It is a "suggestion.")

Line 4 – double-space; there is a change from *outside* the jeep, to
inside. We are focusing on the character, Joe Chaco.

Line 5 – New characters are always capitalized.

Line 6 – The character speaking is always capitalized and placed
in the center of the page.

Line 7 – Stage directions for the actor are written in parentheses
under the name of the character speaking. Always single-spaced.
Don't abuse this; use only when necessary.

Line 8 – Dialogue is placed in the center of the page, so the character speaking forms a block in the middle of the page surrounded by
description from margin to margin. Several lines of dialogue are
always single-spaced.

Line 9 – Stage directions also include what characters do within
the scene. Reactions, silent and otherwise.

Line 10 – Sound effects, or music effects, are always capitalized.
Don't overdo effects. The last step in the filmmaking process is to give
the film to the music and effects editors. The film is "locked," that is,
the picture track cannot be changed or altered. The editors skim

through the script looking for music and effects cues, and you can help them by putting references to music or sound effects in capitals.

Film deals with two systems – the *film*, what we see, and the *sound*, what we hear. The film portion is complete before it goes to sound, and then the two are put together in sync. It is a long and complicated process.

Line 11 – If you choose to indicate the end of a scene you may write "CUT TO:" or "DISSOLVE TO:" (*dissolve* means two images overlapping each other; one fades out as the other fades in) or 'FADE OUT," used to indicate a fade to black. It should be noted that optical effects like "fades" or "dissolves" are really a film decision, made by the director or film editor. It is not the writer's decision.

That's all there is to basic screenplay form. It's simple.

It's a new form for most people who want to write screenplays, so give yourself time to "learn" how to write it. Don't be afraid to make mistakes. It takes a while to get used to it, and the more you do, the easier it gets. Sometimes I have students simply write, or type, ten pages of a screenplay just to get the "feel" of the form. If you want, you can get screenwriting software to remove the doubt or confusion. Final Draft is the best software around and is used by many famous professionals like Tom Hanks, Alan Ball, Steven Bochco, Julie Taymor, James L. Brooks, Anthony Minghella and others.

I once had a student who was a TV reporter for CBS News. He wanted to write a screenplay, but refused to learn the form. He wrote his script like a news story, even using the same paper. When I brought that to his attention, he said he'd change it after he finished the first draft. That was the way he wrote, he explained, and did not feel comfortable writing in any other style. And he wasn't going to change it. As it happened, he never finished writing his screenplay.

If you're going to write a screenplay, do it right! Write in screenplay form from the beginning. It's to your advantage.

The word CAMERA is rarely used in the contemporary screenplay. If your script is 120 pages long, there should be no more than a few references to CAMERA. Maybe ten. "But," people say, "if you don't use the word CAMERA and the shot is what the CAMERA sees, how do you write the shot description?"

The rule is: FIND THE SUBJECT OF YOUR SHOT!

What does the CAMERA, or the eye in the middle of your forehead, see? What takes place within the frame of each shot?

If Bill walks out of his apartment to his car, what is the subject of the shot?

Bill? The apartment? The car?

Bill is the subject of the shot.

If Bill gets in his car and drives down the street, what is the subject of the shot? Bill, the car, or the street?

The car is, unless you want the scene to take place inside the car: INT. CAR – DAY. Moving or not moving.

Once you determine the subject of the shot, you're ready to describe the visual action that takes place within the shot.

I've compiled a list of terms to replace the word CAMERA in your screenplay. If you're ever in doubt about whether to use the word CAMERA, *do not use it*. Find another term to replace it. These general terms used in shot descriptions will allow you to write your screenplay simply, effectively, and visually.

SCREENPLAY TERMS

(to replace the word CAMERA)

RULE: FIND THE SUBJECT OF YOUR SHOT.

1. ANGLE ON

A person, place, or thing – ANGLE ON BILL (the subject of the shot) leaving his apartment building.

2. FAVORING

Also a person, place, or thing – FAVORING (subject of the shot) BILL as he leaves his apartment.

3. ANOTHER ANGLE

A variation of a SHOT – ANOTHER ANGLE of Bill walking out of his apartment.

4. WIDER ANGLE

A change of focus in a scene – You go from an ANGLE ON Bill to a WIDER ANGLE which now includes Bill and his surroundings.

5. NEW ANGLE

Another variation on a shot, often used to "break up the page" for a more "cinematic look" – A NEW ANGLE of Bill and Jane dancing at a party.

6. POV

A person's POINT OF VIEW, how something looks to him – ANGLE ON Bill, dancing with Jane, and from JANE'S POV Bill is smiling, having a good time. This could also be considered the CAMERA'S POV.

7. REVERSE ANGLE

A change in perspective, usually the opposite of the POV shot – For example, Bill's POV as he looks at Jane, and a REVERSE ANGLE of Jane looking at Bill – that is, what *she* sees.

8. OVER THE SHOULDER SHOT

Often used for POV and REVERSE ANGLE shots. Usually the back of a character's head is in the foreground of the *frame* and *what* he is looking at is the background of the frame. The *frame* is the boundary line of what the CAMERA sees – sometimes referred to as the "frame line."

9. MOVING SHOT

Focuses on the movement of a shot – A MOVING SHOT of the jeep racing across the desert. Bill walking Jane to the door. Ted *moves* to answer the phone. All you have to indicate is MOVING SHOT. Forget about trucking shots, pans, tilts, dollies, zooms, cranes.

10. CLOSE SHOT

What it says – close. Used sparingly, for emphasis. A CLOSE SHOT of Bill as he stares at Jane's roommate. When Jake Gittes, in *Chinatown*, has a knife in his nose, Robert Townes indicates a CLOSE SHOT. It is one of the few times he uses the term throughout the entire screenplay.

11. INSERT (of something)

A close shot of "something" – either a photograph, newspaper story, headline, face of a clock, watch, or telephone number is "inserted" into the scene.

Knowing these terms will help you write a screenplay from the position of choice and security – so you know what you're doing without the need of specific CAMERA directions.

Take a look at contemporary screenplay form. Here are the first nine pages of my screenplay *The Run*, an action film as yet unproduced. The opening is an action sequence. It is the story of a man setting out to break the Water Speed Record in a rocket boat.

Examine the form; look for the subject in each shot, and how each shot presents an individual mosaic within the tapestry of the sequence.

The "first time around" refers to the title of the individual sequence; it is the first attempt at breaking the Water Speed Record.

(page 1 of screenplay)
　　"THE RUN"

　　"first time around"

　　EXT. BANKS LANE, WASHINGTON – JUST BEFORE
　　DAWN

　　A SERIES OF ANGLES

A few hours before dawn. Some stars and a full moon are pinned to the early-morning sky.

BANKS LANE is a long sleeve of water nestled against the concrete walls of the Grand Coulee Dam. The water reflects the shimmering reflection of the moon. All is quiet. Peaceful. Hold.

Then, we HEAR the high-pitched ROAR of a truck. And, we:

CUT TO:

HEADLIGHTS – MOVING

A pickup truck moved INTO FRAME. PULL BACK to reveal the truck hauling a large trailer, the puzzling-shaped cargo covered with a tarpaulin. It could be anything – a piece of modern sculpture, a missile, a space capsule. As a matter of fact, it's all three.

A CARAVAN

of seven vehicles moves slowly along the winding, tree-lined highway. A pickup truck and station wagon lead the group. Another station wagon is followed by a truck and trailer. Bringing up the rear are two large camper trailers and a toolvan. They bear the insignia "Saga Men's Cologne."

INT. LEAD STATION WAGON

Three people are in the wagon. The radio plays softly, a Country & Western tune.

STRUT BOWMAN drives, a lean and expressive Texan who happens to be the best sheet-metal man and mechanical wizard west of the Mississippi.

JACK RYAN sits next to the window staring moodily into the predawn darkness.

(2)

Strong-willed and stubborn, he is considered by many to be a flamboyant boat designer, a crackpot genius, or a daredevil race driver; all three are true.

ROGER DALTON sits in the back seat. A quiet man, he wears glasses and looks like the rocket systems analyst he is.

THE VEHICLES

wind their way along the wood-lined highway heading toward the Grand Coulee Dam and the sleeve of water known as Banks Lake. (Formerly, it was known as Franklin D. Roosevelt Lake.)

EXT. BANKS LAKE – DAWN

The sky lightens as the caravan moves to the far side, the vehicles looking like a column of fireflies parading before the dawn.

THE BOATHOUSE AREA

The cars pull in and park. The lead truck pulls to a stop and a few CREW MEMBERS jump out. Others follow and the activity begins.

A long Quonset hut has been erected near the water. The BOATHOUSE, as it's known, houses the work area and is complete with work benches, lights, and tool area. The two campers park nearby.

A FEW CREWMEN

jump out and begin unloading various equipment, taking it into the work area.

THE STATION WAGON

Strut parks the wagon; Ryan is the first out, followed by Roger. He walks into the boathouse.

A TV CONTROL VAN

from "Sports World," as well as some local Seattle sportscasters, begin setting up their equipment.

THE OFFICIALS AND TIMERS

all with the initials FIA emblazoned on their shirts, set up electronic timing devices, timing boards, digital consoles, and floating timing buoys. Video images from the TV Control Monitor are assembled into a montage of activity. The "feel" of this sequence should begin slowly, like someone waking up, then gradually build into a rhythm of a tense and exciting rocket-launch sequence.

(3)

INT. CAMPER LIVING QUARTERS – JUST AFTER DAWN

Jack Ryan puts on his asbestos racing suit and Strut helps him lace it up. He steps into his cover suit, the name of "Saga Men's Cologne" clearly seen. Strut fixes something on the suit, and the two men exchance a glance.

Over this, we HEAR the voice of the:

TV ANNOUNCER (VO)

This is Jack Ryan. Most of you already know the story – Ryan, one of the most innovative racing designers of high-speed water vehicles, son of the wealthy industrialist Timothy Ryan, was approached by Saga Men's Colognes to build a racing boat that would break the Water Speed Record of 286 miles an hour held by Leigh Taylor. Ryan did that and more: He designed and built the world's first rocket boat – that's right, rocket boat – revolutionary in concept and design –

THE BOATHOUSE

Moving out of the boathouse, mounted on two specially constructed mounts, is the rocket boat, "Prototype I," a gleaming, missile-like boat that looks like a Delta-winged aircraft. It is beautifully designed, a piece of sculpture. The crew members guide the boat onto the launching track, disappearing into the water. Over this, the TV announcer continues.

TV ANNOUNCER (VO, contd.)

Just how fast it will go is unknown –
some people claim it won't even work!
But Jack Ryan says this boat can easily
break the 400 mi/hr barrier. Well, Ryan
designed and built this boat, Prototype I,
and took it to the sponsor.

And, irony of ironies – Saga couldn't
get anyone to drive the rocket boat – no
one was willing to attempt the record in
it – it was too radical, unsafe. That's
when Ryan, the former hydroplane racer,
stepped in and said, "I'll do it!"

INT. TV CONTROL VAN BOOTH

We see a bank of TV monitor screens. MOVE IN to a
screen where the TV ANNOUNCER is interviewing
Jack Ryan at a press conference.

(4)

RYAN (on TV screen)

You see, I built this boat, piece by piece
– I know it like the back of my hand. If I
thought there was the slightest chance
of failure, or that I might possibly hurt
myself, or kill myself – if I didn't think it
was completely safe, I wouldn't do it!
Somebody's got to do it and it might as
well be me! I mean, that's what this life's
all about, isn't it? Taking risks?

TV ANNOUNCER (on screen)

Are you scared?

RYAN (on screen)

Of course – but I know I can do the job.
If I didn't, I wouldn't be here. It's my
choice and I'm confident I'm going to set
a new Water Speed Record and live long
enough to give you a chance to interview
me after I do it!

He laughs.

OLIVIA

Ryan's wife, standing nervously alone on the side-
lines, biting her lip. She's scared and she shows it.

EXT. TV CONTROL VAN – EARLY MORNING

The TV ANNOUNCER from the Ryan interview stands
near the Control Van, the lake in b.g.

TV ANNOUNCER

Several years ago, Jack Ryan was a
highly successful hydroplane racer. He
gave it up after an accident put him in
hospital – some of you remember that –

THE START AREA

A finger-like dock stretches into the water.
A tow-boat is tied to it.

(5)

PROTOTYPE I

sits on top of the water being fueled; two oxygen
tanks connected with long polythene tubing
disappear into the engine. Roger supervises the
fueling.

RYAN

Jack Ryan steps out of the camper and walks toward
the rocket boat. Strut is with him.

> **TV ANNOUNCER (VO)**
> So, here we are – at Banks Lake in east-
> ern Washington, right next to the Grand
> Coulee Dam – where Jack Ryan
> becomes the first man in history to
> attempt setting a new Water Speed
> Record in a rocket boat.

AT THE START SITE

Ryan walks down the dock and steps into the boat.

AT TIMING CONTROL

A series of digital timing mechanisms race wildly, end
at zero across the board.

INT. TV CONTROL BOARD IN VAN

The DIRECTOR sits in front of the TV Monitor
Console and prepares for the TV broadcast. Eight

screens are banked in front of him, each with a different image: crew, finish line, lake, timing buoys, crowd, etc. One screen follows Ryan as he prepares for the run.

TV ANNOUNCER (VO)
Working with Ryan are his two coworkers – Strut Bowman, the mechanical engineer –

STRUT

in the tow-boat, walkie-talkie in hand, watching Ryan carefully.

TV ANNOUNCER (VO)
– and Roger Dalton, a rocket systems analyst, and one of the scientists from the Jet Propulsion Lab responsible for putting a man on the moon –

ROGER

checking fuel gauges and other details. Everything's ready.

(6)

RYAN

is buckled into the cockpit. Strut is in the tow-boat, nearby.

INT. ROCKET BOAT COCKPIT

Ryan checks the three gauges on the control panel in front of him. He flicks a toggle switch marked "fuel flow"; a needle jumps into position and holds. He clicks another toggle switch marked "water flow," and another needle is activated. A red button switch lights up and we see the word "armed." Ryan puts his hand on the steering wheel, positions one finger next to the "eject" button.

RYAN

He checks the gauges, takes a few deep breaths. He's ready.

TV ANNOUNCER (VO)
Ryan appears ready –

A SERIES OF ANGLES

of the countdown. Crews, timers, and spectators quiet down; electronic devices hold at zero; the TV camera crew is focused on Prototype I, poised like a bird on the edge of flight.

STRUT

watches Ryan, waits for him to give the "thumbs-up" signal.

RYAN

All we see are eyes peering out of a crash helmet. Concentration high, intention high.

THE TIMING COMPLEX

The timers wait, all eyes riveted on the timing
mechanisms and the boat on the lake.

THE LAKE

is quiet, the metric-mile course marked out with three
timing buoys.

AT THE FINISH LINE

Roger and two crewmen stand looking down course,
watching the dot that is the boat.

THE TV CREW

waits, the air heavy with tense anticipation.

(7)

RYAN'S POV

He stares down course, the "armed" button clearly
seen in foreground.

STRUT

checks and double-checks final details. Ryan's
ready. He checks the timers – they're ready. It's a
"go." He gives "thumbs-up" to Ryan and waits for
Ryan's signal.

RYAN

returns "thumbs-up."

STRUT

talks into the walkie-talkie.

> **STRUT**
> Timing sequence ready –
> *(he begins his countdown)*
> 10, 9, 8 – 5, 4, 3, 2, 1, 0 –

THE TIMING BUOY

flashes three lights sequentially, red, yellow, then
green.

RYAN

flips the "on" switch and suddenly

THE ROCKET BOAT

explodes into motion, the finger-like flame searing the
surface of the water as it leaps forward.

THE BOAT

literally flies toward the end of the lake like a
missile, hovering several inches above the water
as the hydrofoil tyres skim along the water at over
300 mi/hr.

THIS INTERCUT

with Strut, Olivia, the timers, Roger at the finish line, the TV Monitor screens in the TV control van.

RYAN'S POV

The periphery landscape is distorted, flattened as the world plunges into silence and high-speed visual images.

THE BOAT

streaks by as the

(8)

DIGITAL NUMBERS

of the timing mechanisms race toward infinity.

VARIOUS ANGLES

as the boat hurtles toward the finish line. Crew, timers, spectators, watch in breathless wonder.

RYAN

holds onto the steering wheel when suddenly we see his hands "twitch" slightly as the boat vibrates.

                    TV ANNOUNCER (VO)
            It's a solid run –

THE TIMING CONSOLE

The digital numbers spin at a dizzying speed.

RYAN'S POV

The boat shimmies, builds into a pronounced vibration jarring the entire landscape view. Something is terribly wrong.

FROM THE SHORE

We see the rooster tail becoming irregular and choppy.

STRUT AND OLIVIA

watch the boat shaking violently.

A SERIES OF QUICK CUTS

intercut between spectators and boat. Prototype I veers off course, Ryan frozen at the wheel.

>   **TV ANNOUNCER (VO)**
>   Wait a minute – something's not –
>   something's wrong – the boat's shaking –

PROTOTYPE I

lists to one side.

RYAN

pushes the eject button.

>   **TV ANNOUNCER (VO)**
>   *(hysterical)*

Ryan can't hold it! Oh, my God! He's
crashing – Ryan's crashing – oh, my God
–

(9)

THE COCKPIT

ejects, arches high into the air, the parachute trailing
behind it.

THE CAPSULE

heads towards the water.

STRUT, THE CREW, TIMERS, OLIVIA

watch horrified, disbelieving.

THE BOAT

tips over, smashes into the water, careens out of
control, then cartwheels over and over again, until it
disintegrates before our very eyes.

TV ANNOUNCER (VO)
Ryan's ejected – but wait a minute – the
chute's not opening – oh, my God – how
could this happen – what a tragedy!

VARIOUS ANGLES

as the parachute attached to the capsule fails to
open. Ryan, encased in the plastic cockpit, hits the
water at over 300 mi/hr.

The capsule bounces and skips across the
water like a stone on a pond. We can only guess
what's happening to Ryan inside. The capsule
speeds more than a mile before it finally comes
to a stop.

Silence. The world seems frozen in time. And then:

Ambulance SIRENS shatter the silence, and all hell
breaks loose as people move toward the lifeless
figure of Jack Ryan floating helplessly in the water.
Hold, then:
CUT TO:

Notice how each shot describes the action, and the terms on the list
are used to give it a "cinematic" look without resorting to excessive
CAMERA instruction.

Write something in screenplay form. Remember to find the "subject"
of the shot. Many times it's helpful to get a screenplay and simply type
or write ten pages of it. Any ten pages will do, simply to get the "feel"
of writing in screenplay form.

Allow yourself some time to learn how to do it; it may be uncomfortable at first, but it gets easier.

THE PROBLEM SHEET

OK, Fasten Your Seat Belts
- The action goes nonstop
- Action scenes are too detailed, with too much description
- No transitions between scenes
- Story line is thin and episodic
- The stakes are not high enough

✎ The action is dull and boring, and goes from interior to interior to interior

✎ The scenes are too expository, and the characters explain too much

✎ The characters are too thin, and do not reveal anything about themselves

OK, BUCKLE YOUR SEAT BELTS, HERE IT COMES ... That's the line that begins the Third Act of *Terminator 2: Judgment Day*, one of the most significant action films of modern times. Not only is the action singular and the characters sound but it is the uniqueness of James Cameron's vision that drives the film into our consciousness. The same holds true with any great film, whether it be an action-adventure, science-fiction, or mystery thriller, or simply a great action sequence nailed into the scenario of a good drama or detective story.

The action film is a significant staple of our movie fare, and at least half of a major studio's production schedule is devoted to developing and nurturing this particular brand of entertainment. And, since the advent of the computer-graphic revolution, it has become more popular. Writing the action film, or even an action sequence, is really an art unto itself. So many times I read screenplays whose pages are filled with nonstop action – in fact, there is so much action that it becomes dull and repetitive with little or no characterization. The reader, and the viewer, are overwhelmed and numb. Sometimes, it's a good action script with strong individual action sequences, but the premise is weak and derivative of earlier films. In other words, we've seen it all before. It needs a "new look," or a more interesting concept, and when that happens you're in trouble.

Why? Because there are problems. Either with the plot, or the characters, or the action itself. Some writers have a natural ability to write action films, and there are others who are more comfortable writing character, but it's important to note that before you can write any kind of action film, or sequence, it's essential to understand what an action film is, what it's nature is. I had a student who wrote a screenplay about a navy pilot sent on a mission to a foreign country to rescue a kidnapped scientist being held hostage. It's a good premise, and there are several opportunities to create some notable action sequences and keep the story moving forward at a fast pace. So that's what he did, and his entire screenplay was one action sequence after another; the story moved like lightning, but it didn't work at all. What he didn't do was create an interesting main character. Because he didn't know his main character, most of the dialogue consisted of expository elements designed to keep the story moving forward. It didn't work. We didn't know anything about this person sent to rescue the scientist, had no idea about his thoughts or feelings, or about the forces working on his life.

This is not all that uncommon. When you're writing an action screenplay, the focus must be on the action *and* character; the two must reside and interact with each other. Otherwise there are going to be problems. What usually happens is that the action overpowers the story and diminishes the characters, resulting in a screenplay that, no matter how well written, is flat and uninteresting. There has to be an appropriate balance of peaks and valleys, places in the material where the reader and audience can pause and catch their collective breath.

So, what do we have to know in order to avoid creating these problems in an action screenplay? Let's start from the top. *Action* is defined in the dictionary as "a movement or a series of movements," or "the state of being in motion." Writing an action script, or sequence, is a definite skill, and good action scripts are written with color, pacing, suspense, tension, and, in most cases, humor. Remember the Bruce Willis character mumbling to himself in *Die Hard* (Steven de Souza) or the bus making the leap across the enormous freeway chasm in *Speed* (Graham Yost)? We remember good action films like *Jurassic Park* or *The Fugitive* (David Twohy) or *The Hunt for Red October* (Larry Ferguson and Donald Stewart) by the uniqueness of the action, but we usually forget all the cool car chases and explosions that occupy the majority of action films that fill our theaters. They all look alike.

The key to writing any action film lies in writing the action sequence. (Plot and character come later.) In an action film like *Terminator 2: Judgment Day*, for example, the entire film is structured and anchored by six major action sequences. After the introduction of Terminator, the T-1000, and John and Sarah, the *first* major sequence is where young John Connor is rescued by Terminator; *two*, Terminator and John break his mother out of prison; *three*, the "rest period" at Enrique's gas station where they load up with weapons; *four*, Sarah's attempt to kill Miles Dyson, creator of the microchip that makes possible the future Age of Machines; *five*, the siege at Cyberdyne Systems; and sequence *six*, their breakout and chase, winding up in the steel factory. The entire Third Act is literally one long nonstop action sequence. These key sequences *hold* (the function of the structure) the entire story together, but within this structural framework James Cameron and William Wisher have created a dynamic and intriguing premise, as well as some interesting characters. That, along with the special effects, is what makes this a truly memorable action film. And let's not forget that at the Mid-Point there is the "rest period" at the abandoned gas station so we can "breathe" and learn more about the characters. Then we're off and running again.

What is it that makes a good action film great? The electricity of the action sequences. Remember the chase scene from *Bullitt*? Or "the walk" at the end of *The Wild Bunch*? Or Butch and Sundance jumping into the river's gorge after being relentlessly chased by the Super Posse in *Butch Cassidy and the Sundance Kid*? The list goes on and on.

The key word in writing a great action sequence is the way it's *designed*. A sequence, remember, *is a series of scenes connected by one single idea, with a beginning, middle, and end*. A sequence is usually a complete entity, held together by one *single idea*: a chase sequence, wedding sequence, party sequence, fight sequence, love sequence, storm sequence. As mentioned earlier, *Twister* is a film that is really four major sequences, held together by the characters racing from one to the next. And, of course, each new sequence is more intense than the last.

If your script doesn't seem to be working as well as it should, or you have some problem areas in terms of pacing, or it seems dull and boring, you might think about adding some kind of action sequence to keep the story moving and the tension taut. Examine the material and see whether the proposed action will blend in with your original concept. Your script is only a start point; sometimes you have to make some drastic creative choices to allow you to fix your film. But always remember that *you can't just throw in an action sequence because your story line drags or sags, or is dull and boring*. To approach any action film or sequence, the material has to be designed for and incorporated into your story line and be executed to the best of your ability.

I think it's essential that every screenwriter should know how to write a good action sequence, no matter what kind of film he or she is working on.

David Koepp, who wrote *Mission: Impossible*, *Jurassic Park*, and *The Lost World*, to name a few, says that the key to writing a good action sequence "is finding more ways to say that someone runs. You tend to use a lot of adjectives. For example: He runs to hide behind the rock. He races over to the rock. He scrambles over to the rock. He crawls frantically on his belly over to the rock … Those are the things that drive me crazy. Hurries, trots, sprints, dives, leaps, jumps, barrels, slams. The word *slams*, that'll appear a lot in your action script.

"In an action scene," Koepp continues, "the reader is sometimes forcing their eyes along because what's tremendously entertaining to watch on film is not necessarily so thrilling to read. I think the challenge is to make that stuff fly by at the pace you would like it to fly by in the movie. So you've constantly got to find ways to make the action sequences readable and easy for the reader to picture in his mind."

So what's the best way to write an action sequence?

Design it, choreograph the action from the beginning, through the middle, and to the end. Choose your words carefully when you're writing. Action is not written on the page with a lot of long and beautifully styled sentences. Writing an action sequence has got to be intense, visual. The reader must see the action as if he or she were seeing it on the screen. We're dealing with moving images that hopefully keep you glued to the edge of your seat, filled with excitement, or fear, or great expectation, locked in that great "community of emotion" that unites everybody in the darkened movie theater. Just look at the great action sequences: *Bullitt*, *The French Connection*, *Psycho*, *Terminator 2*, *Lord of the Rings: The Two Towers*, the long walk and final shootout from *The Wild Bunch*. These are all action sequences that have been designed and choreographed with immense care and strict attention to detail.

Sometimes people tend to write too little, and then the action line becomes thin and doesn't carry the gripping intensity that you must have in a good action sequence.

Suppose, for example, your screenplay is slow, it drags and sags, and seems dull and boring. If you re-examine the material, it may be possible to insert some kind of action into the narrative that pumps up the story line. But you must be careful that the action you want to insert belongs in the tone and style of the script. Often the easy way out, a car chase, or a kiss, or a shootout, or a murder attempt, draws attention to itself and therefore will not work.

Here's an example of an excellent action scene; it's lean, clean, and tight, totally effective, extremely visual, and not bogged down with details. This is a little piece out of *Jurassic Park*, by David Koepp. The scene takes place on the island off Costa Rica just as it has been hit by a violent tropical storm, and the security systems have been shut down by an employee trying to smuggle out dinosaur embryos. The two remote-controlled electric cars, one with the two children and the attorney Gennaro, the other with the Sam Neill and Jeff Goldblum characters, are stalled next to the massive electric fence that keeps the dinosaurs enclosed in their restricted area. The power is out all over the island, and the kids are scared, nervous.

> Tim pulls off the goggles and looks at two clear
> plastic cups of water that sit in recessed holes on the

dashboard. As he watches, the water in the glasses vibrates, making concentric circles –

– then it stops –

– and then it vibrates again. Rhythmically.

Like from footsteps.

BOOM. BOOM. BOOM.

Gennaro's eyes snap open as he feels it too.
He looks up at the rearview mirror.

There is a security pass hanging from it that is bouncing slightly, swaying from side to side.

As Gennaro watches, his image bounces too, vibrating in the rearview mirror.

BOOM. BOOM. BOOM.

> **GENNARO**
> (not entirely convinced)
> M-Maybe it's the power trying to come
> back on.

Tim jumps into the back seat and puts the night goggles on again. He turns and looks out the side window. He can see the area where the goat is tethered. Or was tethered. The chain is still there, but the goat is gone.

BANG!

They all jump, and Lex SCREAMS as something hits the Plexiglas sunroof of the Explorer, hard. They look up. It's a disembodied goat leg.

GENNARO

Oh, Jesus. Jesus.

Tim whips around to look out the side window again. His mouth pops open, but no sound comes out. Through the goggles he sees an animal claw, a huge one, gripping the cables of the "electrified" fence.

Tim whips the goggles off and presses forward, against the window. He looks up, up, then cranes his head back farther, to look out the sunroof. Past the goat's leg, he can see –

Tyrannosaurus rex. It stands maybe twenty-five feet high, forty feet long from nose to tail, with an enormous, boxlike head that must be five feet long by itself. The remains of the goat are hanging out of the rex's mouth. It tilts its head back and swallows the animal in one big gulp.

Well, there it is ... Quite impressive. The sequence is the beginning of the action that will carry us through to the end of the film. We literally see the action as it unfolds, step by step, bit by bit. Notice how visual it is, and how short the sentences are, almost staccato in their presentation, and how much "white space" is on the page. This is the way a good action sequence should read.

The reader and the characters experience the same thing at the same time. We are bonded together, "one on one," so we can experience what the characters are experiencing.

Take a look at the sequence dynamics: there is a definite beginning, middle, and end to the action. Each visual moment builds the action line, incident to incident.

We open at the beginning, with the cups on the dashboard vibrating. We know something's going on here, we just don't know what.

Notice how visual it is, then look at how the writing of the sequence builds upon the fear and terror of the characters. "BOOM. BOOM. BOOM." Relentlessly, each sound expands and heightens the moment, stimulating the antennae of our imaginations. The writing style, besides being visual, uses short, clipped words or phrases. No long, beautifully formed sentences here. And of course, Spielberg is a master at putting this kind of sequence on film. A perfect example is the opening sequence of *Close Encounters of the Third Kind*.

So far everything remains unseen, which heightens the fear and causes us to expect the worst. The goat is another visual aid that amplifies the tension and pacing. Generally, a good action sequence builds slowly, setting things up, drawing us into the excitement so the action gets faster and faster. Good pacing allows the tension to build upon itself, no matter whether it's a chase sequence like *Speed*, a thriller sequence like *Seven*, the killing of Harlan in *Thelma & Louise*, or the tense waiting period for the emergency action message to arrive in *Crimson Tide*.

A good action sequence builds image by image, word by word. Notice after the goat has vanished and the chain is swinging freely, suddenly there's a BANG! and we literally jump in our collective seats. Then, we see the "disembodied goat leg." That's when the fear starts rising among the characters, and that's when our palms begin sweating and our mouths become dry, waiting for and dreading what we know is coming … Tyrannosaurus rex.

It's just good writing. Sometimes writers will try to cover a weakness in character writing by inserting action sequences, thus avoiding any attempt at characterization. Sometimes the action sequences are written up in such detail that it looks like there's a blanket of words on the page, and any attempt to create a good reading experience is simply lost in the excess verbiage.

Writing a good action film, or a good action sequence, can often create as many problems as it solves. But if you find that your script drags and sags, and needs an extra shot of something, consider some kind of action sequence that can be incorporated into the story line to visually expand the attributes of your character.

Action and character, joined together, can often sharpen the focus of your screenplay and make it a better reading experience. And that's what it's all about.

ADAPTATION 14

Adapting a novel, book, play, or article into a screenplay is the same as writing an original screenplay. "To adapt" means to transpose from one medium to another. *Adaptation* is defined as the ability "to make fit or suitable by changing, or adjusting" – modifying something to create a change in structure, function, and form, which produces a better adjustment.

Put another way, a novel is a novel, a play a play, a screenplay a screenplay. Adapting a book into a screenplay means to change one (a book) into another (a screenplay), not superimpose one onto the other. Not a filmed novel or a filmed stage play. They are two different forms. An apple and an orange.

When you *adapt* a novel, play, article, or even a song into a screenplay, you are changing one form into another. You are writing a screenplay *based on other material*.

In essence, however, you are still writing an original screenplay. And you must approach it the same way.

A novel usually deals with the internal life of someone, the character's thoughts, feelings, emotions, and memories occurring within the *mindscape* of dramatic action. In a novel, you can write the same scene in a sentence, a paragraph, a page, or chapter, describing the internal dialogue, the thoughts, feelings, and impressions of the character. A novel usually takes place inside the character's head.

A play, on the other hand, is told in words, and thoughts, feelings, and events are described in dialogue on a stage locked within the boundaries of the proscenium arch. A plays deals with the *language* of dramatic action.

The screenplay deals with *externals*, with details – the ticking of a clock, a child playing in an empty street, a car turning the corner. A screenplay is a story told with pictures, placed within the context of dramatic structure.

Jean-Luc Godard, the innovative French film director who did *Breathless*, *Weekend*, *Vivre sa Vie*, says that film is evolving its own language, and that we have to learn how to read the picture.

An adaptation must be viewed as an original screenplay. It only *starts* from the novel, book, play, article, or song. That is *source* material, the starting point. Nothing more.

When you adapt a novel, you are not obligated to remain faithful to the original material.

All the President's Men is a good example. Adapted by William Goldman from the book by Bernstein and Woodward (about Watergate, lest we forget), there were several dramatic choices that had to be made immediately. In an interview at Sherwood Oaks, Goldman says that it was a difficult adaptation. "I have to approach very complicated material in a simple way without making it seem simple-minded. I had to make a story where there wasn't one. It was always a question of trying to figure out what the legitimate story was.

"For example, the movie ends halfway through the book. We made a decision to end it there, on the Haldeman mistake, rather than show Woodward and Bernstein going on to their greater glory. The audience already knew they had been proven right and gone on and gotten rich and famous and were the media darlings. To try and end *All the President's Men* on an up-beat note would have been a mistake. So we ended it there, on the Haldeman mistake, a little more than halfway through the book. The most important thing about the screenplay was setting up the structure. I had to make sure we found out what we wanted to find out when we wanted to find it out. If the audience is confused, we've lost them."

Goldman opens with the break-in at the Watergate Complex, a taut, suspenseful sequence, and after the capture of the men introduces Woodward (Robert Redford) at the preliminary hearing. He *sees* the high-class attorney in the courtroom, becomes suspicious and then involved. When Bernstein (Dustin Hoffman) joins him on the story (plot point 1), they succeed in unraveling the thread of mystery and intrigue that leads to the downfall of the President of the United States.

The original material is source material. What you do with it to fashion it into a screenplay is up to you. You might have to add characters, scenes, incidents, and events. Don't just copy a novel into a screenplay; make it visual, a story told with pictures.

Goldman does this in *Marathon Man*. He adapted his own novel: "People ask me if I wrote it as a screenplay first and I tell them no. Not at all. It was a novel first, and the fact that it was bought for the movies is purely coincidental.

"*Marathon Man* is a very complicated screenplay. The novel is an interior novel; most of the action takes place inside the kid's head. The only scene that plays directly in the book *and* the movie is the scene with Olivier in the diamond district. That is an exterior scene. I didn't have to do very much to it because it always played. It worked in the book, it worked in the screenplay, and it worked on film."

When you adapt a novel into a screenplay you are not obligated to remain true to the original material. Not too long ago I adapted a novel into a screenplay. I had to start from scratch. It was a disaster book about a meteorologist who discovers a new ice age approaching. No one believes him, of course, and when the weather changes it's too late. The new ice age begins. The meteorologist and a group of other scientists are sent to examine the glacier in Iceland, but the ship freezes in the ice. The novel ends with the main character freezing to death.

That was the book. A disaster story of 650 pages that's a downer.

I decided to keep the main character, but I wanted to place him in emotional conflict for more dramatic value. So I made him a politically outspoken professor who was being considered for tenure at NYU. His "irresponsible" statements about the impending ice age could possibly jeopardize his appointment.

Then I had to figure out what to do about the story. I needed to change the ending into an "upbeat" or positive one. I wanted them to live, not die in the frozen ice. So I had to construct new elements *based* on the novel. I began knowing I wanted an exciting opening. I went through the book and on page 287 found the main character traveling to the glacier in Iceland to measure glacial movement. I decided to open there, on the vast ice plain. A visual element. As they descend deep into the heart of the glacier an earthquake occurs, causing an avalanche. They barely make it out alive. It's a strong, visual sequence and sets up the story appropriately.

When the professor returns to New York and presents his findings to his superiors, they don't believe him. The first blizzard of the year, the warning, then becomes the plot point at the end of Act I. It happens on Halloween (my idea) because it's possible and is a good visual sequence.

The shape of things to come.

The second act was another problem. I reduced most of the action to three major sequences: one, the main character organizes a world-wide network of scientists to try and solve the problem; two, New York City freezes; and three, the people finally accept the truth and try to formulate a plan. I strung these sequences together with incidents from the book, knowing I had to avoid all disaster-movie clichés; there was no market for disaster movies at the time. As mentioned, the original ending didn't work and had to be changed. I ended up with a futuristic survival story.

I changed the action so that when the scientist's boat freezes in the ice (the plot point at the end of Act II), I have the main character, along with his scientist girlfriend and seven others, leave the boat to try and adapt to conditions of the ice the way the Eskimos have over the last thousand years.

Act III, then, is all new. The characters travel in a cell of nine people, hunting caribou, throwing off the remnants of the twentieth century. I end the screenplay with the meteorologist's girlfriend giving birth to their child.

It worked very well.

When you adapt a novel into a screenplay, it must be a visual experience. That's your job as a screenwriter. You must remain true only to the *integrity* of the *source material*.

There are exceptions, of course. Perhaps the most unique exception is the script written by John Huston for *The Maltese Falcon*. Huston had finished adapting the script of *High Sierra* with Humphrey Bogart and Ida Lupino from the book by W. R. Burnett. The film was very successful, and Huston was given the opportunity to write and direct his first feature. He decided to remake *The Maltese Falcon* by Dashiell Hammett. The Sam Spade detective story had been filmed twice before by Warner Bros., once as a comedy in 1931, with Ricardo Cortez and Bebe Daniels, and again in 1936, as *Satan Met a Lady* with Warren William and Bette Davis. Both films failed.

Huston liked the feel of the book. He thought he could capture its integrity on film, making it a hard-boiled, gritty detective story in tune with Hammett's style. Just before he left on vacation, he gave the book to his secretary and told her to go through it breaking down the written narrative into screenplay form, labeling each scene as either interior or exterior, and describing the basic action using dialogue from the book. Then he left for Mexico.

While he was away, the script somehow found its way into the hands of Jack L. Warner. "I love it. You've really captured the flavor of this book," he told the startled writer/director. "Shoot it just as it is – with my blessing!"

Huston did just that, and the result is an American film classic.

William Goldman talks about the difficulties he had writing *Butch*

Cassidy and the Sundance Kid: "First of all, Western research is dull because most of it's inaccurate. The writers that write Westerns are in the business of perpetuating myths that are false to begin with. It's hard to find out what really happned."

Goldman spent eight years researching Butch Cassidy, and occasionally he would find "a book or some articles or a piece about Butch. There was nothing about Sundance; he was an unknown figure until he went to South America with Butch."

Goldman found it necessary to distort history to get Butch and Sundance to leave the country and go to South America. These two outlaws were the last of their breed. Times were changing, and the Western outlaw could no longer pull the same kind of jobs he'd been doing since the end of the Civil War.

"In the movie," Goldman says, "Butch and Sundance rob some trains, then a super posse forms and chases them relentlessly. They jump off a cliff when they find out they can't lose them and go to South America. But in real life, when Butch Cassidy heard about the super posse, he took off. He just left. He knew it was the end; he couldn't beat them …

"I felt I had to justify why my hero leaves and runs away so I tried to make the super posse as implacable as I could so the audience'd be rooting for them to get the hell out of there.

"Most of the movie was made up. I used certain facts. They *did* rob a couple of trains, they *did* take too much dynamite and blow the car to pieces; the same guy Woodcock *was* on both trains, they *did* go to New York, they *did* go to South America, they *did* die in a shoot-out in Bolivia. Other than that, it's all bits and pieces, all made up."

In *The Lord of the Rings: The Two Towers*, Part II of the trilogy, the book traces the paths of each member of the Fellowship travels. But the movie couldn't do that so they intercut between each of the stories to make it a unified flow of action.

"History," T. S. Eliot once observed, "is but a contrived corridor." If you are writing a historial screenplay, you do not have to be accurate about the people involved, only to the historical event and the result of that event.

If you have to add new scenes, do it. If necessary add a sequence of events that will personalize the story while leading it to an accurate historical result. *Napoleon*, by the French filmmaker Abel Gance, originally made in 1927 and in recent years excavated by Kevin Brownlow and presented by Francis Ford Coppola, is an extraordinary illustration of how to use history as a springboard. The film traces Napoleon's early life (Gance dramatizes the child's remarkable military ability in a snowfight. Action is character, remember!), and then jumps to 1789 to show six years of the French Revolution, ending with Napoleon assuming command of the French Army. The film ends with the magnificent triptych sequence (a three-screen process) where Napoleon leads the French Army into Italy.

Don't be *too* free with history, however.

In a recent European screenwriting workshop, a French student wrote a film about Napoleon being transported from Waterloo to St. Helena. He made it into a romantic swashbuckler, an action-adventure story filled with historical inaccuracies and blatantly fictitious events. He failed to prepare or research his story sufficiently for it to be anything but a good example of bad writing.

Adapting a play into a screenplay must be approached in the same manner. You're dealing with a different *form* but utilizing the same principles.

A play is told through dialogue and deals with the *language* of dramatic action. Characters talk about how they feel, memories, emotions, events. Talking heads. The stage, the sets, the background, are forever fixed within the restrictions of the proscenium arch.

There was a time in Shakespeare's career when he cursed the restrictions of the stage, calling it "an unworthy scaffold" and "this wooden *O*," and begged the audience to "eke out the performance with your mind." He knew the stage couldn't capture the vast spectacle of two armies stationed against an empty sky on the rolling plains of England. Only when he completed *Hamlet* did he transcend the limitations of the stage and create great stage art.

When you adapt a play into a screenplay, you've got to visualize events that are referred to or spoken about. Plays deal with language and dramatic dialogue. In *A Streetcar Named Desire* or *Cat on a Hot Tin Roof* by Tennessee Williams, Arthur Miller's *Death of a Salesman*, or Eugene O'Neill's *Long Day's Journey Into Night*, the action takes place on stage, in sets, the actors talking to themselves or each other. Take a look at any play, whether it be a contemporary play by Sam Shepard like *Curse of the Starving Class*, or Edward Albee's *Who's Afraid of Virginia Woolf*.

Because the action of a play is spoken, you've got to open it up to add a visual dimension. You might have to add scenes and dialogue that are only referred to in the text, then structure, design, and write them in such a way that they lead you into the main scenes that occur on stage. Search the dialogue for ways to expand the action visually.

A good example is the Australian film *Breaker Morant*. The play, written by Kenneth Ross (who wrote *Day of the Jackal*), then adapted and directed by the Australian filmmaker Bruce Beresford, tells the story of an Australian military commando who is accused, court-martialed, and finally executed for killing the enemy in "an unorthodox and uncivilized fashion" (guerrilla warfare) during the Boer War (1900). He becomes a political victim, a pawn in the game of war, an Australian sacrifice to the English Colonial system at the turn of the century. The play takes place in the courtroom, but the film opens the action to include flashbacks of battles as well as scenes from the soldier's personal life. The result is a stunning and thought-provoking film.

Play and film stand on their own, a tribute to both playwright and filmmaker.

Screenplays dealing with people, either alive or dead – biographical scripts – must be selective and focused in order to be effective. *Young Winston*, for example, written by Carl Foreman, deals with only a few incidents in the life of Winston Churchill before he was elected Prime Minister.

Your character's life is only the beginning. Be selective! Choose only a few incidents or events from your character's life, then structure them into a dramatic story line. *Coalminer's Daughter* by Tom Rickman, *Laurence of Arabia* written by Robert Bolt, and *Citizen Kane* (loosely adapted from the life of William Randolph Hearst) by Orson Welles and Herman Mankiewicz, are good examples of a few incidents in a character's life laid out and structured in dramatic fashion.

How you approach your subject's life determines the basic story line: without a story line you've got no story; without a story you've got no screenplay.

A short time ago, one of my students obtained the motion-picture rights to the life of the first woman editor on a major metropolitan newspaper. She tried to get everything into the story – the early years "because they were *so* interesting"; her marriage and children "because she had such an unusual approach"; her early years as a reporter when she covered several major stories "because they were *so* exciting"; and getting the job of editor and several stories because "that's what she's famous for."

I tried to convince her to focus only on a few events in the woman's life, but she was too tied into the subject to see anything objectively. So I gave her an exercise. I told her to write her story line in a few pages. She came back with twenty-six pages and was only halfway through her character's life! She didn't have a story, she had a chronology, and it was boring. I told her it wasn't working, and suggested she focus on one or two of the stories in the editor's career. A week later, she came back saying she had been unable to choose which ones were the right ones. Overwhelmed by indecision, she became despondent and depressed and finally gave up in despair. She called me one day in tears, and I urged her to get back into the material, to choose three of the most interesting events in the woman's life (writing, remember, *is* choice and selection), and if need be, to talk to the woman about what *she* thought were the most interesting aspects of *her* life and career. She did and managed to create a story line based on the newspaper story she covered that led to her appointment as the first woman editor. It became the "hook" or basis of the screenplay.

You only have 120 pages to tell your story. Choose your events carefully so they highlight and illustrate your script with good visual and dramatic components. The screenplay should be based on the dramatic needs of your story. Source material *is*, after all, source material. It is a starting point, not an end in itself.

Journalists seem to have a hard time learning this. They often have a difficult time with a screenplay based on an article. I don't know why, except perhaps that the methods of constructing a dramatic story line in film are exactly the opposite of those in journalism.

A journalist approaches his/her assignment by getting facts and gathering information, by doing text research as well as interviewing people related to the piece. Once they have all the facts, they can figure out the story. The more facts a journalist can collect, the more information he has; he can use some, all, or none of it. Once he's collected the facts, he searches for the "hook" or "angle" of the piece, and then writes the story using only those facts that highlight and support the material.

That's good journalism.

But writing a screenplay is exactly the opposite. You approach a script with an *idea*, a *subject*, an action and character, then weave a story line that will dramatize it. Once you have the basic story line – three guys holding up the Chase Manhattan Bank – you expand it; you do research, create characters, do character biographies, interview people if need be, collect all the missing facts and information that build and support your story. If you need something for the story, make it up!

The facts *support* the story in a screenplay; you might even say they create the story.

In screenwriting, you go from general to specific; you find the story first, then collect facts. In journalism, you go from specific to general; you collect the facts first, then find the story.

A well-known journalist was writing a screenplay based on a controversial article he had written for a national magazine. All the facts were at his disposal, yet he found it extremely difficult to let go of the article and dramatize the elements he needed to make it a good screenplay. He got stuck in finding the "right" facts and the "right" details, and then couldn't get beyond the first thirty pages of the screenplay. He got bogged down, went into a panic, then shelved what might have been a very good screenplay.

He couldn't let the article be the article and the screenplay the screenplay. He wanted to be faithful to the other material, and it just doesn't work.

Many people want to write a screenplay or teleplay based on a magazine or newspaper article. If you're going to adapt an article into a screenplay, you've got to approach it from a screenwriter's point of view. What's the story about? Who's the main character? What's the ending? Is it about a man who was captured, tried, and then acquitted for murder only to discover after the trial that he was really guilty? Is it about a young man who designs, builds, and races cars and becomes a champion? About a doctor finding a cure for diabetes? About incest? *Who* is it about? *What* is it about? When you answer those questions, you can lay it out in dramatic structure.

There are many legal problems if you adapt a screenplay or teleplay from an article or story. First of all, you must obtain permission to write a script: that means getting the rights from the people involved, negotiating with the author, and possibly with the magazine or newspaper. Most people are willing to cooperate in trying to bring their stories to the screen or TV. An entertainment attorney who specializes in these matters, or a literary agent, should be consulted if you're serious.

Don't get bogged down with the legalities, however. If you don't want to deal with it now, don't deal with it. Write the script or outline first. Something attracted you to the material. What is it? Explore it. You might decide to write the script based on the article or story and then see how it turns out. If it's good, you may want to show it to the people involved. If you *don't do it*, you'll never know how it would have turned out. And that's what it's all about.

We've discussed adapting novels, plays, and articles into screenplays, and still the question must be asked: What *is* the fine art of adaptation?

Answer: NOT being true to the original. A book is a book, a play is a play, an article an article, a screenplay a screenplay. An adaptation is always an original screenplay. They are different forms.

Just like apples and oranges.

Open a novel at random and read a few pages. Notice how the narrative action is described. Does it take place inside the character's head? Is it told with dialogue? What about description? Take a play and do the same thing. Notice how the characters talk about themselves or the action of the play. Talking heads. Then read a few pages of a screenplay (any that are excerpted in this text will do) and notice how the screenplay deals with *external* details and events, what the character *sees*.

THE PROBLEM SHEET

Another Time, Another Place: Bridging Time and Action
- The script is too long
- The story is episodic, too expository
- Too many things happen, with no focus in the story line
- Things happen too fast
- Too many characters
- The main character is too weak, overpowered by other characters
- Scenes are too long, too complicated
- Too many subplots
- There seem to be two stories in one
- Too many things have to be explained

A look at the *Problem Sheet* reveals a lot of common problems that plague screenplays. Many times I'll read a screenplay and within the first ten pages I can make a fairly accurate "read" of the material. I look for a lean, clean, visual style, with an economy of story, the characters and their actions clear and concise. If there are too many characters, or too much action, or too many long-winded scenes, the chances are the script will be overlong, say more than 145 pages. If that's the case, the story line might be too broad, too expansive, too big in scope, resulting in the main character not being clearly defined; or there may be too many characters, or too many scenes where the main character is not involved, or a story line that covers too much time and too much action.

Scripts that span a number of years, like *The Shawshank Redemption*, are very difficult to write because the time frame is very long and there may be too many incidents that have to be covered and explained. There's too much going on. So when you're working on a subject that covers a long period of time, you have to know what problems you're going to be confronting.

Apollo 13 is a script like this. The story is a chronological time line that covers seven days, and what makes it difficult to write is that a series of events must happen that includes a multitude of details, and each one is contingent upon the others. I understand that the first few drafts of *Apollo 13* were more than 200 pages long. So what do you have to do to make it work effectively? If you're not true to the "history" of the story, the circumstances and events, you're bound to break the "willing suspension of disbelief" and nobody will buy it. It's just not "real" or believable and this becomes apparent immediately. The music is there, but that's about it.

So how do you approach the *historical film* or the period piece? A script based on actual characters and events? There are many ways to approach the *historical screenplay*. First, of course, you have to do the textual research, reading books, magazines, or newspapers of the time and subject, finding out all you can about the period, as well as the people and the forces of time. Personal diaries or novels of that period are also a good source. Once you've done the research, then you can place the historical facts into a progression of events that become the structural foundation of the screenplay.

Then you have to decide how you're going to end it. What incident or event will resolve your story line most effectively? Is it based on an actual incident whose ending we already know, like *Apollo 13*, *All the President's Men* (William Goldman), or *Nixon*? Or will you base the ending on some kind of commentary using a scrawl over the end of credits, as in *Dances With Wolves*? In other words, how true do you have to be to history? And the answer is simple. Be true to the facts, and the events of history, but the motivations that drive the characters can be created and entirely fictional.

Immortal Beloved (Bernard Rose) is a script like this: if you know anything at all about Beethoven's life, you'll know that the events shown were obviously fabricated; if you look for "the real" Beethoven in that script, you'll have a hard time finding him.

If you happen to be writing a script like this, a historical or period piece, and you find that your script is too long, and too episodic, or you have too many characters, or too much seems to be going on, the first question you have to ask yourself is not "What do I keep in?" but *"What do I leave out?"*

It's *the* major creative decision that must be made before you even begin to approach the story, or the rewrite. If you don't ask yourself this question, it often leads to difficulties and raises many problems, most notably *selectivity*. What events *do I need* to tell the story in the most visually effective way, and then what can I leave out?

One of the ways to solve this particular problem is by using *transitions*. The passage of time and the link between the scenes and sequences has to be conceived visually, for moving the action from one scene to the next requires a visual transition. *Transitions* bridge time and move the action forward quickly, visually. Whether you're writing an original screenplay, or adapting a novel, play, magazine, or news article, each piece of film, each scene or sequence, must bridge a particular *time* to a particular *place* in order to move the story forward. To go from Point A to Point B in a screenplay requires making transitions that connect the two. If you don't make those transitions, then you may wind up with many of the symptoms that are on the *Problem Sheet*.

There are four major ways to make *transitions*: cutting from *picture to picture*, *sound to sound*, *music to music*, *or special effect to special effect*. There can be dissolves, fadeouts, and *smash cuts*.

It wasn't too long ago that the screenwriter depended on the director or film editor to create these visual transitions, but more recently most of the working screenwriters have taken the responsibility to write the required transitions from scene to scene. One of the recognizable traits of the modern screenwriter is his or her ability to write good visual transitions. And over recent years there has been an evolution in the style and sophistication of the art of transition. Even a script like *Pulp Fiction*, which is sequential and episodic, uses effective transitions so the five episodes that make up the screenplay seem to be connected into a single story line. The title page even proclaims the script is really "three stories about one story." If Tarantino and Avary had not created those transitions, the script would have been disjointed and episodic and not worked as well as it does.

As far as I am concerned, it is the screenwriter's responsibility to write these transitional scenes that move the story forward and bridge time and action. Writing good transitions is also a very good way to solve a number of problems.

Transitions have always been an integral part of the screenwriting process. From the earliest days of silent movies the craft of filmmaking has always been the same: to tell a story in pictures, building it from beginning to end with little bits and pieces of film. That's what a screenplay is: a story told with pictures.

In *The Shawshank Redemption*, for example, the passage of time is handled incredibly well. Only one shot is needed to tell us the passage of time: the large posters of Rita Hayworth, Marilyn Monroe, and Raquel Welch visually indicate that several decades have passed by. That, and some music on the soundtrack. In *How to Make an American Quilt* a young woman of twenty-six is kneeling down looking at a book and we hear her in voice-over narration: "How do two separate people fuse into this thing called a couple? And if your love is that strong, then how do you still keep a little room for yourself …?" That's what the whole film is about, and when Finn stands up we match-cut to her as a little girl of five or six years standing up looking at the woman in the quilting bee as her narration leads us directly into the story line.

Why are transitions so important? Because when you're reading a script, or seeing a movie, it has to flow smoothly across the time period that is usually not more than two hours. The story line has to be a seamless parade of images across the page or screen, and time becomes a relative phenomenon; days and years and decades can be condensed into seconds, a few seconds stretched into minutes, as a leap is made from one image to another. That's one of the things that make *The Shawshank Redemption* such a remarkable movie; the passage of time does not draw attention to itself. It becomes an integral part of the fabric of the screenplay.

Transitions can be as varied and as multiple as the colors in a kaleidoscope. In *The Silence of the Lambs*, for example, the screenwriter, Ted Tally, generally plays the last line of one scene over the first line of the next. The dialogue is used to bridge time and action and shows one way that *sound* can be the link connecting two different scenes. Tally ends one scene with a question, then opens the next scene by answering that question.

This kind of overlapping transition scene has been done many times before, of course, most notably in *Julia*, Alvin Sargent's Academy Award-winning screenplay adapted from Lillian Hellman's *Pentimento*. But the way Tally approached his transitions pushes the boundaries of the medium in such a way that we're not even aware of them. If you're watching a movie and become aware of the visual transitions, or feel that "arty" influence of the director in each scene, chances are it's not a very good film.

Every screenplay has its own particular style and form in terms of transitions. An action film usually has short, quick transitions, because the film moves forward at a very rapid pace and we have to be swept up into the action. But in a character-driven piece the transitions could possibly come from silence, or looks between the characters, or dialogue. There is never *any one right way* to make transitions. *The only criterion is whether it works or not.*

There may be times when you're so engrossed in putting the story down on paper that you don't even think about the transitional flow of the script. But when you finish the first or second draft, you find that you've written a screenplay that may be 145 pages or longer. During the actual screenwriting process that's OK, but afterwards you're going to have to do a lot of work to cut it to a proper length. A 140-plus page screenplay is only accepted if it's by William Goldman, Quentin Tarantino, David Koepp, or Eric Roth.

If your screenplay is too long, and you feel there's too much going on, too many things happening, or too many characters, look for ways to bridge the time and action. Transitions solve so many problems in screenwriting and sometimes the bridge to another time, or another place, can be as simple as changing the character's clothes, or using matchcuts, or changing the weather, or using holidays to condense the time and action.

One of the most interesting films to use transitions as an integral part of the story is *Pulp Fiction*. This is a unique film in many respects, but what's especially interesting is the way Tarantino and Roger Avary created the transitions to keep the film flowing smoothly in one single time line.

As the title-page reads, *Pulp Fiction* is really "three stories about one story." The first page of the screenplay is "The Table of Contents," and states that there is a Prologue, where the holdup begins (with Tim Roth and Amanda Plummer) then a story called "Vincent and Marcellus Wallace's Wife," another called "The Gold Watch," and the last story, "Vincent, Jules, Jimmie, and the Wolf" (in the film the title's been changed to "The Bonnie Situation"), which leads us into the Epilogue and the conclusion of the robbery. The use of a Prologue, which opens the script, and the Epilogue, which closes it, is called a *"bookend"* device; the opening scene or sequence leads into the story and the last part of the scene or sequence closes it. *The Bridges of Madison County* (Richard LaGravenese) is another example of the use of a "bookend" opening and closing. Despite all the five specific episodes that make up the script of *Pulp Fiction*, it really seems like one story. Why?

Because of the transitions.

All the transitions in this screenplay are character driven, and the reason the film works so effectively is that the three stories are woven together with these characters. Even though it is "three stories about one story," the focal point always seems to be Vincent, the John Travolta character.

The film opens in the restaurant with Tim Roth – Pumpkin – and his girlfriend, Honeybunny (Amanda Plummer); they pull out their guns and the robbery begins. We freeze at this point, then cut to Vincent and Jules driving somewhere having one of their many weighty and lengthy discussions about the difference between McDonald's restaurants here and abroad. They seem like two nice guys until they open the trunk, pull out several guns, and make their way inside an apartment building. Their actions seem to contradict their dialogue, which makes them interesting and colorful characters. They walk up the stairs, stake out a room, all the time continuing their discussion about the moral and ethical complications of a "foot massage." Especially Marcellus's wife Mai's foot massage which left the "masseur" with a very "severe speech problem."

It is this attitude of casual nonchalance that is so effective in the film. There have been all kinds of essays and comments and literary debates about *Pulp Fiction*, and they reveal the extent to which movies have become the social fingerprints of our time.

The two hitmen force their way inside the room and confront four young men who tried to rip off Marcellus Wallace and not deliver what they said they were going to deliver, the mysterious briefcase with the light inside, and the combination 666, the devil's numbers. (In

Hitchcockian terms, the briefcase and what's inside would be called the "McGuffin.") As Jules quotes from the Bible (another nice character touch), Vincent and Jules kill three of the four guys in a very explosive scene. When Brett, one of the four, leaps out of the bathroom with his gun blazing, *missing* Vincent and Jules, it becomes "a fucking miracle," and then we cut to:

Marcellus's bar, where the "boss" is telling Butch (Bruce Willis), a boxer, to take a fall in the fifth round of his fight. Butch agrees, reluctantly, to deliberately lose the fight, then goes to the bar for a pack of cigarettes and is joined by Vincent who has just arrived (wearing the funny clothes he wears in the story #3), and the two exchange some words. They don't like each other. Vincent is called in to the boss, Marcellus, who gives him an order: take his wife out to dinner.

At this point we have a choice; in terms of story we can either follow Butch, or Vincent. We follow Vincent. We set up the encounter between Vincent and Mia when he scores some "great" heroin, and then follow him as he takes Mia out to dinner in a long and bizarre sequence, ending with her overdosing on heroin. Vincent saves her, they say their goodbyes to a "memorable" evening, and we go into:

The second story, titled "The Gold Watch." The transition between these two stories is simply to Fade Out at the end of the Vincent/Mia sequence, and Fade In on a flashback sequence of a young Butch being told the story of his father's gold watch that he had carried up his ass for more than six years in a Vietnamese POW camp. When the young boy reaches to take the watch, Butch wakes up in his dressing room just before the fight. We know Butch was supposed to take a fall, but we actually don't see the fight; we cut to the taxi driver listening to the results. We hear on the driver's radio that a fighter has died, then we see Butch leap into a Dumpster, then into the cab and make his way to a motel, where his girlfriend is waiting for him.

She has forgotten the gold watch at his apartment. Furious, he realizes he must go back and retrieve it, even though it may cost him his life. He has double-crossed Marcellus and he knows there will be a contract on him (executed by Vincent and Jules). Sure enough, when he returns to the apartment and retrieves the sacred watch, Vincent emerges from the bathroom and Butch blows him away. Which is perhaps the most arresting moment in the film, because the scene is out of its normal time frame. It's a nonlinear action. And, occurring as it does in the middle of the script, it breaks the normal linear thread of the story line. This "nonlinear" structure is what has been so instrumental in the success of the film, and became the inspiration for many others coming up in the latter part of the nineties.

Butch escapes in his little VW and at a stoplight sees Marcellus and literally runs over him in his efforts to get away. In the ensuing somewhat comedic escape, both men are captured by two goon brothers, Ned and Zed, who lock them up in order to sodomize them. Butch escapes, but decides he cannot let Marcellus remain in the hands of these two goonies. He rescues him, again at the peril of his own life, and when Marcellus grants him a pardon, he promises to leave with his girlfriend, never to be seen again. As Mia and Vincent have agreed to reveal nothing about what happened at dinner, Marcellus and Butch make an agreement not to say anything about this incident. Life is a compromise.

Which then brings us to the third story, "Vincent, Jules, Jimmie, and the Wolf," though in the film the title's been changed to "The Bonnie Situation." Bonnie is Jimmie's wife, the nurse who is expected home within the hour. And Jimmie (played by Tarantino) is not going to jeopardize his marriage by his wife finding a dead man in the garage. It's a situation that needs to be handled by the Wolf, the Harvey Keitel character whom we heard Marcellus mention at the end of the previous story.

The story begins at the end of the opening section after the Prologue, in what is really an overlapping scene from another point of view. When Jules kills the first man, the character Brett, whom we have not seen before, has been in the bathroom, a gun in hand. He listens to Jules spouting the Bible in the living room and then we hear gunshots. Muttering to himself, Brett leaps out of the bathroom firing six times at Jules and Vincent and misses each time; the bullets thud harmlessly into the wall. As Jules says, "It's a fuckin' miracle," and he becomes obsessed with the fact that they're still alive. "This is some serious shit," he says as they drive away, the other character, Marvin, being held "captive" in the back seat. They become engrossed in an illuminating conversation, Jules declaring that they've survived "only by divine intervention"; Vincent disagrees, and when he turns to get Marvin's opinion, the gun he's holding accidentally fires and Marvin's head is blown all over the car.

In a panic Jules calls his friend Jimmie and they go there to clean up the car and get rid of the body. A quick call to Marcellus produces "The Wolf" and he comes to their rescue and saves the day. The job done, the body and the car both disposed of, the two of them are hungry and go get some breakfast.

That, of course, is the transition that leads to the coffee shop that Tim Roth and his girlfriend are going to rob. As they are having breakfast and continuing their discussion, Vincent goes to the bathroom, and when he's gone the robbery begins, so we begin this action a little bit before it ended in the Prologue. Another nice use of nonlinear structure. The two of them thwart the holdup, permit Pumpkin and Honeybunny to leave, and then leave themselves. The end.

This nonlinear structure works very well within the framework of the three stories, Epilogue, and Prologue. It is really what makes the film so interesting and appealing. Just for the sake of an exercise we could put these three stories, along with the Prologue and Epilogue, into a linear story line. We might open with Vincent and Jules on their way to kill the kids who were trying to rip off Marcellus. They leave, accidentally kill Marvin, go to the "Jules, Vincent, Jimmie and the Wolf" sequence, which would be followed by their breakfast, leading to the Prologue and Epilogue. We follow them to the Marcellus bar scene of the first story, where Vincent and Butch meet; we would follow Vincent to Mia and their night out, then end with Butch and the gold watch, with Vinnie's death and Butch's escape. Yes, it would work well, but it certainly would not be as effective as it is now.

It is the transitions between these stories that really hold it all together; they make the screenplay work, bridging both linear time and narrative line. All the characters are introduced and set up from the beginning, and these characters are the links that connect the three stories, even though they are told in a nonlinear way. The "wackiness" of the characters (their discussions and the dialogue are wonderful), along with the bizarre humor of the stories, makes *Pulp Fiction* the entertaining and highly influential film it is and, I think, will continue to be.

Different kinds of films require different kinds of transitions. An action or action-adventure film like *Apollo 13* or *Mission: Impossible* (David Koepp and Robert Towne), requires swift transitions, sharp, dynamic bridges that keep the pace flowing fast and smooth, so the reader and view are swept into a torrent of movement. Look at *Twister*, simply a one-line story of storm chasers; it is the four storm sequences that really hold the film together. So everything in the story acts as a transition leading into the next storm.

A character piece, like *Pulp Fiction* or *The Bridges of Madison County*, requires a different kind of transitional connection, a smooth and careful sculpting of transitions. In a comedy the transitions from one scene to the next might be capped with one-liners, but they must be character driven or humor driven in order to move the story forward in a funny and seamless way.

Transitions in a biographical or historical screenplay present a problem of selectivity. How do you weave what might be a number of historical incidents into a 120-page screenplay? If you simply string the character's life story, or a series of events, in chronological order, it becomes nothing more than a filmed essay; first this happens, then that happens, then this other thing happens, and so on until the character dies or something significant takes place that leads to an ending we already know. As in *Nixon*, or *Apollo 13*, or *Gandhi*.

Some years ago, I had the opportunity of working with a Brazilian writer-director on a screenplay about the famous Brazilian composer

Villa-Lobos. The writer did not want simply to show a biographical chronology of events, so he chose to write the screenplay like a free-association collage, fragmented bits and pieces of the composer's life presented in a nonlinear fashion like some kind of a visual jigsaw puzzle. That way, he explained to me, he hoped to make the composer's life both visual and interesting. But, he confided, he felt very insecure about the script; he didn't know whether it worked or not.

When I first read the material, I thought it an interesting presentation, but unfortunately, the script didn't work; it was a hard and difficult read because I didn't know what was going on; I didn't know *what* the story was about and it was hard to get a grasp of the main character.

My problem was "how to fix it," how to keep the writer's style and subject matter intact but also to tell the story of the composer, the subject of the script. At first I thought this was a structural problem, but when I went back over the material, trying to isolate and define the historical moments of the character's life, I realized that the main character seemed to disappear off the page; that's when I realized that it was really a problem of *Character*, because the events of his life seemed to overshadow him. The women in his life seemed to dominate him, the smaller characters seemed larger than he was, and there seemed to be too many events going on.

When I took it apart, I saw the screenplay really focused on five major periods of the composer's life, and it was these "parts" that were broken up and placed in various sections of the screenplay. I had the impression that *the main character got lost on the page,* for he literally disappeared from the action, even though it was his story and he was the main character. The main character always seemed to be reacting to the events of his life, and not creating them. The main character in a screenplay always has to be active; he or she must *cause* things to happen.

A biographical film like *Gandhi*, for example, covers only a few events of his life, yet the conflict the character confronts and endures is encapsulated in two or three events and they become the structural foundation the script is built upon. The film covers only three major periods in Gandhi's life: as a young attorney fighting for social causes; then formulating and embracing his philosophy and practice of "passive resistance"; then trying to mend the Hindu-Muslim disputes. Gandhi's murder and death "bookend" the film, very much like the bookend Prologue and Epilogue in *Pulp Fiction*.

The Brazilian script, as fragmented as it was, really dealt with these five periods of the composer's life: his childhood, his struggles to get his music performed; the two women in his life; his world fame; and his final acceptance of old age.

As I started going through the script again, I found that I could isolate and define these five areas of his life, but there seemed to be several key scenes missing, scenes needed to highlight and accent those periods of the composer's life. And it was these key scenes, I felt – discovering the source of his inspiration, meeting his second wife, overcoming those incredible obstacles to get his music performed, and so on – which became the Plot Points, or anchors, the basic glue that held the script together.

Good transitions in a screenplay should never really be noticed; they should disappear into the visual narrative like the individual threads that make up a piece of cloth.

Transitions become an essential tool in the Problem-Solving process. If your script is too long, look for whole chunks of action, or full sequences, to omit and then find some kind of transition to tie the remainder together and bridge the action. Sometimes you can cover a longer period of time by using a *montage*.

A montage is a sequence, a series of scenes connected by one single idea with a definite beginning, middle, and end. The purpose of a montage is to cover a lot of time, or a lot of events, in a very short period of time. In the Brazilian screenplay we used several montages in order to move the story forward quickly. We numbered the shots: 1) walking along the beach; 2) at dinner alone; 3) working hard at the piano, sheet music spread all around him on the floor; 4) walking into an office; 5) in another office arguing violently with a short, fat bureaucrat, wearing different clothes from the previous shot; 6) walking angrily out of another building, on another day, wearing the same crumpled suit with a different tie, and so on. The montage served a very specific purpose within the screenplay, yet conceived as one single action carried out over a period of several days.

Perhaps the best transition ever put on film was the marriage montage in *Citizen Kane* (Orson Welles and Herman Mankiewicz). The sequence starts after the marriage of Kane and his first wife, as they sit at the breakfast table having an intimate conversation. There is a *swish pan* (the camera swishes out the frame) and we see them in different clothes talking and reading the paper. *Swish pan* and we see them at a slightly larger table having a very heated discussion. *Swish pan* to them having a more vocal argument about him spending so much time at the office. *Swish pan* to them at a much larger table, both silent, both reading the paper; she asks him something and he simply grunts a reply. *Swish pan* to them at a very long table eating in total silence. It tells us so much in so little, using pictures instead of words. It's an incredible sequence that is probably the best portrait of the disintegration of a marriage ever conceived.

15

ON COLLABORATION

While I was attending the University of California at Berkeley, I had the privilege of working with Jean Renoir, the great French film director. It was an extraordinary experience. Son of the great painter Auguste Renoir and creator of two of the greatest films ever made, *Grand Illusion* and *Rules of the Game*, Renoir was a man who loved film with religious passion.

He loved to talk, and we loved listening to him for hours on end, talking about the relationship between art and film. Because of his background and tradition, Renoir felt that film, though a great art, was not a "true" art in the sense that writing, painting, or music is, because too many people are directly involved in its making. The filmmaker can write, direct, and produce his own film, Renoir used to say, but he can't act all the parts; he can be the cameraman (Renoir loved to paint with light), but he can't develop the film. He sends it to a special film laboratory for that, and sometimes it doesn't come back the way he wants it.

"One person can't do everything," Renoir used to say. "True art is in the *doing* of it."

Renoir was right. Film is a collaborative medium. The filmmaker depends on others to bring his vision to the screen. The technical skills required to make a movie are extremely specialized. And the state of the art is constantly improving.

The only thing you can do by yourself is write a screenplay. All you need is pen and paper, or a typewriter or computer, and a certain amount of time. You can write it alone or with someone.

It's your choice.

Screenwriters collaborate all the time. If a producer has an idea and commissions you to write it, you will be in a collaboration with the producer and director. In *Raiders of the Lost Ark*, for example, Lawrence Kasdan, the screenwriter (*The Empire Strikes Back*, writer/director of *Body Heat*), met with George Lucas and Steven Spielberg. Lucas wanted to use the name of his dog, Indiana Jones, for the hero (Harrison Ford), and he knew what the last scene of the movie would be: a vast military basement warehouse filled with thousands of crates of confiscated secrets, much like *Citizen Kane*'s basement was filled with huge crates of art. That's all Lucas knew about *Raiders* at the time. Spielberg wanted to add a mystical dimension. They spent two weeks locked in an office, and when the three of them emerged, they had worked out a general story line. Then Lucas and Spielberg left to work on other projects, and Kasdan went into his office and wrote *Raiders of the Lost Ark*.

That's a typical collaboration in Hollywood. Everybody works for the finished product.

Writers collaborate for different reasons. Some think it's easier to work with someone else. Most comedy writers work in teams, especially television writers, and shows like *Saturday Night Live* have a staff of five or ten writers working on each episode. A comedy writer has to be both gag man and audience – a laugh is a laugh. Only the gifted few like Woody Allen or Neil Simon can sit in a room alone and know what's funny and what isn't.

There are three basic stages in the collaborative process. One, establishing the ground rules of the collaboration; two, the preparation needed to write the screenplay; and three, the actual writing itself. All three are essential. If you decide to collaborate, you better go into it with your eyes open. For example, do you like your potential collaborator? You're going to be working with that person for several hours a day for many months, so you had better enjoy being with him or her. Otherwise, you're starting off with problems.

Collaboration is a relationship. It's a fifty-fifty proposition. Two or more people are working together to create an end product, a screenplay. That's the aim, goal, and purpose of your collaboration, and that's where all your energy should be directed. Collaborators tend to lose sight of that very quickly.

They get bogged down in "being right" and various ego struggles, so it's best you ask yourself some questions first. For example, why are *you* collaborating? Why is your *partner* collaborating? What's the reason you're choosing to work with somebody else? Because it's easier? Safer? Not as lonely?

What do you think collaborating with someone on a screenplay looks like? Most people have a picture of one person sitting at a desk in front of a typewriter, typing like crazy, while his partner paces the room rapidly, snapping out words and phrases like a chef preparing a meal. You know, a "writing team." A talker and a typist.

Is that the way you see it? It may have been that way at one time, during the twenties and thirties with writing teams like Moss Hart and George S. Kaufman, but it's not that way anymore.

Everyone works differently. We all have our own style, our own pace, our likes and dislikes. I think the best example of a collaboration is the musical collaboration between Elton John and Bernie Taupin. At the height of their fame, Bernie Taupin would write a set of lyrics, then mail them to Elton John, somewhere in the world, who would then lay down the music, arrange it, and finally record it.

That's the exception, not the rule.

If you want to collaborate, you must be willing to find the right way to work – the right style, the right methods, the right working procedure. Try different things out, make mistakes, go through the collaborative process by trial and error until you find the best way for you and your partner. "The sequences tried that *don't* work," my film-editor friend said, "are the ones that show you what *does* work."

There are no rules when it comes to collaboration. You get to create them, to make them up as you go along. Just like a marriage. You've got to create it, sustain it, and maintain it. You're dealing with someone else all the time. Collaboration is a fifty-fifty proposition with an equal division of labor.

There are four basic positions in collaboration: writer, researcher, typist, and editor. No position is *more* equal than another.

What does your collaboration look like to *you* and *your partner*? What are your goals? Your expectations? What do *you* see yourself doing in the collaboration? What is *your partner* going to do?

Open up a dialogue. Who's going to do the typing? Where are you going to work? When? Who's going to do what?

Talk about it. Discuss it.

Lay down the ground rules. What's the division of labor? You might list the things that have to be done, two or three trips to the library, three, possibly more, interviews. Organize and divide up the tasks. I like to do this, so I'll do this, you do that, and so on. Do things you like to do. If you like to use the library, do it; if your partner likes to interview people, let him do it. It's all part of the writing process.

What does the work schedule look like? Do you have full-time jobs? When are you going to get together? Where? Make sure it's convenient for both of you. If you have a job or a family or are in a relationship, sometimes it gets difficult. Deal with it.

Are you a morning person, an afternoon person, or an evening person? That is, do you work the best in the morning, the afternoon, or the evening? If you don't know, try it one way and see what happens. If it's working, stay with it. If not, try it another way. See what works best for both of you. Support each other. You're both working for the same thing, the completed screenplay.

You'll need a couple of weeks simply to explore and organize a work schedule that supports both of you.

Don't be afraid to try something that doesn't work. Go for it! Make mistakes. Create your collaboration by trial and error. And don't plan on doing any serious writing until the ground rules are set.

The last thing you're going to do is write.

Before you can do that, you've got to prepare the material.

What kind of story are you writing? Is it going to be an action-adventure story with a strong love interest or a love story with a strong action-adventure interest? You better find out. Is it a contemporary story or a historical story? Is it a period piece? What do you have to do to research it? Spend one or two days at the library or several days? Do you have to interview any people? Or sit in on a legal proceeding? And then – who's going to type it up?

Collaboration is a fifty-fifty division of labor.

Who's going to do what?

Talk about it. Work it out. What do you *like* to do? What do you do *best*? Do you like collecting facts and data and then organizing them for background material? Do you work best talking or writing? Find out. If you don't like it, you can always change it.

The same thing with the story. Work on the story together. Verbalize the story line in a few sentences. What is the subject of your story? What's the action? Who's the main character? What's it about? Is your story about an archeologist assigned to recover the lost ark just before World War II? Who is the main character? What is the dramatic need of your character?

Write the character biographies. You may want to talk about each character with your collaborator, and then write one biography while your partner writes another. Or you may write the biographies, and your collaborator edit them. Know your characters. Talk about them, about who they are and where they come from. Feed the pot. The more you put in, the more you can take out.

After you do the character work, structure the story line. What's the ending, the resolution of your story? Do you know the opening? The plot points at the end of Acts I and II?

If you don't, who does?

Lay your story out so you know where you're going. When you know your ending, the opening, and the two plot points, you're ready to expand your story line in a scene progression using 3 x 5 cards. Discuss it. Talk about it. Argue about it. Just make sure you know your story. You may agree or disagree about it. You may want it one way, your partner another. If you can't resolve it, write it both ways. See which works the best. Work towards the finished product, the screenplay.

It's possible to spend anywhere from three to six weeks or more preparing your material – the research, the characters, building a story line, and creating the mechanics of your collaboration. It's an interesting experience because you're building another kind of relationship. Magic at times, hell at others.

When you're ready to write, things sometimes get crazy. Be prepared. How are you going to put it down on paper? What are the mechanics involved? Who says what, and why is that word better than this word? Who says so? *I'm* right and you're wrong is one point of view. The other point of view, of course, is you're wrong and I'm right.

Collaboration means working together.

The key to collaboration, or any relationship, is communication. You've got to talk to each other. Without communication, there's no collaboration. Only misunderstanding and disagreement. That's nowhere. You two are working together to write and complete a screenplay. There will be times when you'll want to chuck it and walk away. You might think it's not worth it. You may be right. Usually, it's just some of your psychological "stuff" coming up. You know, all the stuff we have to contend with on a day-to-day basis, the fears, insecurities, guilts, judgments, and so on. Deal with it! Writing is learning more about yourself. Be willing to make mistakes, to learn from each other what is working and what isn't.

There are many ways of working, and you're going to have to find your own way. You may work together, with one of you sitting at the typewriter or pad, and the two of you laying out words and ideas. This works well for some people. You will agree on some things, disagree on others; you win some, you lose some. It's a good opportunity to learn about negotiation and compromise in a working relationship.

Another method is to work in thirty-page units. You write Act I, and your partner edits it. Your partner writes Act II, and you edit it. You write Act III, and your partner edits it. This way you see what your partner is writing and can act as editor.

When I work in collaboration, we both decide upon story and characters. The first thing we do is conceive a Mission Statement for each project. What do we want to achieve or accomplish with the screenplay? For example, in one script, a science-fiction epic adventure, we wanted to create an "engaging, edge-of-the-seat page turner." Then we made an agreement to "serve the material." When the preliminary work is done, we work in thirty-page units. My collaborator will write Act I, and we'll talk by phone to handle any problems that might arise.

When the first act is done, a fairly tight and clean words-on-paper draft, I read and edit it. Is it working? Do we need another scene here? Does the dialogue have to be clarified? Expanded? Sharpened? Is the dramatic premise clearly staged? By words and picture? Are we setting it up properly? I may add some lines or a scene here and there, and occasionally sketch in certain visual aspects.

Sometimes you have to criticize your partner's work. How are you going to tell him that his writing is terrible, that he better throw it away and start over! You better think about what you're going to say. Realise you're dealing with your partner's feelings based on your *judgments*. "Judge not lest ye be judged." You've got to respect and support (hopefully) the other person. First determine *what* you want to say, then decide *how* to say it the best. If you want to say something, say it to yourself first. How would you feel if your partner told you what you're going to tell him?

Collaboration is a learning experience.

Sometimes changes have to be made in Act I before moving on to Act II. The process is exactly the same. Writing is writing. Bring the material to a semi-rough stage, then move on. You can always polish it. Don't worry about making your pages perfect. You're going to change it anyway, so don't worry about how good it is. It may not be very good. So what? Just get it down, then you can work on it to make it better.

Once you complete the first words-on-paper stage, go back and read it. See what you've got. You should be able to see it as a whole and obtain some kind of overview or perspective on the material. You might need to add some new scenes, create a new character, possibly telescope two scenes into one. Do it!

It's all part of the writing process.

If you're married and want to collaborate with your spouse, other factors are involved. When things get difficult, for example, you simply can't walk away from the collaboration. It's part of the marriage. If the marriage is in trouble, your collaboration will only magnify what's gone wrong with it. You can't be an ostrich and pretend it isn't there. You've got to deal with it.

For example, some married friends of mine, both professional journalists, decided to write a screenplay together. At the same time, she was in between assignments and he was in the middle of one. She had time on her hands, so she decided to get a head start and began the research. She went to the library, read books, interviewed people, then typed up the material. She didn't mind because "someone's got to do it!"

He had completed his assignment by the time the research was done. They took a few days off, then got down to work. The first thing he said was "Let's see what you've got." Then he proceeded to appraise the material as if it were *his* assignment and the work had been done by a researcher, not his collaborator, not his wife! She was angry, but said nothing. She had done *all* the work, and now he was going to come in and *save* the project!

That's how it began. It got worse. They didn't talk about *how* they were going to work together, only that they *would* work together. No ground rules were established, no decisions made about who does what or when, and no work schedule had been set up.

She works in the morning and writes fast, throwing words down quickly with lots of blank spaces, then goes back and rewrites three or four times until it's right. He works at night, writing slowly, crafting each word and phrase with delicate precision; the first draft is almost a final one.

When they began working together they had no idea about what to expect from each other. She had collaborated once before, but he never had. They both had expectations about what the other would do, but didn't communicate them to each other.

They set up their schedule so she would write the first act – that was the material she had researched – and he would write Act II.

She got down to work. She was a little insecure – it was her *first* screenplay – and she worked hard to overcome the form and resistance. She wrote the first ten pages, then asked him to read them. She didn't know if she was on the right track or not. Was she setting up the story correctly? Was it what they had discussed and talked about? Were the characters real people in real situations? Her concern was natural.

He was working on the second scene of Act II when she gave him the first ten pages. He didn't want to look at them because he was having *his* problems and was just beginning to find his style. The scene was a difficult one; and he'd been working on it for several days.

He took the pages, then put them aside and went back to work, saying nothing to his wife. She gave him a few days to read the material. When he didn't read it, she became angry, so he promised he would read them that night. That satisfied her, at least for the moment.

She got up early the next morning. He was still sleeping, having worked late the night before. She made coffee and tried to work for a while. But it was no use. She wanted to know what her husband, her "collaborator," thought about the pages she had written. What was taking him so long?

The more she thought about it, the more impatient she became. She had to know. Finally, she made a decision; what he didn't know wouldn't hurt him. Quietly she crept into his office and softly closed the door behind her.

She went to his desk and started rifling his papers to see what comments, if any, he had made on her first ten pages. She finally found them, but there was nothing on them – no marks, no comments, no nothing. He didn't read them! Angry, she started to read his pages to see what he was so hung up about.

That's when she heard the noise on the stairs. The door suddenly burst open, and her husband stood framed in the doorway yelling, "Get away from that desk!" She tried to explain, but he didn't listen. He accused her of spying, of meddling, of invading his privacy. She erupted, and all the anger and tension and withheld communication came pouring out. They went at it, fighting tooth and nail, no holds barred. It *all* came out; resentment, frustration, fear, anxiety, insecurity. It was a screaming match. Even the dog started barking. At the peak of their "collaboration" he picked her up bodily, dragged her across the floor, and literally threw her out of the office, slamming the door in her face. She took off her shoe and stood there pounding on the door. Her heelmarks are still etched into his office door.

Now they can laugh about it.

It wasn't funny then. They didn't speak for days.

They learned a great deal from the experience. They learned that fighting doesn't work in a collaboration. They learned to work together and communicate on a more personal and professional level. They learned to criticize each other in a positive and supportive way without fear and restraint. They learned to respect each other. They learned that every person has a right to his or her own writing style, and you can't change it, only support it. She learned to respect the way he styles and fashions words into polished prose. He learned to admire and respect the way she worked – fast, clean, and accurate, always getting the job done. They learned how to ask for help from each other, something that was difficult for both of them. They learned from each other.

When they completed the screenplay, they felt a sense of satisfaction and achievement in what they had accomplished.

Collaboration means "working together."

That's what it's all about.

If you decide to collaborate, design the writing experience into three stages: the ground rules, the preparation, and the mechanics of writing the material.

AFTER IT'S WRITTEN

16

What do you do with your screenplay after you've completed it?

First, you've got to find out whether it "works" or not; whether you should engrave it in stone or paper the walls with it. You need some kind of feedback to see whether you wrote what you set out to write.

At this moment you don't know whether it works or not; you can't see it; you're too close to it.

Hopefully your writing copy is fairly clean, so you can make a copy. Keep the original. Never, never, never give your original to anyone.

Give your script to two friends, close friends, friends you can trust, friends who will tell you the truth, friends who are not afraid to tell you: "I hate it. What you've written is weak and unreal, the characters flat and one-dimensional, the story contrived and predictable." Someone who will not be afraid to hurt your feelings.

You'll find most people won't tell you the truth about your script. They'll tell you what *they think* you want to hear: "It's good; I liked it! I really did. You've got some nice things in it. I think it's 'commercial,'" whatever that means! People mean well, but they don't realise they're hurting you more by not telling you the truth.

In Hollywood, nobody tells you what they really think; they tell you they like it, but "it's not something we want to do at the present time"; or, "we have something like this in development."

That's not going to help you. You want someone to tell you what they really think about your script, so choose the people you give it to carefully.

After they've read it, listen to what they say. Don't defend what you've written, don't *pretend* to listen to what they say and leave feeling righteous, indignant, or hurt.

See whether they've caught the "intention" of what you wanted to write. Listen to their observations from the point of view that they *might be right*, not that they *are* right. They'll have observations, criticisms, suggestions, opinions, judgments. *Are* they right? Question them; press them on it. Do their suggestions or ideas make sense? Do they add to your screenplay? Enhance it? Go over the story with them. Find out what they like, dislike, what works for them, what doesn't.

You want the best script you can write. If you feel their suggestions can improve your screenplay, use them. Changes must be made from choice, and you must be comfortable with those changes. This is your story, and you'll know whether the changes work or not.

If you want to make any changes, make them. You've spent several months working on the script, so do it right. If you sell your material, you're going to have to make changes anyway; for the producer, director, and stars. Changes are changes; nobody likes them. But we all do them.

At this point, you still can't see your screenplay objectively. If you want another opinion "just in case," be prepared to get confused. If you give it to four people, for example, they'll all disagree. One person will like the holdup of the Chase Manhattan Bank, another won't. One person will say they like the holdup, but not the *result* of the holdup (they either get away or don't); and the other one wonders why you didn't write a love story.

It doesn't work. Two people you can trust.

When you're satisfied with the script, you're ready to go to the typist. Your script must be clean, neat, and professional-looking. You can either type it yourself, or have it done by a professional typist. If you can, let a typist do the final copy. If you type it yourself you may find a tendency to "chip away" at it and change something that shouldn't be changed.

The *form* of your screenplay must be correct. Don't expect the typist to do it for you. It's not a typist's job. The pages you give the typist should be clean enough to read. Crossed-out lines, notations penciled in the margins, or pasted-up strips of paper are all OK. Just make sure the typist can read them. Look around for a typist who will do a good job at a reasonable rate of pay. Remember that the master copy will always be longer than your version; it is not worth having the typist crowd the page to save a few dollars. A neat and well laid-out typescript is going to impress!

Do not number your scenes. Final shooting scripts have numbers running down the left margin. They indicate scene breakdowns compiled by the *production manager*, not the writer. When a script is bought, and the director and cast are signed, a production manager is hired. The production manager and director will go over the script, scene by scene, shot by shot. Once locations are established, the production manager and his secretary will make a production board, a large foldout folio with each scene, interior or exterior, specifically notated on their cardboard strips. When the production board is completed and the scenes are notated and approved by the director, the production secretary types the numbers of each scene on each page for a shot-by-shot breakdown. These numbers are used to identify each shot, so when the film (maybe 3–500,000 feet of it) is processed, and catalogued, every piece of film will be identified. It is not the writer's job to number the scenes.

A word about the title page. Many new or inexperienced writers feel they should include statements, registration, or copyright information, various quotes, dates, or whatever on the title page. They want to present "The Title," an original screenplay for an "epic production of a major motion picture for an all-star cast," by John Doe.

Don't do it. The title page is the title page. It should be simple and direct; "The Title" should be in the middle of the page, "a screenplay by John Doe" placed directly under it and in the lower right hand corner your address or phone number. Several times, as head of the story department, I would receive material from new writers without any information about where I could reach them. Those scripts were held for two months, then dumped into the waste basket.

You don't need to include copyright or registration information on the title page. But it is essential for you to protect your material. In the UK your work has automatic copyright protection under the Copyright Designs and Patents Act of 1988. Obviously your copyright position is strengthened if you can prove authorship of your screenplay and the date by which it was written. You can demonstrate proof and date of your authorship by posting your work to yourself by registered delivery but you must not open the sealed package except under controlled conditions and with witnesses. Alternatively, and probably better, you can deposit a hardcopy of it at your bank or lawyer. Then there can be no argument about what you have written and by what date. For more information, contact:

The Writers Guild of Great Britain,
15 Britania Street, London, WC1X 9JN
020 7833 0777 or www.writersguild.org.uk

In the US however, it's more complicated. There are three legal ways to claim ownership of your screenplay:

ONE

Obtain copyright forms from the Library of Congress.

Registrar of Copyright, Library of Congress,
Washington, D.C. 20540

TWO

Place a copy of your screenplay in an envelope, and send it to yourself, special delivery, return receipt requested. Make sure the postmark shows clearly.

When you receive the envelope file it away. DO NOT OPEN IT!

THREE

Perhaps the easiest and most effective way to register your material is with the Writers Guild of America, West or East. The Writers Guild provides a registration service that "provides evidence of the writer's prior claim to authorship of the literary material involved and the date of its completion."

Costs for registering material with the WGA are quite reasonable – contact them to find out what their current charges are. They take a clean copy of your screenplay, microfilm it, and store it in a safe place for ten years.

Your receipt is "evidence," or "proof," you've written what you say you've written. If someone does plagiarize your material, your attorney will subpoena the Custodian of Records of the WGA and they will appear on your behalf.

You may register your script by mail: Send a clean copy of your script with a check for the proper amount to the Registration Office:

Writers Guild of America, West, 7060 W Third St,
Los Angeles, CA 90048-4329
(323) 951-4000

If you like you can register your screenplay on-line at the Writers Guild: www.wga.org and go to the registration page. Cost is $10 for members of the Guild and $20 for non-members. Several years ago, a friend of mine wrote a treatment for a movie about a competitive skier and sent it to Robert Redford. Redford's company returned the material with a "thanks, but no thanks" letter.

A year or so later she went to see a movie titled *Downhill Racer*, starring Robert Redford. She claimed it was her story.

She went to court and won a large settlement because she could prove "prior access"; her story was registered with the Writers Guild of America, and she had the "thanks, but no thanks" letter from Redford's company.

Nobody did anything "intentional" in this situation. They refused her idea, for whatever reason, and when they were looking for a subject for a film someone "had an idea" about a "downhill racer."

James Salter was called in and wrote an excellent screenplay; the film was made and released. As directed by Michael Ritchie, it's a fine film, one sadly neglected by its distributor and the viewing public.

Once you've got your "master copy" photocopy ten copies. A lot of people don't return material; especially with the rising cost of postage. (Sending a self-addressed, stamped envelope with your material simply lets the producer or story editor know that you're a novice screenwriter. Don't do it. The chances are it won't be returned anyway.) So: ten copies. You'll register one. That leaves nine. If you're fortunate enough to get an agent to represent you, he'll want five copies immediately. That leaves you with four.

Make sure your screenplay is bound with paper fasteners; do not submit it loose. Put a simple cover on it, a cover that lends itself to the screenplay. Do not use a fancy, embossed leatherette cover. Make sure your script is on 8½ x 11 (A4 size) paper, and not 8½ x 14, legal size.

You've got "one shot" with your script, so make it count. One shot means this: at Cinemobile, every submission received was logged in a card file and cross-indexed by title and author. The material was read, evaluated, and written up in synopsis form. The reader's comments were carefully registered, then filed away.

If you submit your screenplay to a studio or production company, and they read it and reject it, and then you decide to rewrite it and resubmit it, chances are it won't be read. The reader will read the original synopsis and return it to you. Change the title, or use a pseudonym. No one reads the same material twice.

Do not send a synopsis of your script along with your material; it will not be read. If it is, it will be to your disadvantage. All our decisions were usually based on the reader's comments. If the synopsis had an interesting premise, we glanced through the first ten pages and then made a decision.

Some story editors at studios, networks, or production companies will accept unsolicited material only if you sign a release that permits them to read it. For the most part, studios will return your screenplay unopened and unread. Like insurance companies, they've been "burned" by plagiarism suits a few too many times and they don't want to deal with it. I don't blame them.

Then how do you "get it" to people? Since most people in Hollywood don't accept unsolicited material – that is, they don't accept material unless it's submitted through an authorized literary agent, an agent who has signed the Artists-Managers Agreement drawn up by the WGA – the question then becomes: How do you get an agent?

I hear that question over and over again. If you're going to sell your script for a cool million and have Ben Affleck and Julia Roberts star in it, you need a literary agent. So, how do you get an agent?

First, you must have a completed screenplay. An outline, or treatment, doesn't work. Then, contact the Writers Guild of America, West or East. Ask them, by mail or phone, to send you the list of agents who are signatory to the Artist-Managers Agreement. They'll send you a list of scores or agents. Those agents who are willing to read unsolicited material from new writers are indicated.

List several of them. Contact them by mail or phone; ask if they would be interested in reading a screenplay by a new writer. Give your background, sell yourself.

Most of them will say "no." Try some more. They'll say "no," too. Try some more.

People are always looking for material. That's the irony and truth.

There is a dearth of salable material in Hollywood. The opportunities for new screenwriters are enormous.

Many times you'll talk to the agent's secretary or assistant. Sometimes they'll read your screenplay; if they like it they'll recommend it to the agent. Let anyone who wants to read your script read it. A good script does not go unfound.

Good material does not get away from the readers in Hollywood. They can spot potential movie material within ten pages. If your script is good and worthy of production, it's going to be found. "How" is another matter.

It's a survival process. Your screenplay is entering the raging current of the Hollywood river, and like salmon swimming upstream to spawn, only a few make it.

Many screenplays are registered each year with the Writers Guild of America, West, in Los Angeles. Last year alone, more than 75,000 screenplays were registered. The registration office sometimes receives hundreds of submissions a day.

Do you know how many movies are made by studios and independent production companies each year? Not that many! Between 400 and 500 last year. And the number of studio productions is *decreasing* while the number of people writing screenplays is *increasing*. The cost of making a movie today is astronomical – several thousand dollars a minute. That's why a "medium" budget movie in Hollywood costs somewhere between $60 and $80 million and the cost of prints and advertising is mind-boggling.

Figure it out. Keep your dreams and reality separate. They're two different worlds.

If an agent likes your material, he still may not be able to sell it. But he will be able to show your screenplay as a sample of your writing ability. If a producer or story editor likes your work, you may be able to get a "development deal" from a studio or producer to write an original, or adapt one of their ideas or books into a screenplay. Everybody's looking for writers, no matter what "they" say.

Give the agent three to six weeks to read your material. If you don't receive a reply from him or her within that period of time, call.

If you submit your script to a large, well-known agency, like William Morris, or ICM, the established agents will ignore it. But they have readers and trainee agents there and they might read it.

If you're fortunate, you might find someone who likes your work and wants to represent you.

Who is the best agent?

The agent who likes *your* work and wants to represent you.

If you contact eight agents, you'll be lucky to find one who likes it. You can submit your script to more than one agent at a time.

A literary agent gets a ten-percent commission of whatever he or she sells.

What kind of a deal can you expect to make if someone wants to buy your screenplay?

Prices for a screenplay vary for the Writers Guild minimum. A Writers Guild minimum is broken down into two categories: a high-budget movie that costs more than $5 million to make and a low-budget film that costs less than $5 million. At this writing, the WGA minimum for a high-budget film is $97,068; for a low-budget, $51,105. These minimums will increase each time a new contract is negotiated.

An "eyeball" price for a screenplay is five percent of the budget. If you sell the script, you'll probably receive a "percentage of the profits," at least on paper. You'll get anywhere from two and a half to five percent of the producer's net, whatever you can get.

If someone wants to buy your script they will probably *option* it for a year. With an option, someone pays you for the exclusive right to get a "deal" or raise financing for a certain period of time, usually a year. The option price may be five to ten percent of the purchase price.

Let's take a one-year period for a low-budget film.

The purchase price is WGA minimum, say $50,000, so they option your material for $5,000. That means you have a balance left of about $45,000: $50,000 purchase price minus the $5,000 option.

If a *production-distribution* agreement is made with a "money source," you'll receive the balance in full, or a certain amount applied against the total. A production-distribution agreement is when a financially responsible money source – a studio, or production funding company – agrees to finance and distribute the movie. When the p/d agreement is reached, they may make an additional payment, and perhaps pay the balance of the purchase price on the "first day of principal photography." That is, the first day of shooting.

That may be more than a year after you receive your option money. This is a standard type "step-deal" in Hollywood. The money numbers may vary, the procedure will not.

If you do get an offer on your script, let someone represent you. Either an agent or an attorney. An attorney will either charge by the hour or receive five percent of your earnings from the project.

You can obtain an option for a book or novel just like a screenplay. If you want to adapt a book or novel, you must obtain the motion-picture and theatrical rights to it.

To find out if the material is available, call the publisher of the hardbound edition. Ask, either by mail or phone, for the subsidiary rights department. Ask if the motion-picture and theatrical rights are available. If they are, they'll tell you or refer you to the literary agent who represents the author. Contact them. The agent will tell you whether the rights are available or not.

If you decide to adapt the material without obtaining the motion-picture rights, you might find you've been wasting your time; the rights are not available, someone owns them. If you can find out who has the rights, they might be willing to read your screenplay. Or they might not.

If you want to adapt the material simply as an exercise for yourself, do it. Just be sure you know what you're doing so you're not wasting your time.

It costs so much to make a movie today that everyone wants to minimize the risk; that's why money paid to a writer is termed "front money," or "risk money."

No one likes to take a risk. And the motion-picture business is one of the biggest crap shoots around. No one knows whether a film is going to "go through the roof," like *Star Wars* or *Titanic*. People are reluctant to put up a lot of front money. Do you know anyone who spends money easily? Including yourself? Studios, production companies, and independent producers are no exception.

Option money comes out of the producer's pocket; they want to minimize the risks. Don't expect a lot of money for your material the first time out. It doesn't work that way.

Most screenwriters don't sell. John Milius wrote his first screenplay several years ago, a piece called *The Last Resort*.

It still hasn't sold. Nobody wants to buy it, and Milius doesn't care to rewrite it. Yet it clearly reveals John Milius's unique gift for telling a story visually. Milius is a "natural" filmmaker, like Spielberg, or Kubrick, men "born to film." Though unsold, *The Last Resort* began his career.

There are a few exceptions. Bob Getchell's *Alice Doesn't Live Here Anymore* was a first screenplay. Rob Thompson's *Hearts of the West* was a first effort that he managed to get to Tony Bill, long a champion of the new writer, and the movie got made.

These are the exceptions, not the rule.

When you really get down to it, you're writing your screenplay for yourself first, for money second.

Only a handful of well-known and established writers in Hollywood get enormous sums of money for their screenplays. There are now almost 10,000 members of the Writers Guild, West, and only a few are employed to write screenplays. And less than a handful earn six figures a year. Those that do, earn every penny of it.

Don't set up unreal expectations for yourself.

Just write your screenplay.

Then worry about how much money you're going to make.

IN CONCLUSION 17

Whatever problem you might have, whether it's one of *Plot*, *Character*, or *Structure*, know that if you created the problem, then you can solve it. Don't be afraid to rethink the material, don't be afraid to rewrite. Anthony Minghella (*The English Patient*) told me he did twenty-one rewrites on the material, and he was still rewriting in the editing room while they were cutting the film. It's not how many times you need to rewrite the material, *it's what you need to do in order to make the material the best it can be*. That means being able to recognize, define, and then solve whatever problem you might have.

If there's one quality I feel is the most essential within the cauldron of *Problem Solving*, it's patience. If you become impatient with the material, impatient with yourself, impatient with a lack of progress, impatient with how many times you have to rewrite the same material, impatient with the results, just put your impatience aside and keep to the task at hand. Your job, your responsibility, is to make the material the best it can be, regardless of how long it takes. I know people who write their first draft, dabble a little on some scenes, then send it out into the world. It's not ready, and it comes back with the results that you would expect. Nobody's interested, everyone has an idea on how to make it better, and you hit the wall of rejection that is so debilitating it's possible you'll put the script on the shelf somewhere and never go back to it.

There's another side to this coin. The more people you give your script to read, the more diverse and contradictory the opinions will be about what you have to add, change, or delete in a rewrite. So many times writers give their material to people to read and the opinions and criticisms they receive are so diverse, so contradictory, and alter the story line so much, they don't even recognize the material any more. That's because it's not their story any more.

If you make changes that you don't feel are right for your screenplay, that's when it becomes a real problem, indeed a nightmare. It never works. The only thing that works, in terms of your material, is whether you feel satisfied with it when you put it out into the world. Deep down inside, when you're one-on-one, you have to know that you've done the best job you can do, at least at this time. Only you can know that for certain. Only you can trust your own instincts, your own creative Self.

As I've said many times over, everybody's a writer; everybody has an opinion about how to make your script better, how to sharpen the characters, how to make it more "commercial," how to be more acceptable to the current temper or trend of the times.

There will be occasions when someone will make a particular comment or observation that strikes a chord, or a feeling, within you. That's what you're looking for, that's what you have to follow as you walk along the path of *Problem Solving*; that's the only map you can follow, that's the spark of truth and light that illuminates your own creative vision.

Are you willing to do what has to be done to make your screenplay the best it can be? Are you willing to be true to your own vision? Are you willing to sit down and honor your own inner voice, and mine, whatever problems the material might have and turn them into a workable solution? A solution that becomes an opportunity for your own growth and expansion, a solution, whether you know it or not, that will only sharpen your skills as a screenwriter?

Problem solving is really two sides of the same coin, a process that contains both sacrifice and commitment, for it's either a challenge or an obligation.

Writing is a personal responsibility; either you do it or you don't. "*The world is as you see it*," reads the ancient scripture. Either you see it as an opportunity, or a burden. Either you honor your own creative vision, or you don't.

It's your choice.

A PERSONAL NOTE

18

Over the last few years there's been a significant evolution going on in the world of film and understanding the role of dramatic structure has become the focus of an intense debate. The discussion rages between conventional and unconventional methods of story telling. I find these debates good because they may inspire conversations of discovery, new points of departure in the evolution of film. The essence of structure will not change; only the form, the way the story is put together, will change. And if that leads to new ways of telling stories with pictures, then I've accomplished what I set out to do. So while we may be through with the past, the past is not through with us.

Today, as I sit in a darkened theater, I'm sustained with an unbridled hope and optimism. I don't know whether I'm looking for answers to my own questions about life, or whether I'm sitting in the dark silently giving thanks that I'm not up there on that monster screen confronting the struggles and challenges I'm seeing. Yet, I know in those reflected images, I may glean an insight, an awareness, that might embrace the personal meaning of my life.

I think about this as I look back upon the footprints of my life. I see where I began my journey, gaze over the ground I've covered, the trails I've traversed, and understand it's not the destination that is so important; it is the journey itself that is both the goal and the purpose.

Everybody's a writer.

That's what you'll find out. Everybody you tell about your screenplay will have a suggestion, a comment, or a better idea about it. Then, they'll tell you about the great idea *they* have for a screenplay.

It's one thing to *say* you're going to write a screenplay, it's another to *do* it.

Don't make judgments about what you've written. It might take years for you to "see" your script objectively. If at all. Judgments of "good" or "bad," or comparisons between this and that are meaningless within the creative experience.

It is what it is.

Hollywood is a "dream factory"; a town of talkers. Go to any of the various hangouts around town and you'll hear people talking about the scripts they're going to write, the movies they're going to produce, and the deals they're going to make.

It's all talk.

Action is character, right? What a person *does* is what he *is*, not what he says.

Everybody's a writer.

There is a tendency in Hollywood to "second-guess" the writer; the studio, the producer, the director, and the star will make changes in the script that will "improve" it. Most people in Hollywood assume they're "larger" than the original material. "*They*" know what has to be done to "make it better." Directors do this all the time.

A film director can take a great script and make a great film. Or, he can take a great script and make a terrible film. But he can't take a terrible script and make a great film. No way.

Only a few film directors know how to improve a screenplay by visually tightening the story line. They can take a wordy dialogue scene of three to four pages, condense it into a tense and dramatic three-minute scene that "works" with five lines of dialogue, three looks, somebody lighting a cigarette, and an insert of a clock on the wall. Sidney Lumet did this in *Network*. He took a 160-page screenplay, beautifully written and constructed, and visually tightened it into an excellent 120-minute film that captures the integrity of the script by Paddy Chayefsky.

That's the exception, not the rule.

Most directors in Hollywood have no story sense at all. They'll second-guess the writer, making changes in the story line that weaken and distort it, and eventually a lot of money is spent making a lousy film that nobody wants to see.

In the long run, of course, everybody loses; the studios lose money, the director adds a "flop" to his "track record," and the writer takes the rap for writing a poor screenplay.

Everybody's a writer.

Some people will complete their screenplays. Others won't. Writing is hard work, a day-by-day job, and a professional writer is someone who sets out to achieve a goal and then does it. Just like life. Writing is a personal responsibility; either you do it or you don't. And then there's the old "natural law" about survival and evolution.

There are no "overnight success stories" in Hollywood. Like the saying goes, "The overnight success took fifteen years to happen."

Believe it. It's true.

Professional success is measured by persistence and determination. The motto of the McDonald's Corporation is summed up in their poster called "Press On";

Nothing in the world can take the place
of persistence.
Talent will not; nothing is more common
than unsuccessful men with talent.
Genius will not; unrewarded genius
is almost a proverb.
Education will not;
the world is full of educated derelicts.

Persistence and determination alone
are omnipotent.

When you complete your screenplay, you've accomplished a tremendous achievement. You've taken an idea, expanded it into a dramatic or comedic story line, then sat down and spent several weeks or months writing it. From inception through completion. It's a satisfying and rewarding experience. You did what you set out to do.

Wear that proudly.

Talent is God's gift; either you've got it, or you don't. But that doesn't interfere with the experience of writing.

Writing brings its own rewards. Enjoy them.

Pass it on.

INDEX